*To Marcel Durry
Professor at the Sorbonne,
who should have written
this book*

LOVE IN ANCIENT ROME

PIERRE GRIMAL

With a Foreword by
WILLIAM R. NETHERCUT

Translated from the French by
ARTHUR TRAIN, JR.

University of Oklahoma Press
Norman and London

Other books in English by Pierre Grimal

Larousse World Mythology (ed.) (New York, 1981)
Roman Cities (Madison, Wis., 1984)

```
HIGHLAND LAKES LIBRARY
HQ 13 .G713 1986
Grimal, Pierre,
Love in ancient Rome /

                              $ 11.95
```

Library of Congress Cataloging-in-Publication Data

```
Grimal, Pierre, 1912-
   Love in ancient Rome.

   Translation of: L'Amour à Rome.
   Reprint. Originally published: New York : Crown
Publishers, 1967.
   Includes index.
   1. Marriage--Rome.  2. Rome--Social life and
customs.  I. Title.
HQ13.G713  1986         306.8'5'09376         86-40087
ISBN 0-8061-2014-2 (pbk.)
```

Designed by Barbara Lewis

Paperback edition published by the University of Oklahoma Press, Norman, Publishing Division of the University. Manufactured in the U.S.A. Originally published in France under the title *L'Amour à Rome*. Copyright © 1980 by La Société d'Edition Les Belles Lettres. First printing of the University of Oklahoma edition, 1986.

CONTENTS

FOREWORD BY WILLIAM R. NETHERCUT ix

INTRODUCTION xiii

I. LOVE IN THE EARLY DAYS 1
II. LOVE AND RELIGION 26
III. ROMAN MARRIAGE 48
IV. MARRIAGE IN THE GOLDEN AGE 70
V. FREE LOVE 102
VI. LOVE AND THE POETS 136
VII. LOVE AND POLITICS 182
VIII. IMPERIAL AMOURS 246
IX. ROME AND LOVE 292

SELECTED READINGS 307

INDEX 309

FOREWORD

by William R. Nethercut

The past two decades have seen a proliferation of studies which address from a variety of directions the lives and images of women in the ancient world. Within this development the present volume holds a special place.

The appearance in paperback of Otto Kiefer's *Sexual Life in Ancient Rome* (Panther Books, 1969) may serve on two accounts as a point of departure for our discussion. Like Pierre Grimal's *Love in Ancient Rome* (1967), Kiefer's study signaled the presence of a growing public eager to understand with greater intimacy and realism the psychological experiences of a people on whom history and Hollywood have conferred a unique allure. Kiefer's and Grimal's books, along with many others, fix the period in which the investigation of women in antiquity brought new energy to classical scholarship in the United States. At the same time, Kiefer's *Sexual Life in Ancient Rome* was symbolic of the focus which first had attracted readers' curiosity in this century, for it is in the translation of Kiefer by Gilbert Highet and Helen MacInnes in 1934 that we may begin to discern the background for contemporary works on women in Greece and Rome.

Many of the examples which served Kiefer as a basis for generalization would recur as colorful and standard references in subsequent essays; for example, in Ruth Hoffsten's examination (1939) of Roman women of rank as such figures emerge in the writings of imperial historians like Suetonius and Tacitus. The central problem of this research became clear at once: it was too easy to dwell only on the striking antipathy between a Messallina amid her fellow orgiasts and the Republican and virtuous Lucretia. Rome offers us a femininity which seemed to claim immortal renown only by one of two opposed and extreme courses—a stoic submission to sexual abuse or the arch-devices of depravity. Indeed, such a distortion reflects a Roman bias.

The 1950s balanced the bias of those earlier years in several ways. First, little had been said before about women in Greece and other parts of the ancient world, because Rome has always lain closer to our urban fantasies: banquets and wild parties require the press of bodies, and the large and heterogeneous populations of the baths excite us with their variety and diverse possibilities for indulgence; the fertile soil and the fruits of Italy seem more sensual than the rock-strewn hillsides of the Aegean. Finally, in 1951, H. D. F. Kitto presented in *The Greeks* (pp. 219–36), a careful and well-analyzed assessment of the position of Athenian women. Charles Seltman in *Women in Antiquity* (1956), adduced the evidence of vase paintings and literature and studied women not in Athens alone but in all the major city-states of the Greek world, offering for comparison the images we have discovered of women in Egypt and the early Near East. Like Kitto, Seltman focussed his study along broadly cultural rather than narrowly sexual lines.

Two other publications suggest another way whereby in the 1950s we saw a widening of the perceptual field in which earlier scholars had approached women in antiquity. Gilbert Highet, in *Poets in a Landscape* (1957), and Georg Luck, in *The Latin Love Elegy* (1959), explored the relationship between the Roman poets of love—Catullus, Tibullus, Propertius, Ovid—and the mistresses to whom they dedicated their verses. Their emphasis was on women holding power over devoted lovers, on the *domina,* or lady, who commanded her suitor's talent and inspired him intellectually and with love. The male, as a servant, was not seen as one who exploits but as one-half of a reciprocal relationship in which full union was the goal and "marriage" its metaphor. Such a view brings us much closer to the women *and men* of Rome. Each exists magically for the other, creating for us a sense of *humanitas*—the awareness of what human beings can share and make possible for each other as human beings. It is just this emphasis which makes *Love in Ancient Rome* such a pleasure to read. We want to know our Romans as living, truly human, beings. In such a manner they will have more meaning for us than if we look across the centuries at them immobilized in debauchery or, as Paul MacKendrick once wrote, set in stained glass uttering pious platitudes.

It was during the 1960s, as I have said, that we discerned the first full bloom of studies on women in ancient societies. J. P. V. D. Baldson's *Roman Women: Their History and Habits* came out in 1962; its far-ranging summaries of the different aspects of its subject make it a basic text even today. In fairly continuous succession appeared monographs on the festival of the Matronalia and other rituals observed by Rome's daughters (J. Gagé, 1963) and the Roman erotic poets' attitude toward women (S. Lilja, 1965), while shorter studies were directed toward family life among Rome's lower classes (B. Rawson, 1966) or contributed importantly toward clarifying the spread of literacy in Rome and the value set upon the education of Roman women (E. E. Best, 1970). A bibliographical guide by Sarah B. Pomeroy, of great use for the titles in women's studies during the late 1960s and early 70s, was carried in the spring 1973 issue of *Arethusa*. Pomeroy's own book followed soon thereafter: *Goddesses, Whores, Wives and Slaves: Women in Classical Antiquity* (1976). The greater part of that work is given over to Greek society, but three chapters, on the Roman matron, women in the lower classes, and women in the religion of the Romans, draw tightly together the essential information we meet also in Baldson and Grimal. Most recently, Judith P. Hallett's *Fathers and Daughters in Roman Society* (1983) has elicited more fully, through her careful analysis of this key family tie, the contours of a relationship that combined tenderness and tradition.

The scholarly writings of Pierre Grimal, professor for many years in the Sorbonne in Paris, are appreciated by colleagues for their blend of creative new suggestions with a practical mastery of topography and archaeology which has allowed Grimal to confront with particular fruitfulness moments in Roman history which, though of obvious significance, have remained obscure. As a literary critic Grimal is intense with dramatic power, alive to the conflict of light with darkness: no better discussion of Propertius's poetic shaping of Augustan Rome exists than his essays on this author in *Latomus* in 1952. This spiritual fire creates for *Love in Ancient Rome* a distinctive organization: the early chapters do not plunge into sociological paradigms but ask important questions first. What do Rome's legends show us about Woman and Love? What does the name *Venus* allow us to understand about her descendants? Geoffrey Grigson (*The Goddess of Love*, 1976) finds in its etymology a debasement of the vital and beautifying force implied in *Aphrodite: venus* is a *neuter* noun, not feminine at all, and it suggests petition or prayer to accomplish some material end. For his part, Grimal stresses that petition and prayer imply mutuality and respect: love cannot be taken, but must be granted; love is consent. Thus, throughout this book the reader is directed away from the enumeration of specific cases to reflect upon what the Roman conception of law and marriage, or of love, possesses as its deepest assumption.

It has become popular for scholars of quite precise, and sometimes narrow, philosophic persuasions to take Greek or Roman women as a subject. We encounter Marxist interpretations; psychologists of several schools offer their contributions. For the economic historian Woman is quite different from what she appears to be to the feminist. And among feminist scholars degrees of militancy can be distinguished. Love, by contrast, cuts across all lines of this sort and asks that we put aside, along with the all-too-familiar icons of Virtue and Purity or Carnal Abandonment, some of our more monochromatic portraits of the economic or social Woman whom male distortions have misrepresented. It is important, assuredly, to be aware when evidence is coming predominantly from one side, yet it is also striking to see—as Grimal reminds us—how Rome's men changed their image of love and of their relationship to women. In this respect *Love in Ancient Rome* underlines the innovative comedy of Terence as against the comic philosophy of Plautus; the traditional nature of Aeneas's liaison with Dido, as against the very un-Roman love of Nisus for Euryalus in Vergil's *Aeneid,* a love that can be set beside the sacrificial commitment of the love poets to their mistresses; and finally, the new sense of love that Isis comes to communicate in Apuleius's tale of bodily and spiritual transformation, circa A.D. 200, at a time when wedding scenes appeared on sarcophagi to symbolize an initiation into sacred mysteries and as an image of immortality. This evolution in the expression of love as conceived by the male is an essential element in the equation for Woman that today's students of the classical past are seeking, and it deserves highlighting within Grimal's presentation.

The time is right for us to ease our eyes away from a picture that has perhaps become somewhat uneven or roughened from the encrustation of academic or philosophic vogues. A portion shines clearly—the most important part. Nothing can be more impressive as an affirmation of self-value, reflecting credit upon a man equal to the esteem it bespeaks in a woman who evaluates their relationship, than the words of Tibullus's Sulpicia quoted by Pierre Grimal: she learned, in loving one whom society could not approve, that "she was worthy of him, and *he was worthy of her.*"

INTRODUCTION

ANCIENT Rome and Roman love have a bad reputation. The indulgent smile that is standard for Greece and Greek love is not granted Rome. The complacency with which the Romans themselves denounced the vices they saw practiced around them, and the arguments of the Christian writers, who wanted to arraign a society they wished to reform according to the dictates of Holy Grace, resulted in increasing the amount of unfavorable evidence and in obscuring all the facts that might incline us to a more moderate judgment.

And then it is hard not to feel somewhat disconcerted by the gap between the emphasis on virtue that is an inseparable part of the concept of Republican Rome, and what we glimpse of the realities of daily life from reading the poets, novelists, and historians, and also from observing the figures on monuments—which do not always keep within the bounds of decency. It seems to us that the Romans betrayed their ideals. We would reproach them less if they had abandoned themselves more straightforwardly to the lusts of the flesh. We delude ourselves into thinking that a beautiful statue of Aphrodite is "purer" than the nudities of the Roman Venuses, as if Rome had soiled the "spiritual" sensuality of Hellenism by a hypocritical Puritanism. All this is what has tarnished the reputation of Rome. The orgies of Nero have become proverbial. Messalina, Nero's first cousin, has come down to us as a symbol of debauchery. When we think of love in Rome, that is what occurs to us first—and not without a certain self-satisfaction.

But—and it is as true of this more or less instinctive opinion as of all hasty impressions—it is backed up only by generalizations.

The real truth is infinitely more complex and subtle. To begin with, our judgment of Rome is based on comparison with a purer moral standard—or at least we think it is—but if we say that, we have already committed an anachronism. Next, it is dangerous to start with a judgment. It would be more productive to start with an attempt at understanding, difficult, no doubt, but necessary if we want our judgment to be fair. And finally, we may come to realize that it is not in the least necessary to judge; understanding is all that we require.

The Roman era is not a simple historical phenomenon; it covers ten centuries. Are we to be surprised if, during those thousand years, morals and moral values changed, and if persons did not love in the days of Apuleius as they did in the days of Romulus?

The emotion of love is not a simple fact. Never, in any civilization, has it been depreciated to the level of the merely physical relationship between the sexes. Society intervenes to impose laws, restrictions, and even fashions. Today we know the role that the love instinct plays in the personal life of a human being, a role often not acknowledged by him, but that rules over the entire range of his feelings. Love elaborates myths for everyone, including the social group. What we should do is to observe the life of these myths, whose significance we must try to discover if we want to reach what might be called the unconscious "substratum" of a given society. To that extent, the observed facts do not call for a judgment; they are really so many signs of a spiritual reality from which they emanate. At each stage, this reality constituted a "moment" in human history.

Rome began as a patriarchal society—not a pure one, but one allied to other social structures. It is only natural that in this society, since the earliest epochs, different types of sexual morality were intermingled. Each group behaved differently according to its conformation. From early times separate religious currents can be discerned, each of which had a specific influence on modes of love. And the whole history of Roman customs is the growth of this complex system, still further complicated by the effect of even more numerous and powerful outside influences.

At the end of the Republic, Rome tended to abdicate its own personality. It was no longer anything more than the center of an immense Empire. People of every race and nation abounded in the cities, bringing with them their customs, beliefs, and prejudices. In addition, the material wealth in the hands of the aristocracy continued to increase steadily; luxury and the abundance of slaves brought about emotional situations that could not fail to have an effect on human hearts. Passion is not the same in a poor society in the daily grip of the need to find at least barely adequate sustenance, as it is in a city where everything is easy, where money can procure anything, and enable persons to transform their wildest dreams into reality. If we consider the unbelievable wealth of Imperial Rome, we will be surprised not so much that there are some examples of corrupt practices as that there are not more. The moral sense, the "virtue" of the Romans must have been very strong to have resisted the temptation to give way to vice in its infinite ramifications.

At its best period, Greece never possessed much in the way of financial resources. It was the treasure of the Orient, flowing into Rome, which corrupted not everybody, but a certain number, the weakest, and it is a miracle that there were still Romans to be scandalized by them.

As in other countries, the story of love in Rome tends to be scattered throughout an infinite number of affairs and relationships. It would seem that everyone loves in his own way, and that each love is unique. It is possible nevertheless to discern the outline of a "Roman" development of the art of love. The course of each human destiny—the only reality we can grasp directly—was in effect willed by the person living it out, who, usually consciously, modeled it on the ideals and myths by which he was surrounded.

A man and a woman have an idea of themselves, of their reciprocal role, that has been largely forced on them, and these desires will conform to that idea without their wishing them to. A woman in love wants to be for the partner a person who will touch his emotions, the person she thinks he longs for, whom she considers suitable for him. In this love parade, men do not lag behind either. The comedy that is acted by the two sexes for each other, neither wholly conscious nor wholly involuntary, takes its style and its theme from models imposed from the outside. But each one, to the extent that he can, puts a little of himself into it. From wanting to be like his model he can grow to be like him, but never identical. Thus, from generation to generation, the ideal is modified, and grandchildren do not love exactly the same way their grandparents did!

Rome did not escape this law, which is the law of every life. Its fundamental conservatism never had the power, fortunately, to stop the growth and change either of customs or feelings. The models chosen by Roman lovers at different epochs naturally changed. In the early days the influence of the family was predominant, at least among the patricians. We should ask ourselves what effect that discipline had on the relationship of young husbands and wives, and on men's conduct when they were beyond the reach of family tyranny.

Religion too dominated sexual life. Its control, exercised through the rites, was at first more "magical" than moral. Though the myths came somewhat later, they made their appearance fairly early on the Italian scene. The authority of the state acted at first as a kind of filter, then, little by little, the myths invaded the city and men's consciences—and the latter were sometimes troubled by them. We shall see, for example, how the growth of the Dionysian mysteries was on the point of effecting a veritable upheaval at the beginning of the eleventh century before Christ.

Other invasions by religion, if less dramatic, were no less important. It was in this way, at the end of the historical period we are trying to reconstruct, that the religion of Isis conquered Rome. We can guess that this religion would not have been known so favorably in the Roman world had it not been found to correspond to a conception of love-life resulting from a natural evolution of

INTRODUCTION xvii

Roman customs. But it helped crystallize and spread a mystique of femininity, the germ of which had been present in Rome for a long time, but that had lacked the sanction of religion.

Another question that is sometimes raised, apropos of Roman customs, is to what extent pagan legends were able to influence them. Did not the mythology developed by Greek culture degenerate, in clumsy Roman hands, to the point of changing into a cult of immorality? It would be a little naïve to think so. The Romans could always distinguish between fables and real morals. It is certain that the scenes evoked by the Greek myths, repeated everywhere, brimful of amorous escapades, could inject an erotic atmosphere into everyday life. But the same is no less true of the Greek world, in which it seems that familiarity with the love attributed to the gods had the result rather of conferring a dignity, a spirituality, on human love that would otherwise have been more difficult to attain. To deny the existence of love is not to suppress it; the example of the myths mitigated the allure of evildoing.

That is not to say either that the Romans always indulged in complete sexual liberty. Like men of every time they were also familiar with repression. But they never established a hard-and-fast bond between the act of love and moral turpitude. To love, under certain circumstances, was not lawful. But to love, as such, was to obey the gods, and achieve one of the requisites of the human condition. Chastity could be required by the rites in certain cases, but it was not a good thing in itself, not even a desirable thing, it was rather an impairment of what was good and desirable. What were chiefly regarded as moral virtues were self-control, self-discipline, and moderation in the pursuit of pleasure. But among the gifts of the gods to men, love is always to be found.

One of the outstanding traits of Roman civilization is its unremitting regard for the right and for the law. Jurists could not refrain from legislating about love, and an entire code regulating the relationship between the sexes is to be found on their statute books. We will have to take notice of that in due course, but we will find that the law has never tried to take into consideration anything more than the consequences of love, not the choice of its objects. All men and all women have always kept their complete freedom, and Roman marriage remains up to the end an obligation freely entered into.

Many men and women remained faithful to that obligation even during the times that are called the most corrupt. And finally we will reach the point where we ask ourselves whether the so-called "corruption" of Roman customs is not the reward of a victory: may not the extreme license which we find in certain periods among certain persons be the consequence of the liberation of individuals, particularly women, who were, not without hesitation and reservations, accorded the right to love?

In any case we may be sure that Rome did not die because of immorality, and that the amorous verses of its poets did more to elevate and refine the human psyche than the example of Messalina, Tiberius, or Nero did to corrupt it.

LOVE IN ANCIENT ROME

I

LOVE IN THE EARLY DAYS

IF it is true that the legends of a people or a race reveal to us its deepest characteristics and the aspirations of its soul, the legends of Rome, because of the prominence they give to stories of love, suggest that these hardy world conquerors kept hidden within themselves a tenderness that had more influence than they were willing to admit.

The history of their capital begins with a love story: the sudden passion conceived by the god Mars for the vestal virgin Rhea Silvia. But if we go back still farther, to the time when the future of the occidental world was at stake beneath the walls of Troy, we again find that a love story influenced the course of destiny at the end of which the beginnings of Rome are to be found. This romance of early times is recounted in a Homeric saga.

Anchises watched his flocks on Mount Ida in Phrygia. He was a nephew of King Laomedon, who ruled over the country of Troy. He was handsome. In those days princes and sometimes kings did not disdain to watch over sheep. Now the goddess Aphrodite had seen Anchises, and was consumed with love for him. In the grip of passion, Aphrodite could not resist. Without hesitating, she sought out the handsome shepherd, and told him a long rigmarole which she made up as she went along. She was, she said, a daughter of the King of Phrygia. The god Hermes had kidnapped her and taken her up into the mountains. How tragic it would be if no one came to her aid! Anchises was most sympathetic; a certain tenderness crept into their conversation. That very night the handsome shepherd obtained the favors of the goddess disguised as a mortal. Once her desires were satisfied Aphrodite did not keep up the deception. She disclosed her divine origin, and announced to Anchises that she would soon present him with a son. But she formally charged him to tell no one that the child's mother was the Goddess of Love. Otherwise Zeus, annoyed at having the secret of the gods discovered, would strike down the blabbermouth with his thunderbolts.

As it turned out, a few years later drink got the better of Anchises on one occasion and loosened his tongue. Boasting, he revealed to his companions the divine origin of his son, little Aeneas. Zeus, being a parent himself and proud of his children, decided that it was punishment enough to make Anchises lame (according to some accounts, to make him blind), but let him go on living. Later, after the capture of Troy, Anchises left his fatherland, borne on his son's shoulders, and together they followed the little band of Trojan exiles as far as Sicily, where, apparently, the old man died.

This legend was highly popular in the whole Mediterranean basin, and had reached Italy by the beginning of the sixth century B.C., if not earlier. The image of Aeneas carrying the elderly Anchises on his shoulders was a familiar one to the faithful who made pilgrimages to the Etruscan sanctuary at Veii a few miles north of Rome. It was well known to the Romans as well, who from a very early epoch claimed to have originated in Troy. Truth to tell, the Romans preferred to trace their ancestry back to Aeneas rather than Venus. To attribute their origin to a whim of passion was disturbing. They preferred to ascribe it to a calmer, more tender feeling, which they called "piety," of which Aeneas was the permanent symbol—made up of filial affection, a devotion to those dear to one so strong as to approximate heroism, and the awareness of a transcendental duty, anterior to any human law, the manifestation of a divine order. This piety they looked on as one of the most profound requisites of the moral life.

The son of Aphrodite, having lost his fatherland, his house, and his wealth, chose to save only his father, his household gods, and his own son, little Ascanius. As for his wife Creusa, he had been obliged—swayed by a duty beyond human love—to resign himself to leaving her in the doomed city.

In other times, decorum would have obliged Aeneas to pay more attention to his wife's safety, perhaps to choose it in preference to that of his father. The commentators of Virgil, who related the legend in the Aeneid, were not inclined to reproach Aeneas for what they call his negligence in regard to Creusa. In any case Virgil neither could nor wished to change the legend. All he did was to introduce certain human emotions which were not depicted in it: Aeneas' suffering, the risks he willingly ran in trying to save the unfortunate woman. But the meaning of the account remains clear: the hero's piety toward Anchises and Ascanius is a duty toward the gods. In sacrificing Creusa, his heart alone was involved; if he chose her in preference to those of his own race, he would be guilty, and remiss in regard to the established pattern of his world.

Still another time, in the course of his interminable voyage to the Promised Land, Aeneas had to sacrifice the feelings of tenderness in his heart. His momentary entanglement with Queen Dido has the same significance as his involuntary abandon of Creusa.

After the storm that drove his ships onto the African coast, Aeneas thought his trials were at an end. At the spot where he landed, people were building a city. A Queen, lately arrived from Sidon, was laying the foundations of an empire. Well informed of the events in Troy, she welcomed the shipwrecked voyagers cordially, moved to pity by their misfortunes, and impressed by their courage. Fate had not spared her either. She had seen her own brother murder the man she had married and whom she loved more than anyone in the world. She herself had fled her country to escape a more than likely death, and now she was trying to create a new homeland for herself among the barbaric Numidians. Thus the Queen and the Trojans had many feelings in common. The same nostalgia for the East, for a civilization that seemed all the more precious since the land of Africa and the eastern Mediterranean had nothing to offer but wild forests and nomadic peoples without towns and without laws. The same urge to build a human oasis in that desert, a capital which would have its gods, temples, and open squares, a collective existence in which human qualities and virtues could grow and flower. Moreover, Dido, who was an enterprising Queen, was just as alone as Aeneas in the role she had carved out for herself: each was leading a people, and both were condemned to solitude.

So the two of them were immediately and irresistibly tempted to share their lot. It was hardly necessary for the gods to intervene. A single opportunity was all that was needed, a hunt, a storm in the mountains that separated Dido and Aeneas from their followers, a grotto in which they took refuge—and there they were, united, like Aphrodite and Anchises before them. Dido even thought she could descry the flame of the wedding torches in the lightning that illuminated the grotto from time to time. She cherished the illusion that the gods approved the bond she was so glad to accept.

As for Aeneas, he simply let her love him. He felt neither shame nor fear at incurring an obligation to which his whole being had consented. He played his role as husband and King in entire good faith—up to the day when the gods reminded him that this was not where his mission called him; this was not his Promised Land. Was he willing to refuse his son Ascanius and their common race the good fortune which destiny was saving for them? And once again, torn by distress, the son of Venus sacrificed his human love to his duty. He left. Dido, when he told her he was determined to go, showered reproaches on him. This flight from her love threw her into despair. He knew it, and still abandoned her. Ravaged by anger and shame because for a while she had thought Aeneas could really take the place of her husband, and because in abandoning herself to him she felt that she had broken her vows, Dido decided that she must die. At the highest part of her palace roof she built a huge bonfire—to serve as her funeral pyre, and its flames lit up the sky as the Trojans' ships fled north.

The "Romance of Dido," which takes up a whole volume of the

Aeneid—the fourth—was probably not made up by Virgil; apparently the old poet Naevius knew it two centuries earlier. It belongs to the Roman tradition rather than that launched by Virgil himself. There is no doubt that the poet or writer who contrived it showed that he was aware of the deepest moral requisites of his race. For this reason the tale deserves the attention of those who plan to analyze the attitude of the Romans toward love. It is significant, in effect, that the hero from whom Rome proudly traces its descent twice subordinated his heart's desires to his duty; that he chose, long before this celebrated saying became current: "to change his ideas rather than the pattern of his world." Yet he was the son of Venus! In order to remain faithful to his heritage, should he not have put the "rights" of passion above duty? Did he not owe his birth to the whim of a woman in love, or still better, the whim of the Goddess of Love herself?

But the Romans thought that a caprice of Venus could not be merely a vagary. Since Venus was a goddess, all her actions were related to the workings of divine providence. In giving herself to Anchises she carried out in the flesh the will of Fate, whereas the whim of a mortal in love is blind and subject to chance. Moreover Venus was just as capable of "playing politics" as Juno, the defender of legitimate marriage, the patron goddess of Queen Dido, and an enemy of Aeneas.

For once Venus and Juno cooperated; both drew Aeneas and Dido together. Juno figured that having put the Queen into the arms of Aeneas, he would be encumbered by her forever. As for Venus, she saw through the trick while continuing to play her part, but in private she mocked her rival's delusions. She knew the limits of her own domain. She realized that an amorous episode, especially one in which passion was satisfied, would not subjugate a man's will, especially if he were a Roman. She laughed at Dido's pangs of love, since she herself had experienced them. (Dido, who was a woman, not a goddess, might die of them—though more from anger and shame than from love.) Aeneas, who was of Venus' own blood lineage, would survive. And what does the life of one woman amount to when the stake is the founding of Rome?

This was Virgil's intention. As the poet and thinker no doubt most subtly responsive to the intimate exigencies of the Roman soul, he presented at the dawn of recorded history a story of love shared and then surmounted. He did not do this in order to comply with a prevailing literary mode, since all the poets of his century sang of love and made it the principal theme of their verses, but because he wished to embody in his hero the intrinsic conflict of a man torn between his will and his fleshly lust, between the "world pattern" and the imperious impulses of his own being, between the divine element that transcended them and the tender susceptibilities that prolonged them. He wanted also to show that that same hero, triumphing over his suffering, subordinated his love to his duty, in a way that came naturally to him.

In the first days there were many other love stories. Virgil abandoned his hero on the eve of his victory over the Italian barbarians, but the traditional accounts of the historians before Virgil give us an idea of the events that followed, or at least of those that were part of the legend.

In the realm of myth a whole series of dramatic episodes had come into existence, that supposedly took place in the city and in the palaces built by the Trojans as soon as they settled down in Latium. We do not know exactly how these legends grow. They have many features in common with Greek literature and especially Greek tragedy. Nevertheless they correspond to a given idea of romantic and family love that was convincing to the Romans, since they reconstructed the events of their earliest, most distant history around them.

King Latinus, who ruled over the natives when Aeneas arrived, had given him his daughter Lavinia in marriage. It was a purely political union. As frequently happened in legends having to do with Greek colonization, the marriage of a daughter—an only daughter!—of a native King with the leader of the foreign invaders was supposed to mark the beginning of an era of peace and collaboration between the two peoples, who until then had been hostile to each other. As son-in-law of the King, Aeneas quite naturally succeeded him as the leader of the issue of the numerous marriages which took place between Trojans and the inhabitants of Latium following that between Aeneas and Lavinia.

Thus the Romans agreed that a daughter could confer on her husband a kind of right to the kingdom—or, more usually, to her father's heritage. And in effect during the classical period we see sons and sons-in-law equally close to great personages, growing in stature in the shadow of the latter and benefiting from their political influence. If it is true, as we shall see, that a young woman after her marriage becomes part of her husband's household, the story of Aeneas and Lavinia will keep us from forgetting that the husband also will revolve around his father-in-law. The new ties of this type which he assumes will to a considerable extent weaken those binding him to the family in which he was born.

The marriage of Aeneas and Lavinia was not very happy. Roman tradition has it that she was jealous of her husband's past. News travels rapidly from one shore of the Mediterranean to another, and she heard of what had happened in Africa. She soon learned that Queen Dido had been abandoned and that she was dead. Womanlike, she suspected that all the tenderness and regret had not been wiped from Aeneas' heart. And when a fugitive appeared, and, declaring that she was Anna, sister of the unfortunate Dido, requested the hospitality of their home, Lavinia became a prey to the darkest suspicion.

Immediately a palace tragedy took place. As she could not prevent Aeneas from acting in a kindly way toward Anna, who had been obliged to flee Carthage after a disastrous war, she sought a way to get rid of her. Fortunately the gods were on the alert. Anna was warned in a dream to be on her guard against the pitfalls prepared by Lavinia. She fled in the middle of the night. In the morning, when the King's men went to look for her, they saw that her tracks led straight to the river Numicius and stopped there. At that moment a form rose from the water, revealing that the young woman had been married to a river god, and that she had become a nymph, to whom a cult might appropriately be dedicated.

The events that followed the death of Aeneas—or rather, his transfiguration, for a rumor spread that he had been taken up into heaven by the gods—suggested that all was far from well in the royal family. Lavinia was hostile to Ascanius, son of Aeneas and Creusa. To avoid her mute antagonism, Ascanius decided to leave Lavinium, and, going up the Tiber, founded the city of Alba Longa, which was to serve as the birthplace of the city of Rome.

Thus we see that the Romans liked to situate in the palace and in the very family of their most distant hero, conspiracies of jealousy, of the partition of power, in fact all the intrigues which can rend a noble house fighting against itself because it is the result of a succession of unions of different persons and peoples. It is significant that these tales grew up around the person of Lavinia, who is so neglected in Virgil's poem. But that does not mean that the poet himself did not want to put the figure of a passionate woman at the beginning of the story of the race.

To this end he chose Queen Amata, wife of King Latinus. She was much younger than her husband, and she had chosen as a son-in-law not Aeneas, the stranger she hated, but a young King, Turnus, who ruled over the Rutules. When Latinus tried to give Lavinia to Aeneas, Amata urged Turnus to take up arms. Latinus had to accept a war between his people, drawn into it by the Rutules and the Trojan immigrants. When Aeneas won, Amata, beside herself with fury, committed suicide. A symbol of violence, possessed by all the devils of anger and pride, she was the unconscious and pliable instrument of Juno's hatred.

The feelings that legend ascribed to Lavinia, and those that the Aeneid attributed to her mother Amata, if they were appropriate, perhaps, to the heroines of Greek tragedies, like Medea or Hecuba, are still more suitable to the Roman women whose personalities we will come to know. Considered officially simply as companions, they desired nonetheless to play a preponderating role in the exercise and transmission of power from which they were excluded by custom and by law. We look in vain in the legends of early Roman days for a feminine personality who was reasonable, whose heart was not motivated by passion, and, even more strongly than the desire to love, by political interest and the will to dominate. Resigned, it would appear, to accepting the husbands that had been chosen for them, once they became mothers they assumed all the authority they could grasp, manifested an indomitable will, intrigued without scruple, and fought without mercy. As soon as their ambitions, their dreams of power, were threatened or opposed in the slightest, their fury was unleashed.

Even Dido herself, of whose melancholy charm the commentators of Virgil have repeatedly spoken, thereby showing complete ignorance of what Virgil was driving at, subordinated her tender feelings to her will. She refused to comprehend the true vocation of the man she claimed to love. All she saw was the wreck of her hopes; she condemned herself to die on account of the blow to her pride. Finally, let us not forget, reading Book IV of the Aeneid, that the tender emotion that impels one person toward another, the sacrifice of one's life for the loved one and not against him, will not be found in the heroines of Virgil, but in the relationship of two men, two lovers, Nisus and Euryalus, one of whom was a hero and the other a fool.

The time had now come when Rome herself was to see the light of day at last. Rhea Silvia was the daughter of Numitor, King of Alba. But Numitor was a fallen King, since he had been dethroned by his brother Amulius. In the hope of wiping out the legitimate King's whole line, Amulius had condemned Rhea Silvia to perpetual chastity. According to some accounts she was bound by vows to the cult of Vesta, who required her to remain chaste during all the years when she might become a mother. According to others, she was locked up in prison, as Danaë was by her father Acrisios at Argos. Despite these precautions, Rhea came to experience love. It is sometimes alleged that her seducer was none other than Amulius himself. But more often the feat is attributed to the god Mars, who, observing the young girl at the river's edge, fell in love with her and approached her when she was alone.

Rhea gave birth to Romulus and Remus, the twins who founded Rome. Her eventual fate is uncertain. In some legends Amulius had her killed at the same time as he exposed the twins on the banks of the Tiber. In others, she survived, a prisoner like Antiope in the legend of Thebes, until the day when her sons, imitating Amphion and Zetos, rescued her, and, after overthrowing the usurper, restored her to her rightful position. Had she simply submitted to his violent assault? Had she tried to find her children who had been torn from her? No one bothered to find the answer to these questions. She had no more reality, no more density than those heroines of Greek comedy presented to us by Menander and those put on the boards by Plautus and Terence in imitation of him. Seduced before the rise of the curtain, they gave birth to a child toward the end of the play. Even if the whole plot hinges on the fate that awaits them, they themselves do not intervene in any way, and let themselves follow wherever destiny leads.

It was significant, in view of the idea that the Romans had of the place of love in the original city, that Romulus and Remus never really had a mother. It puts them straightway beyond the human pale. The poets are fond of repeating that they suckled only "the hard teats of a she-wolf."

To found a city was man's affair, as if feminine tenderness and love could be no more than a luxury belonging to times of peace. Thus Aeneas could have lived in loving respectability beside Dido had he not been responsible for an entire people, and had it not been his mission to translate the designs of divine providence into reality.

LOVE IN THE EARLY DAYS

Some misguided exponents of the Roman legends have from ancient times claimed that the famous she-wolf who took pity on the exposed twins and fed them with her milk was only a rustic beauty, not at all fierce, whose accommodating attitude to the local shepherds, on the contrary, had won her the appellation of she-wolf, a vulgar name for a prostitute.

This "rationalistic" explanation of a marvelous legend was conceived at a time when no one wanted to believe in miracles anymore, and the Christian writers adopted it with enthusiasm on the one hand and malice on the other. But they did not invent this invidious explanation. From historical times on, historians smirched the reputation of Acca Larentia, the foster-mother of Romulus and Remus, who became one of the innumerable minor divinities of the city. Her deification did not put her beyond the reach of calumny. It must be admitted that from Dido to Lavinia, from Rhea Silvia to Larentia, we find in the legends about the origins of Rome only furious females, insignificant silhouettes, or vulgar prostitutes. Noble disinterested love and serene tenderness are absent. One is inclined to suspect that the women are mentioned only because the men had to have mothers and wet nurses. Either the women are of no account, or, when they do intervene, it is to foment intrigues that lead to tragedies.

But everything abruptly changes with the accounts, apparently more authentic, that go back to the beginnings of the city, and that set out to describe the birth of Roman society rather than the exploits of heroes. This may be because these accounts are less gratuitous. They were invented to give an idea of the state of morals at that time. While it is possible and even easy to find among the Greek legends a thousand convincing models for the dramatic happenings at Lavinium and Alba, we would search the collections in vain for a myth similar to the story of the Sabines. This tale takes us deeper into the Roman soul. We discover one of the essential legends of the City-State.

Romulus' companions, who had collected from all parts of central Italy, had quickly filled the city. They were adventurous young men who until then had not found a niche in any nation. Some were marked for crime. Others were fleeing from importunate creditors. All were looking for a free and active way of life. The refuge established by Romulus on the Capitoline Hill promised impunity. Their muscular strength and feelings of mutual brotherliness were a guarantee of liberty. But they had no women. And the future of the city depended on the offspring of the first colonizers.

In the neighboring areas there were certainly villages in which young girls lived, but their fathers did not care to hand them over in marriage to the newcomers, whose past inspired anything but confidence. So Romulus and his men decided to obtain brides by force. They invited the inhabitants of the villages near Rome to a festival, a series of games to be held in honor of the gods. Everyone gathered in the great Circus, in the valley that formed a kind of natural amphitheatre between the Palatine and Aventine Hills, and provided a splendid track for racing. Just when everyone was watching the arena, Romulus' companions seized all the young girls present and carried them away. Their fathers, since they were guests, carried no arms. They had no other expedient but to invoke the gods, calling on them to witness this violation of human rights, and return home to prepare for revenge. The girls stayed in Rome, where they were distributed among the leading citizens.

Livy, who tells the legend—and who virtually believed it in all its details—emphasizes the despair and particularly the fears of the kidnapped girls. But, he adds, Romulus intervened personally, explaining to each one that the Romans had been forced to take violent action by their neighbors' pride. They would have liked nothing better than to obtain their fiancées through mutual agreement. Now that the latter were in Rome, they would be regarded as legitimate wives, not as captives; they would be accorded every possible mark of esteem, and would be shown every consideration. Deprived of their fatherland and their relatives, they would find both—anew—in Rome. Their husbands would treat them all the more tenderly since they had lost everything. Meanwhile, each man repeated the King's plea to his own companion, and caressed her fondly into the bargain. He tried to excuse his deed on the grounds of the ardor of his love. The Sabine women (for the majority of the kidnapped girls were from Sabine villages) did not resist these eloquent and tender entreaties. Their anger was appeased.

Beneath this idyll, adorned as time went on by the imaginings of historians and poets—who sometimes put it on the stage—there may lie a basis of fact. Raids in force from one village to another to capture women were not unknown in primitive society. It is possible that the first inhabitants of Rome indulged in such practices. It is also possible that this is a legend that perpetuated the almost obliterated memory of a very ancient rite. But the intrinsic reality which it conceals is not fundamentally very important: the Romans, although they attached a certain historical significance to it, looked upon it primarily as a myth, a representation justifying a whole philosophy of marriage. The idea they had of the relationship between man and wife was founded on it. Thus the Romans always had the story of the Sabine women in mind—a subjugation carried out with violence, ending in tenderness.

But the account did not stop there, and its epilogue was no less instructive. Back in their villages, the fathers of the Sabine women put on mourning. Crazed with grief and anger, they sent a delegation to King Titus Tatius, the ruler of the Sabine nation, and persuaded him to take up arms against the Romans, his neighbors so lacking in integrity and respect for law. Soon a strong Sabine army spread out on the plain of the Forum, between the Capitol and the Palatine Hill. The companions of Romulus armed themselves in turn, and the battle started. It was a desperate struggle. At one time the Sabines had the upper hand, at another, the Romans. There were moments when the very existence of Rome was in danger, and Jupiter had to intervene personally to strike a balance between the contestants. Finally, during a lull, a pitiable procession could be seen advancing between the lines. It was made up of the young women who were the innocent cause of the hostilities. With their hair streaming and their garments torn, as befitting supplicants whose destiny was at stake, they begged their fathers and their husbands in turn to desist. Overwhelmed at the unexpected eruption in their midst of those whom they loved most in the world, both sides realized that the war was not only criminal but pointless. An armistice was immediately concluded, after which a treaty was drawn up in due and proper terms: the two peoples decided henceforth to live as one, and to move the seat of government to Rome. The two Kings were to collaborate (as the consuls were to do later), and the population of the new state would be divided into new units, thirty *curiae,* each named after one of the leading Sabine women.

Once again it is hard to tell exactly what reality was hidden behind this legend. No doubt it depicts in dramatic fashion the conflict which might befall newly married women. Perhaps there is also embedded in it a nostalgic reminder of the dual origin of the Roman people. Whatever the meaning of the legend may be, it is a striking fact that the Romans were glad to give women a privileged place and role in the development of the City-State. This tendency alone suffices to show the fundamental difference between Roman society and that described in the Homeric poems. Perhaps at Mycenae women played an important role, but their influence remained a purely personal one. In Rome the entire sex was officially attributed an essential function—and not just the one for which nature intended it, that is, fertility. The fact that so many honors were heaped on women may surprise those who tend to concern themselves only with the legal status of Roman women in ancient times. The birth of Rome, in fact, marked the accession of women to a recognized position, and initiated the recognition of values that were essentially quite foreign to the heroes of the Greek world.

If Romulus' companions kidnapped women, it was because they wanted to ensure that Rome would outlast them. Force can found cities; energy and warlike courage can make them prosperous,

LOVE IN THE EARLY DAYS

but only love can endow them with immortality. That is why the legend of the Sabine women appears to have the force of a "second founding of Rome." Romulus, on the Palatine Hill, could trace the outline of a town, build walls around it, and heap up riches in it, but the City-State as such began only with the Sabine women becoming reconciled to their captivity. Without that, Romulus' achievement could not have endured; their acquiescence alone could anchor Rome to its foundation in terra firma forever.

The Roman mentality, as was its habit, tended to translate this development into legal terms. The legend says that the Romans, when they signed the treaty with the Sabines, guaranteed their wives the conditions of an honorable existence. They would be spared all work of a menial nature; they would have no other tasks than to bring up their children and spin. All the rest would be taken care of by servants and slaves. The basis for the relationship between husbands and wives would be established by contract from now on. It is surprising that its terms were not those usually inflicted by a conqueror. The husbands themselves, in a spirit of gratitude and respect, undertook before the gods to treat with kindness those who had agreed to share their lives.

If the legend of the Sabine women was a key to the true condition of Roman wives, it is nothing more in the eyes of modern historians than the image projected on the past of a state of affairs that they try to explain in other terms. They point out that in the beginning Roman society was influenced by its Etruscan surroundings, and that many traces of matriarchal customs survived among the Etruscans. Even in Rome the history of the early days is not free from them. Thus the succession to the throne was apparently carried on through the female line. Numa Pompilius, who came after Titus Tatius and Romulus, was Tatius' son-in-law, not his son. Later, it would seem that Ancus Martius was a grandson of Numa by way of his mother. While Livy and the Roman tradition in general indicate that their kings were elected, it is still a fact that the choice of the Romans fell twice on descendants, through the female line, of the preceding king. And one cannot fail to point out, either, that Tanaquil, wife of the elder Tarquinius, played an important part not only in her husband's rise to power, but also, after his death, to impose on the citizenry the young Servius, a slave born in her home, who was designated by a number of signs and wonders as the favorite of the gods. Tanaquil was surely of Etruscan origin; in the royal household she seemed to be a veritable priestess, interpreting the will of the gods. It may be that she owed these faculties to the traditions of her race, always concerned with divination and heedful of portents. But it is nonetheless striking that it was a woman who possessed this occult knowledge, and used it with undisputed authority. Truth to tell, Tanaquil had no official status; her prophecies had no standing outside her own home, but the men of her family did not hesitate to adopt them, and to act in accordance with their advice. Finally, through their intermediary, she influenced the acts of the state as a whole. And historians have not shown the slightest trace of resentment at the importance of this role played by a woman.

But the influence of the Etruscan world was certainly not alone in imposing and disseminating an almost religious respect for women in Roman society. A very old legend cites an ancient seeress named Carmenta as one of the first inhabitants of the spot where Rome was to rise. She was probably not Etruscan. According to some traditions she was the mother of Evander, a hero exiled from Arcady, who came to the shores of the Tiber seeking asylum at the time of the Trojan War. She it was, they say, who chose the place where they would settle, a "happy" site where the gods were favorably inclined toward man. In her youth, the accounts go on to tell, she was not called Carmenta, but Niostrate, or Themis, or perhaps Tamandra, which are Greek names. She acquired the name of Carmenta in her old age when she had demonstrated prophetic powers—for the name is probably derived from the Latin word for incantations or "charms," and the inspired chants of prophets. Whatever one may think of the legend itself and the Greek elements that are part of it, one main fact emerges:

The Romans admitted that a woman had been the first, at the foot of the Capitol, to interpret the divine oracles. And the name Carmenta was held in such reverence that it was bestowed on one of the gates of the oldest Roman citadel. In the middle of the Classic period, two altars were devoted to the cult of Carmenta.

All those legends tend to prove that according to the most authentic Roman traditions, women were accorded a kind of religious veneration. Far from being excluded from the religious edifice, they acted as its inspired curators. Many other examples come to mind outside Rome: Pythia at Delphos, or Veleda, or those women on the edge of the Sahara who had long held the secret of sacred inscriptions and rites.

The Etruscan influence, which cannot be denied, fell on fertile ground. There is nothing to prove that the Latin or Sabine social groups existing before the formation of the Roman City-State did not accord a privileged status to women. This would go far to explain the reverence with which they were treated as far back in Roman history as it is possible to go.

It is true that other elements intervene to cloud the image we think we perceive. Roman religion is the result of a highly complex synthesis. The official cults tended to minimize the sacred role of women. Moreover the growth and the solidifying judicial patterns in the City-State helped obscure their real function to such a degree that modern historians seem to take pleasure in insisting that, to a Roman, a woman was hardly a person at all, and was in any case an inferior being who had to be kept under tutelage. While this may be the impression given by the oldest laws, it is not the conclusion to be drawn by simply examining the legends. The Roman woman was tenderly loved by her husband and her children; she was respected by her servants. An aura of mystery always surrounded her. Faith in her intuitions and the omens to be found in her dreams and even in her most innocent remarks made conjugal love a matter of veneration and even a kind of fearful humility as far as the husband was concerned. It must be admitted that all this was sporadic and not always easy to discover. The indications were often ambiguous, and one would be tempted to think each one an individual instance, if it were not for the legends. The latter are a proof of the universal validity of certain feelings, certain tendencies which constitute—and can be called—the racial unconscious. Can one imagine more fertile soil for these latent, unacknowledged feelings than the highly nuanced conversations that take place between a husband and wife, or a mother and her children? In a thousand ways, custom and individual preferences inevitably softened the rigid and necessarily impersonal precepts of the legal experts. Legends are an antidote to legal formulas, showing, as if on a stage, relationships between persons in definite situations, giving them a density, a specific character. The jurist, endlessly pursuing a reality that keeps ahead of him and always eludes him, cannot hope to achieve this result.

Two other love stories are to be found in the early legends. Both are also myths that substantiate the overall design we are trying to trace.

The first is the story of Tarpeia. When Titus Tatius' Sabines attacked Romulus' Romans, who were guilty of having kidnapped their daughters, the citadel of the Capitol was defended by a certain Tarpeius, whose daughter was named Tarpeia. We are not told who her mother was, nor how the Romans, who had to seek wives outside their city, had been able to raise families just the same, but such discrepancies do not bother the makers of myths. All we are told is that Tarpeia was with her father in the citadel when war broke out, and that when the Sabines arrived her curiosity was aroused by the enemy soldiers camped on the plain. Among them was a noble knight, none other than King Tatius. He was young and remarkably handsome in his plumed helmet and brightly colored armor: to make Tarpeia fall in love with him, nothing more was needed. From that moment on all she thought of was how to satisfy her desire. Her country's safety did not count, if only she could become Tatius' wife! Secretly climbing down to the enemy encampment, she entered into conversation with the King, and offered to turn over the citadel to him. She would show him a hidden path, and would unlock a gate, if the Sabines would give her "what they had on their left arms," by which she meant their bracelets and gold rings. She assumed as well that the King would make her his wife out of gratitude. How could he fail to be attracted by this siren who betrayed her father and her country for his sake? Inspired by a combination of love and coy cupidity, she pictured a happy future—the future of an uncomplicated girl who could see no further than a "good marriage."

Titus Tatius feigned to agree to the bargain. He would give her what she asked. Faithful to her promise, Tarpeia led the Sabine scouts up the concealed path to the citadel. The other warriors followed. Soon a large band had collected on the plateau in the darkness. The moment came to begin the attack. Tatius muttered that he wanted to give her the price of her treachery; forewarned, his men hurled their shields of wood and leather at her, dashing her to the ground and killing her. Who could pity her? Had she not received what the Sabines carried "on their left arms"?

Centuries later a pile of half-rotted armor marked the spot where Tatius had refused Tarpeia's love and punished her. It was the infamous rock from which traitors were hurled to their death.

As we read it in the writings of Propertius, the legend of Tarpeia evolved over a long period during which later variations and literary adornments were added to already existing folklore. Propertius made Tarpeia a tragic heroine, a Phaedra, struggling against what she realized was a guilty passion and finally giving way to it, while recognizing that she was damned. These are subtleties that did not exist in the original tale but that do not obscure its meaning. Whatever justification there may be for the legend of Tarpeia—crumbling armor, bloodstained weapons rusting away, trophies dedicated to Vulcan or some other vengeful god, or simply a spot haunted by the memory of some demon—or any other source that hairsplitting modern historians have not been able to ferret out—the story holds a warning for Romans: only men know how to be loyal to their country. Too often women's hearts are at the mercy of the seducer. Tarpeia is the soul mate and sister of Scylla, who, at another time and in another place, Megara, in Greece, betrayed her father for love of the Cretan King Minos. A girl who chooses her lover of her own free will follows only the dictates of her passion, which may bring major catastrophes on her country, her family, and, ultimately, herself.

We do not know just how sincere Tarpeia may have been. But her fidelity to her love should not have prevailed against that other and more essential fidelity owed to the established order and to respect for divine law, which attached the highest value to the preservation of the City-State. The story of Tarpeia is simply a particularly dramatic example of the dangerously criminal nature of an immoderate passion. Titus Tatius, the least romantic, and, like Minos in the story of Scylla, the most just of kings, could only have been horrified by the offer of Tarpeia's love. One may consider it a strange moral law that permitted the Sabine King to accept what was of value in the betrayal, while requiring him to punish cruelly the person who sacrificed everything for him. But to accuse Tatius of hypocrisy would be to make the serious mistake of disregarding one of the most profound religious reactions of the Roman mentality. Any means could be used to destroy the enemy; the state of war implies that very condition: the suspension of all justice. But Tarpeia's act was monstrous, it was what the Romans called a *portentum*—failing to be in accord with the "world order," like the birth of a creature whose body does not conform to the laws of its kind.

Thus, like the parricides who were sewn into a sack and thrown into the deepest water to be wiped from the face of the earth, or the vestal virgins who broke their vows and were walled up in a cave, Tarpeia herself was buried beneath a pile of shields which cut her off from the light of day and concealed her from the eye of Jupiter Fidius, patron god of fidelity, whose abode was the Capitol.

Propertius, like a clever lawyer, attributed a line of reasoning to the young girl that justified her actions in his own eyes. He imagined Tarpeia saying to herself that her marriage to the Sabine King would put an end to his anger against Rome, and become one of the best guarantees of peace. But Propertius well knew that this argument concealed a sophism. The miracle that the Sabine women performed on the battlefield could not be accomplished by Tarpeia. The passion that ruled her, and which she obeyed to the exclusion of everything else, denied her the right to act as an intermediary. It was a destructive emotion that could not in the long run have a beneficial result. The situation of legitimate wives is quite different, since their power comes from their submission to the world pattern. The Roman conscience does not forbid what modern writers would call "the right to love." But this right—that is not in itself based on desire, for desire is lawless and destructive—begins with the fullness of satisfaction. A contented love, by the very strength of the happiness it engenders, is productive, and can be naturally integrated into the world order.

The legend of Lucretia, which also goes back to the early days of Rome, has a similar moral. It is the story, told by Livy, of the violation of a woman's chastity. That act of seduction aroused such indignation among the Romans that they dethroned their King, whose son was the guilty party.

Sextus Tarquinius, son of Tarquinius Superbus, was taking part in the siege of the capital of the Rutules. One evening the noble young warriors sat around discussing the virtue of the wives they had left behind them at home. Each one boasted so emphatically of the faithfulness of his own wife that they all decided to get on their horses and go back to see what was what. In Rome, they found the women of the palace enjoying themselves at a banquet with friends. Going from there to Collatium where one of the group, Tarquinius Collatinus, lived, they found the situation quite different: Lucretia, his young wife, was sitting with her servants before the hearth, spinning wool. When her husband and the nobles accompanying him arrived she made every effort to receive them hospitably. A meal was cooked up on the spur of the moment, and the evening passed pleasantly enough. But Sextus Tarquinius was overcome by a guilty passion the instant he saw Lucretia. So much virtue and so much innocence appealed to his baser instincts. He said nothing at the time, and the following morning returned to camp with the others. But a few days later he returned to Collatium. When he arrived at the young woman's home she received him without distrust, offered him the hospitality of the house, and had a bed prepared in the guest chamber. But as soon as everyone in the house was asleep, Sextus Tarquinius crept stealthily into Lucretia's room. Standing beside her bed, sword in hand, he woke her with the words: "Silence! I am Sextus Tarquinius. I am armed. One word from you, and you will die!"

The young woman implored him to leave her alone. Then Sextus began to speak of love; he tried to win her over by every possible means. Finally he threatened her with a dishonorable death. If she continued to resist, he would kill her. He would then strangle the first slave he could lay his hands on and stretch his naked body out on the bed beside her, so that everyone would think she had been caught in the very act of committing adultery in the most ignominious circumstances, and given the punishment she deserved. The contemplation of this horrible possibility finally overcame Lucretia's resistance. She submitted, and the victorious Sextus left the house before dawn.

As soon as she was alone, Lucretia woke her maidservants, and sent messengers to her husband and her father. Both hastened to her side. She told them the story of her dishonor, and while they tried to console her, saying that she was not to blame in any way, she drew a knife from her bosom and plunged it into her heart.

In this case too, passion was destructive of the existing order. It caused the death not only of the ravisher's victim, but his own, as the result of the political repercussions of the crime.

The Roman people became so indignant at this deed of violence that they deposed the King, whose son had given in to his illicit passion. That day the Republic was born. This does not mean that the seduction of Lucretia was in itself the cause—more or less accidental, as far as politics was concerned—of the King's banishment. What really happened was that the Romans were convinced that Sextus Tarquinius' crime was the inevitable result of the monarchical system. It seemed to them that a regime that put absolute power in the hands of one man inevitably aroused in him, and in all those who benefited from his privileges, a contempt for what everyone held most sacred: his wife's love, his self-respect, and the sanctity of his home. Monarchy, degenerating into tyranny, was sure to founder in violent deeds of disordered passion—the curse laid by the gods on mortals guilty of impiety.

But the story of Lucretia, clear as the moral it illustrates may be, has still another meaning. The young woman, a heroine so far as wifely infidelity was concerned, would not listen to the voices of her father and her husband, who quite reasonably excused what she called her sin. She did not admit any extenuating circumstances. Her body was defiled, her blood polluted. That body must perish, that blood must be shed, even though the soul remained pure.

The strictness shown by this Roman wife—which may seem excessive to us, not to say barbaric—can be explained by her deep conviction that her "sin" was a physical taint that could never be wiped out, separating her from her husband forever and making her unworthy to go back to her place in her home, now ruined. She was convinced that the act of love was valid in the absolute sense, at least for the woman, whose body and soul were held in thrall by it forever. Sextus Tarquinius, by forcing her to submit to his passionate advances, prevented her from keeping faith with her husband. It was of little importance that she was not willing. In her opinion the flesh alone, even without the soul, implicated the entire human being. Nothing was further from her mind than the concept of Platonic love which was to develop later in Rome, and which, there as elsewhere, made possible all sorts of sophistries and compromises by subordinating the body to the soul.

Nor was Lucretia the only person to hold such opinions. For a long time, as we shall see, the Romans instinctively refused to admit that a woman could belong to several men in succession, even when, liberated from her marriage by death or divorce, she had a legal right to do so. The mark of the flesh could not be expunged; it spelled eternal bondage.

Now this is highly significant. Since Roman days, we are familiar with other moral codes that consider the act of love a sin. When she yielded her body to the embraces of her husband, Lucretia, to be sure, did not believe that she defiled her body. She was united in accordance with divine and human laws. Morally, the union was impeccable.

The act of love, however, was not something neutral in itself. Under different conditions, in opposition to these same laws, it became monstrous. The idea of sin was not yet implicit in it, but Rome was moving down the road that led there, to the extent that the Romans admitted that the physical union of two bodies could transform an entire being and place it in permanent jeopardy.

This feeling persisted indefinitely in the soul of Rome, even in those times when Romans seemed to be completely liberated from the ancient obligations of the race.

In Roman eyes legitimate marriage always had a well-nigh sacramental significance, inherent in its nature: it became part of the world pattern, and individual wills were powerless to change it.

That was what Sextus Tarquinius could not understand. A King's son, by birth beyond the reach of the law, he could not curb his unruly passion.

Lucretia and Tarpeia were opposites: the first was the personification of virtue, the second, of shamelessness. But love brought death to both, because each one's being was drawn into a tragic drama of uncontrolled passion.

Thus we see that indications of the Romans' fundamental uneasiness as regards the love instinct can be found in their legends. Their anxiety was all the greater since the love instinct cannot be condemned on an absolute basis, being the very manifestation of life. So the history of the sentiment of love in Roman life will continue to reveal this ambiguity to the end. Sometimes it will be indulgently viewed as the joyous impulse of a vigorous young race, the voluptuous expansion of the human soul. Then again we will find someone yielding to it with a quasi-religious fervor or even with fear, like a votary allowed to participate in mysteries that he expects will involve the deepest part of his being, but the significance of which he does not entirely understand.

II

LOVE AND RELIGION

THE Romans liked to call themselves the most religious of all peoples; they acknowledged and honored more gods than any other race in the world. Thus they could hardly be unaware of the sacred nature of the love instinct, which could transform human beings and draw them out of themselves. Its power, experienced equally by man and every other living creature, held all nature in thrall to its laws. It is not surprising therefore that love had its own gods, its own rites, its own magic. The cult of the gods and the scrupulous observance of rites whose origin was lost in the dark night of the past—all this had as its aim at times to develop and exalt the creative forces of love to the maximum, but at others to harness what was lawless in it, and make that element serve the common weal of the City-State.

In the religion of classical times, the period we know best, thanks to written accounts and other evidence of all kinds, faintly discernible traces of those beliefs and rites frequently survived. This or that observance of a magical character in Ciceronian or Augustan days was nothing more than a survival from folklore. We would have neither record nor recollection of them if antiquarians, eager to collect curious items from the early days, had not devoted a few lines to them in works which unfortunately have come down to us only in fragments. Often too the Christian controversialists, looking for proofs of the immorality or absurdity of the pagan religion, carefully handed down details whose archaic and even primitive character tends to cast doubts on their good faith.

Understandably it is difficult to reconstitute a well-ordered and

LOVE AND RELIGION

perfectly intelligible whole starting from such inadequate materials. It is hard, for instance, to estimate the importance of a given rite; there is a risk of making serious mistakes in perspective when trying to fit each fragment into the aggregate. But what can be reconstituted of the truly ancient "religion of love," in spite of all these difficulties, is not without interest in itself. And especially in Rome the past weighed heavily on the present. The distant early period, even half forgotten, survived because it helped develop Roman sensibility; because it composed a kind of nucleus around which religious forms crystallized, which might otherwise have been quite different.

These archaic vestiges are to be found just about everywhere: in both official and popular religious forms, in marriage ceremonies, and especially in the cults of which women were the devotees. This was only natural, since women had long been considered the chief custodians of the life-giving element of fertility. The function of their half of the population of the City-State was to ensure the survival and continuity of the whole race.

On the Velia, one of the earliest of the Roman hills on which buildings were put up, there once existed a bizarre house of worship whose god was represented in the form of a penis. This god bore the strange name of Mutunus Tutunus. We know of him only from a fragment from Festus, the grammarian, and from four or five allusions to him in the writings of Tertullian, Saint Augustine, Arnobius, and Lactantius. And what they have to tell is far from clear. Apparently up to the time of Augustus, at least, women wearing the *toga praetexta,* went at certain times to crown the image of Mutunus Tutunus with flowers. Who were they? Probably priestesses, as their antique costumes seem to indicate, and married women, no doubt, carrying out what were surely propitiatory rites in the name of all the wives in the City-State.

But Mutunus Tutunus was not to be found in the sanctuary of Velia alone. It is said that he had a place of honor in the bedrooms of ordinary citizens. The day they were married, young brides were supposed to sit on his image, as if they were dedicating the first fruits of their virginity to him. Unfortunately we don't know whether the usage was practiced by everyone, or whether it was a custom going back to early times that no young husband of a later day would have dared require his wife to observe. Possibly this indecent gesture represents the last vestiges of a rite aimed at protecting the husband from the magic dangers he might have incurred by deflowering his wife. There is abundant evidence of such beliefs in the malignant powers of virginity. Anthropologists have observed them in many primitive societies. There are examples of the ritual substitution of another woman for the wife during the wedding night.

There are, of course, other traces of phallic cults. Mutunus Tutunus was not the only example in early-day Roman religion. Thus the vestal virgins, priestesses who acted as custodians of the penates, the Roman household gods, those mysterious talismans which it was a crime to look at, also venerated a representation of the male organ in the temple of which they were in charge. Some writers have assumed that this image in the heart of the Capitol corresponded to the "genius," revered at each domestic hearth as the symbol of the potency of the master of the house. To substantiate this similarity, they cite a weird old tale that was part of the group of legends having to do with King Servius Tullius.

The story goes that in the palace of Tarquin the Elder a serving maid named Ocrisia had intercourse with a penis that mysteriously rose from the ashes on the hearth, and that Servius Tullius was the offspring of this union. This legend, which Livy does not pass on, no doubt because of its peculiar obscenity, helps keep alive the memory of a time when at least one of the household daemons symbolized virility.

The belief in the magic powers of the phallus, which was called *fascinus*, lasted a long time among the common people, especially in the country. It can still be found, like a warning, on the doorsill of several houses in Pompeii, where its obvious function was to protect the dwelling from the evil eye. In the fields, peasants set it up to protect the crops. The same symbol even found a place on the chariots of conquerors, showing the same faith in the beneficent properties of an organ that seemed to be above all "the site of life." The phallus was considered the most effective talisman against malevolent powers, against everything that prevented or hindered the growth and felicitous flowering of all living things: humans, animals, and plants. There was no suggestion of shame attached to it.

From which it should not be inferred that persons were not modest about exposing their bodies. While, at the bath, men were not disturbed by going naked into the steam rooms, they did so only in the presence of strangers. Fathers avoided bathing before their sons or sons-in-law. At all times and in all periods indecent remarks could not be addressed to well-bred persons without causing embarrassment. Custom decreed nevertheless that phalli could be freely worn in public. No doubt its very familiarity prevented people from being shocked.

But the *fascinus* had more properties than warding off spells, which was more or less negative. Among the peasants it became the object of a cult affiliated with the *Liber Pater,* who was at first essentially the god of germination—"he who assures birth and growth." It would seem that the phallus was even a symbol of the god himself in rustic festivals of which Saint Augustine has given a description. "On the days devoted to the celebration of Liber," he wrote, "a replica of this shameful organ was placed with much pomp on a chariot and taken through the countryside, from crossing to crossing, to the city itself. In the city of Lavinium, a whole month was dedicated to Liber. During this time everyone used the most obscene language possible every day, until the phallus was carried in solemn procession across the Forum and put in its sanctuary. A mother from one of the most respected families was then required to place a wreath on it. This was, it seems, the way to obtain Liber's help for a successful sowing, and ward off the evil eye from the fields."

At first the god of all procreation, Liber's attributes became progressively more specialized. At an early stage his identity merged with that of the Greek Dionysus, whose cult and mysterious rites also used the phallus as a talisman. In the formal, well-regulated religion of Republican Rome, he became the protector of vines and vineyards. But—a throwback to ancient times—it was on his feast day, March 17, that Roman youths assumed the toga of manhood, signifying that they could now found a family in their turn and become members of the class of *patres*. In the countryside the archaic form of the Liber cult remained active much longer. Virgil recounts that even in his day, during the *Liberalia*, the peasants gathered in the fields to drink, sing, dance, and make dirty cracks at one another's expense. Obscene language had a ritual function for them as it did for the city-dwellers of Lavinium described by Saint Augustine; it possessed magic powers capable of stimulating nature's forces and helping the consummation of the mysterious processes of the vegetable world. The remarks bandied about grew into more or less ritual rhythmic epithets called "Fescennine verses," which the spectators addressed to those participating in wedding processions or victory celebrations.

On these solemn occasions decency was not good form. Ribaldry of expression was part of the rite. Like the *fascinus* itself, it warded off evil, and stimulated the fertility of newly married couples, intensifying the mysterious forces on which the success of the marriage ceremony depended.

When, toward the end of the third century B.C., the religion of Dionysus spread through Italy, and sects of Bacchantes were organized in many places devoted to his cult, the peasants were quick to adopt these rites so like their own. And the "scourge," as the new religion—which differed to such an extent from their ancestral doctrines—was called by the Roman senators, rapidly overran the country. Moreover, not only did Dionysus promise his votaries happiness in this world, but salvation after death. Such a combination of mysticism and sensuality strongly attracted

LOVE AND RELIGION

people attached to the land, who felt that the mysteries of reproduction were somehow divine in character. The priests serving the new god did not ask them to renounce their own observances; they also contributed insights clarifying the peasants' rites, and giving a mystical permanence to what had only been intuited until then.

There is a dearth of exact information as to what really went on in these Dionysiac "cells." It is said that zealots of both sexes took part in orgies, which is probable. But it is also maintained that these debauches sometimes went as far as the commission of crimes, and that human sacrifices were frequent. Many religions in the process of formation have been the object of such calumnies. Whatever the truth may be, a scandal occurred in the year 186 B.C. that shook all Italy.

The Bacchantes had reached Rome. Bacchanalian rites were permitted at the foot of the Aventine Hill in the sacred grove of the old Roman divinity *Stimula*. At night the disheveled Bacchantes could be seen running to the river with flaming torches, which, report has it, they plunged into the water and pulled out still flaming. And it is recorded that a sinister disclosure was made to the Consul by a courtesan named Hispala Fecenia. Her young lover, Aebutius, she said, was in great danger. His mother, who had remarried, wanted to be rid of him, and planned to have him assassinated by the votaries of Dionysus in the course of a sacred orgy. Having been herself initiated into the Bacchanalian mysteries, Fecenia knew of the dangers incurred. She begged the magistrates to take such steps as might be necessary to save the innocent youth.

The senate was called together forthwith. The two young persons were placed under police protection, and an investigation was begun. Accusations were collected; they were even provoked. Priests of Dionysus were arrested, all nocturnal gatherings were forbidden, and all devotees of the god who did not report to the authorities before a certain date were automatically outlawed. Summary trials began to be held, which resulted in executions. A veritable reign of terror broke out in Rome and other Italian cities. The senatorial decree was distributed everywhere; a copy, engraved on a bronze tablet, has fortunately been preserved. The celebration of the Bacchanalian rites was prohibited. The senators, in order not to risk suppressing traditional, legitimate observances, allowed some exceptions. But in no instance could more than five persons take part in the ceremony—two men and three women. The Bacchantes could no longer bind themselves by an oath of fealty; they could neither possess a common fund nor constitute a hierarchy among themselves. And even for these restricted observances, the permission of the senate was invariably required.

It can be guessed from the terms of the decree that the repressive measures were motivated by political no less than by religious considerations. It was feared, obviously, that a kind of secret society was in the process of formation, a confraternity branching out in every direction, eluding the control of the magistrates, and capable of arousing the religious fanaticism of the peasants. The cult of Dionysus continued, but tempered, and stripped of its orgiastic excesses. In this way it grew more spiritual and also became more intimate: the suppression of the priests had reduced it to an expression of personal devotion. But little by little the god banned by the senators in 186 B.C. regained his followers. This time, however, they were not "little people." The elite of Rome, attracted by the Dionysiac mysticism which in the Orient passed for an official religion, was glad to take over its symbols and its myths. From the beginning of the Empire on, Dionysus was everywhere: statues of him and his companions, symbolizing the fecundating forces of nature, were placed in many gardens. Scenes from the Dionysiac legend appeared on the walls of private houses, especially at Pompeii. The famous frescoes of the "Villa of Mysteries" almost certainly represented an initiation into the rites that revealed the secret of love and life.

One of Bacchus' companions had, to be sure, escaped suppression: the god Priapus, who originated in Lampsacus in Asia

Minor. He, too, as his enormous penis showed, was a daemon of fertility, and had been chosen by the Italian peasants to replace the ancient *fascinus* as protector of their fields and vineyards. Every garden had its Priapus, carved from a tree trunk and daubed with bright red paint. It was supposed to ward off evil, and frighten birds away. It could even be used as a club by the gardener to drive off thieves. This obscene god was rarely taken seriously in the gardens; the tributes paid him were usually tinged with irony. Nevertheless it could be observed that Priapus, in spite of his grotesque aspect, was sometimes the object of a quasi-mystical cult. This explains why he is to be found near tombs, where his presence testifies to faith in resurrection. "Priapus, the abode of life and death," reads one inscription, and this is not the extravagant idea of some zealot, but the widespread conviction that life and death are but interdependent aspects of the same truth. This was the doctrine already expounded by Socrates in *Phaedo*. It originated in beliefs deeply rooted in the soil of Greece. In Rome, too, the daemons of life could often be observed exercising their sway over death. Thus the religion of the people instinctively apprehended the connection between love and death that was to be the preoccupation of many latter-day poets, even in Rome.

This religious cult based on virility, primordial and vital as it seems, was not the only expression of the respect and fear experienced by the Romans face to face with the mystery of existence. The sexual life of women also had its daemons, which held it in thrall. The *genius* of the paterfamilias was balanced by the Juno of the mother. There are fewer indications of the importance of her worship in the home, but it is thought that she is represented by one of the two serpents frequently found near the family altar of each house, especially at Pompeii. On the other hand, while the *genius* has never become identified with one of the great gods, the Juno of each matron has in a sense been absorbed by the goddess of the same name, the wife of Jupiter. It is as if the official religion needed to regulate and assimilate the cult of the individual femininity of mothers, while leaving that of male fertility outside its jurisdiction. There were festivities especially for matrons, such as the *Matronalia,* celebrated March 1 by all married women. Others, like the *Nonae Caprotinae,* celebrated on July seventh, had an archaic flavor that affirmed their antiquity: goat and fig tree played important roles. These rites, which included simulated fights, and such disguises as servants wearing their mistresses' clothes, suggest ancient magic influences. These were associated with the giving of milk, and were doubtless intended to stimulate this function as far as mothers were concerned, and at the same time to protect the latter against its dangers by substituting other women, of less "value," during the critical period.

Each year the Consul's house was the scene of an esoteric celebration, participated in by married women in the presence of the vestal virgins. The divinity honored on that day, toward the beginning of December, was known as *bona dea,* "the good goddess." This ritualistic appellation concealed her true name, which is unknown to us. Men were excluded under the threat of the most dire penalties. It was also forbidden, during these celebrations, to bring into the house the smallest sprig of myrtle or to utter the word "wine." The wine used for the sacrificial libation was called "milk," and the receptacles holding it were called "jars of honey."

To explain these eccentricities it was said that "the good goddess" once married the god Faunus, and that the latter, to punish her for having drunk wine in secret, beat her with myrtle branches so cruelly that she died. And in effect, the taboos that are associated with the cult of the *bona dea* are understandable if one remembers that women were forbidden to drink wine up to a fairly late date, and that myrtle was the favorite plant of Venus, the goddess of love. The *bona dea* was a symbol of the virtues matrons were expected to possess, that is, all those that might be lost under the influence of wine or Venus. No doubt the City-

State wanted to stimulate fertility among mothers, and wished to ensure their coming under the protection of well-disposed divinities. But it also reveals its fear that these same gods might encourage the votaries of the *bona dea* to put the very powers it wished to encourage to immoderate uses.

Rome seems at all times to have been caught between two dangerous possibilities: if the fertility cult was neglected, the well of life might run dry, or—and this was no less alarming a prospect—the performance of these rites might provoke outbursts of lawlessness and fanaticism. The fright of the senators at the outbreak of the Bacchanalian scandals is not an isolated example. Stories told of Venus, patroness of love, are instructive in this respect.

At an early stage the physical traits of the Greek goddess Aphrodite were bestowed on Venus. But the older goddess Venus was apparently quite different from this "daughter of the earth and sky," who originated in the Greek world from a complex synthesis in which Asiatic influences predominated. To tell the truth, modern historical writers on Roman religion do not agree on the character of the older Venus or even on her role in the early days. For a long time she was admired for having started out as a peasant, a rural divinity personifying the charm of spring and orchards in blossom, exercising her sway over vegetable gardens and other fertile spots. After that, according to these authorities, the followers of this rustic Venus attained a higher conception: that she embodied one of the primitive forces of nature, whose power was sometimes brutally exercised on humans. But today writers agree in rejecting this hypothesis.

It is hardly logical to assume that the cult of Venus originated in the religious concept of fertility in general, and did not arrive at human love until it had traveled a long way. Would it not be more sensible to think that the attributes of the goddess evolved in the opposite direction—starting with what is human, and gradually extending to all living things? Is not the power of love felt directly by man in his own heart and in his veins? And does he not have a spontaneous tendency to project what he learns from his own experience beyond himself? To discover Venus in the outer world is to have found her in his own soul.

Another explanation of the Roman Venus has recently been put forward. It is asserted that the goddess was apparently not a daemon of fertility at first. She was the personification of an infinitely more subtle spiritual essence: the magic efficacy of prayer, which alone can bring man the blessing of the gods. Originally, it would seem, Venus was a kind of universal intermediary between humans and gods, obtaining for her faithful devotees the energizing power of the supernatural.

This ingenious assumption can be backed up by sound arguments, but it is too abstract to permit of conclusive proof. One cannot but wonder whether the most distant ancestors of the Roman people, no matter how much talent they had for subtle theological speculation, could spontaneously have deified the force controlling sexual union as they deified the light of day and the intoxicating powers of wine. But the question does not in fact present itself to us in the same terms. It is of little importance here to define theoretically the essential powers of the ancient Venus, since as far back in the history of Rome as we can go, we find her in the well-defined role of guiding and controlling affairs of the heart.

This aspect of the personality of the goddess as history reveals her probably evolved in history itself. Since the seventh century B.C. there was a temple honoring Venus at Lavinium, of which the founder was said to be none other than Aeneas. At Lavinium the Latin Venus—whatever her real character may have been— was influenced by the Greek Aphrodite. The latter was brought into Italy by the Greek colonizers of Campania and also by the Etruscan conquerors who had settled in Latium itself. All Latins made pilgrimages to the temple in Lavinium to render public homage to the goddess. It was from Lavinium that she was brought to Rome, but not without precautions and misgivings.

For the inhabitants of Rome, in effect, Venus personified feminine allure, as she undoubtedly already had at Lavinium. She symbolized the mysterious religious and magic power that lies hidden

LOVE AND RELIGION

in the personality and the body of woman. She was a more disturbing divinity than any other; it is not surprising that the Puritan and conservative Rome of those early days did not erect a temple in her honor for a long time. Desirous of maintaining order and safeguarding morality, the patricians, who in practice were in complete control, suspected this lawless goddess who fomented disturbances and aroused passions. But, as happened later at the time of the Bacchanalian scandals, they had too much respect for any manifestation of the divine not to accept the necessity of paying her the homage of which she could not be deprived without grave risk to the entire City-State.

We do not know exactly what form the first cult of Venus took in the city itself. The first appellation bestowed on her seems somewhat strange. Some fairly late accounts declare that that Venus was honored from very early days at the Capitol; a temple had been erected to her under the name of *Venus Calva*—the "Bald Venus." Who was this odd Venus? Legend gives two contradictory explanations of the cognomen. It was sometimes said that during the siege of Rome by the Gauls, the matrons shut up in the Capitol, with its defenders and a few refugees, cut their hair to supply the necessary cords and ropes for engines of war. In recognition of their sacrifice, it would seem that the state dedicated a postvictory statue to "Bald Venus" to show that the women who sacrificed their hair had not thereby lost their powers of seduction!

Such gallantry is anachronistic. It does not jibe with Roman customs of the fourth century B.C. Moreover it is more than likely that the defenders of the Capitol had no engines of war, and would not have known what to do with the severed tresses of the women. According to the other explanation, the origin of the Bald Venus goes even farther back. In the reign of King Ancus Marcius, the women of Rome, including the Queen herself, were attacked by a strange malady that caused their hair to fall out. To console the Queen, the King had a statue erected which showed her as she looked after the illness. At which point a miracle occurred: the statue had hardly been put in place before the women's hair grew again, more beautiful than before. In gratitude the Romans inaugurated a cult of the Bald Venus, who had in this way manifested her power.

Modern historians are incredulous. They declare that the goddess never existed at all, that she is nothing more than the invention of some student of antiquities. But such drastic skepticism may not be justified. It is possible, no doubt, that the Bald Venus was simply a very ancient statue of a woman, some of whose original features had been destroyed by the ravages of time and the weather, and that the people had grown used to calling her by that name. It is also possible (although the hypothesis cannot be verified, to be sure) that the Romans, wanting to honor Venus but at the same time desiring to divest her of some of her magic power, had conceived the notion of showing her without her hair, one of the most characteristically feminine of her adornments. As an attempt to restrain a dangerous force, it was the first and rather naïve example of a political tendency that was soon to find a stronger expression.

The magistrates in charge of the official religion were convinced that Venus represented a danger. The first temple in the city dedicated to her was erected at the beginning of the third century B.C., in 295 to be exact, to appease her wrath. In that year the Consul's son, Q. Fabius Gurges, decided to build a temple to Venus in the valley of the Great Circus. To finance the project he made use of the fines imposed on high society ladies who had been guilty of *stuprum*—illicit sexual intercourse (but not adultery, for which the punishment was death). They consisted of widows who had compromised themselves, and girls of good family whose misbehavior had for some reason not been punished within the gens.

These wicked acts seem to have been numerous, since the amounts collected sufficed for the construction of a public monument. Fabius Gurges gave the temple the appellation of *Venus Obsequens*—a title translated in modern days sometimes by the

"Compliant Venus," and sometimes, more convincingly, by the "Obedient Venus." One is tempted to suppose—and in fact the assumption goes far beyond a hypothesis—that the consecration of the temple was to propitiate the goddess, to keep her from continuing to incite the ladies of the aristocracy to immoral acts. At all times, in fact, it was a common form of revenge on Venus' part to arouse culpable desires in the hearts of mortals (especially women) who had not been zealous enough in their devotion to the cult or who had somehow offended her. By giving Venus an official place in the city, and still more by giving her a ritualistic title of good omen, they could hope to assuage her anger and induce her to limit her activities to encouraging legitimate affairs of the heart.

But the gods are often very obstinate, and make mock of the obstacles set up by man. During the Second Punic War, when Rome was on the edge of disaster, it became clear that the goddess who seemed more than ever to be the mother of all Romans could no longer be left in a subordinate position. Among other unusual measures decreed at the time, bringing the Venus of Mount Eryx to Rome was decided on. The citizens had experienced the efficacy of its protection.

In the course of the First Punic War, the image of the goddess had proved to their satisfaction that she could protect them effectively. Mount Eryx, where her temple was located, had been the main base of operations against the Carthaginians, and the Romans believed that they owed their victory in large measure to her. Why not give her still another chance?

But this particular Venus was obviously of oriental origin, and her cult was accompanied by rites of which the Roman conscience disapproved. The temple was cared for by the goddess' sacred slaves, for example. They carried on prostitution. The priests declared that the goddess performed miracles daily: the open-air altar before the temple became miraculously covered with dew; the traces of the sacrifices of the previous night disappeared without the intervention of any human hands. And it was believed that each year the goddess left the temple on Mount Eryx to visit Africa, accompanied by her sacred doves, who habitually fluttered about the sanctuary in ever-increasing numbers. After nine days she would return flying through the air like a bird, which occasioned great celebrations throughout Sicily.

To bring such a divinity into Rome and give her the rights to the city was a serious matter. The senate had always hesitated to come to a decision, despite the debt of gratitude the Republic owed this turbulent deity, who protected dens of vice and addled men's wits. But faced with immediate danger, they did not hesitate. Their desire was to regard Venus simply as Aeneas' mother, and, in order to show her even greater respect, they set up her image in the Capitol, on the sacred hill ruled over by the great and good Jupiter, the Empire's leading deity.

There was probably another reason for introducing the new cult. According to Roman tradition, Venus was the companion of Mars, the very god whose help had not been forthcoming during the first battles of the war. The homage paid to his "beloved" could not fail to touch his heart. To make sure, the decree prescribing the adoption of the Mount Eryx Venus was accompanied by a solemn vow addressed to Mars.

The goddess of Mount Eryx remained an object of suspicion just the same. It is highly characteristic of the Roman mentality that on the Capitol, beside the unruly Sicilian, they erected a temple in honor of *Mens,* that is, mind, clear understanding, of which the city had such need in times of danger. It seems that the senate, anxious to keep its religious politics in balance, wished to make evident at the Capitol, toward which all eyes were turned, two opposite yet complementary aspects of religion: the orgiastic side of the cult of the Sicilian, that delirium that she could rouse in men's hearts, would have its antidote in the totally cerebral religion of *Mens*. The Fathers were wise enough to realize that manifold influences were brought to bear on the souls of men, and that the key to harmony lay in a multiplication of gods.

It was none the less true that bringing the Mount Eryx Venus to

Rome, no matter what precautions were taken, was to introduce into the city the goddess of sensual passion, which thereby received official, almost legal, sanction at the expense of conventional morals.

At the same time the cult of another Venus could be seen rapidly expanding as a kind of antidote. She was more in conformity with what could be expected of a Roman Venus. As soon as the defeats administered to the invader Hannibal had made him less redoubtable, the senate decided to dedicate a statue to a new Venus, whom they called *Venus verticordia,* that is to say, "who turns hearts," or rather, "who turns them away" from dangerous passions. The Fathers wanted to drive thoughts of dissipation from the minds of virgins and married women, and replace them with respect for propriety. It was a propriety that many had abandoned, swept along by the licentiousness resulting from the inevitable relaxation of moral standards in the course of an interminable war.

The choice to consecrate the statue fell on a certain Sulpicia, the wife of Senator Q. Fulvius Flaccus—no doubt it was felt that she would endow it with her attributes—who was selected after a veritable virtue-contest. The senators listed a hundred women of the aristocracy with blameless reputations. From this hundred, ten were drawn by lot, and the merits of each were carefully weighed. Finally Sulpicia was unanimously selected, and she became the symbol in the people's eyes of all the virtues the senators intended to hold up as exemplary.

Less than a century later, in 114 B.C., an unprecedented scandal was to cause a moral storm. Three vestal virgins, who broke their vows, were convicted of incest, and according to custom, condemned to be buried alive. Such an event had always been considered a bad omen. To ward off ill effects it was decided to increase the honors paid to *Venus verticordia,* whose protection had clearly been revealed to be insufficient. A temple to her was built—its exact location is unknown—and consecrated on April 1, a day usually dedicated to Juno: thus the month of April (which, from earliest times, had been completely under the patronage of Venus) began with a feast celebrated by the matrons in honor of the "Legitimate Venus." Later in the month, on the 23rd, the courtesans made their devotions to the other Venus, the Sicilian, who was given a new temple, far from the Capitol, near the Porta Collina in one of the outermost quarters of the city.

Thus two Venuses shared the devotion of the faithful from then on. But it was the passionate and stormy goddess who was to regain her sway over men's consciences. During the last days of the Republic it was to her that they turned, as the moral code began to lose its earlier rigidity. The three men who successively held the destinies of Rome in their hands, Sulla, Pompey, and Caesar, appealed to her, and placed themselves under her protection. As time went on she became one of the chief goddesses of the City-State. Under the Empire she reached the point of identification with the divinity of Rome itself, symbolized by a temple dedicated to both by the Emperor Hadrian on the hill of Velia.

There are several reasons for this major stroke of good fortune for the goddess, some of which have nothing to do with Roman religious tradition and are only remotely connected with her true role of Queen of Love. But these accidents of history would never have occurred if the Roman Venus had not been ready to accept her new functions and her augmented dignity, conferred on her from the beginning of the first century B.C. As Roman supremacy spread in the East, the influence of the Greek Aphrodite increased. It can easily be shown that Venus appropriated many of the functions of her oriental counterpart. But it also seems clear that the growth of her dominion had been prepared for much earlier by certain preexisting attributes.

For a long time the Italian Venus had tended to be the patroness of everything joyful, of everything exuberant, of all youth—and that is perhaps one of the reasons for the distrust as well as the attraction she engendered in the Roman psyche. The Roman temperament was greatly drawn to "gravity" but was also captivated by every manifestation of the joyous efflorescence of life.

It is significant that from very early days the Romans had allocated the month of April, when spring bursts forth, to Venus, and also that they scheduled the consecration of her temple, and her annual festival during the days of the *Vinalia* which were dedicated to wine. And it should not be forgotten either that the courtesans, the principal devotees of the Mount Eryx Venus—now at the apogee of her triumph—danced in public, unveiled, on the feast day of Flora! Everything indicates that the austere discipline imposed by the Roman senate on popular religious observance had suddenly cracked, allowing the reappearance of a whole cult of Venus which had been masked by repercussion, but not wiped out by it.

At the beginning of the first century B.C., Venus had many votaries who begged her to make them successful in all they undertook, not only in love, but in war, in commerce, and in games of chance. Dice players called the best combination that could turn up, the "throw of Venus." And Sulla, lucky victor over Mithridates, when in the East took the surname of "Epaphrodite" or "Favorite of Venus." A few years later Pompey, after decisively defeating this same Mithridates, dedicated a temple to *Venus Victrix* (Victorious Venus) at the top of the open-air theatre he built in the Plain of Mars.

But on the eve of the Battle of Pharsalus, Pompey's Venus had to bow before another, *Venus Genetrix,* to whom Caesar had appealed. The latter, who, like all the members of the Julia gens, boasted of his descent from Aeneas, had a good excuse for appropriating Venus for his own benefit. The double precedent set by Sulla and Pompey proves that his motive was neither family pride nor a whim. In the people's eyes the patronage of Venus spelled a guarantee of happiness and success; it bestowed a kind of personal aura on those favored by the goddess, which no other divinity could confer.

Thanks to the protection of *Venus Genetrix*, Caesar took with him to Rome what had been so lacking in the dark hours of the past: divine gladness and a pledge of good luck. So, even before he had conclusively established himself as the head of the state, he decided to erect a magnificent temple in the center of the Forum in honor of her whom he called his mother.

A proof of the power of Venus and the profound echoes her cult aroused in the Roman soul can be found in Lucretius' prologue to his poem, *De Rerum Natura*. Calling upon her as mother of the Aeneades, he asked for peace for his people. She alone could induce Mars to restrain his anger. In her arms, sated with love, he could bring to an end the somber rigors of war.

These pages, clearly marked by religious fervor, often surprise commentators who remember that the Epicurean doctrine, which Lucretius wished to expound, had a strong reputation for impiety, not to say atheism (although it was actually unfounded). But Lucretius was a Roman first, a philosopher second. He understood the mentality of his fellow citizens, and wished to speak their language so they in turn could understand him. He knew that one of their profoundest aspirations led them to glorify all the powers of life, even if official restraint sometimes hid their exuberance, and imposed an appearance of austerity belied by the facts. The poet was appealing to this sentiment, to this comprehension of life. By giving the name of Venus to the strongest motivation he discerned in the world of men—the common attraction human beings have for one another, that universal sympathy without which Creation would remain immobile and inert—Lucretius was sure of being understood. The name of the goddess sufficed to enable his hearers to perceive all the grandeur and truth of a philosophy that exalted and transformed the unruly sentiment everyone feels in his own heart into a cosmic principle. Neither Sulla, nor Pompey, nor Caesar would have thought of putting himself under the protection of Venus if the goddess had been only an empty abstraction. Lucretius would not have chosen such an unusual way of symbolizing the Epicurean doctrine at the beginning of his poem, if he had not been sure of awakening a responsive echo in the souls of those he hoped to convert.

It is interesting to note that it was when the Empire was coming into existence, when Rome was beginning truly to fulfill her mission of playing a universal role, that the Goddess of Love established her sway over human hearts and souls. No longer was Venus the daemon of the flesh, if she was ever really nothing more than that. Now she was recognized as cosmic principle and life generator, having overcome the early Puritanism that had affected the laws of the City-State for so long, but with an influence in business and politics as well. The cult of Venus is linked to an immense development that traces its course before our eyes at this turning point in history. The old moral standards, narrowly circumscribed by social requirements, were suddenly swept away. Individual feelings won out over collective restraint. Ancestral traditions gave place to a more human code—looser, some will say—whose aim would no longer be to build up the City-State, but would tend to confirm the status of each individual, his true position in the universe.

The beliefs and rituals of the whole of Italy, of the entire Mediterranean world, now converged on Rome. Sulla's Venus, even if fundamentally she conformed to the national religious tradition, owed much to the Greek Aphrodite and perhaps even more to the Syrian Astarte. The Venus whose praises Lucretius sang personified the metaphysical abstractions of the ancient Ionian philosophers. Popular devotion, in turn, tended to attribute even greater power to her. The festivities held in her honor in southern Italy attracted enormous throngs. Vigils were held during which young girls destined to be married poured out ardent prayers to her as they waited for love to well up in their hearts.

An unknown poet—perhaps it was none other than the historian Florus, or perhaps an obscure contemporary of Statius, composed a quite lively hymn for one of the vigils held at Hybla, not far from Catana, in Sicily. Whether it was simply a literary exercise, or a more or less liturgical chant sung during the sacred night by a chorus of young girls, is not known for sure. But the Venus extolled in these lines reaches an exalted level. She becomes the soul of the world; human loves take on a new dignity and acquire their full significance in a myth that identifies them with the mystery of creation.

"Tomorrow," writes the poet, "is the day on which for the first time the Ether celebrates its wedding. To create the mists of spring the whole year 'round, the father has poured himself like a loving rain into the bosom of his fertile spouse; united to her great body, he was destined to give birth to all creatures. It is Venus who, with her delicate breath, penetrates the blood and the soul, to exercise her mysterious powers on the faculty of reproduction. Across the heavens, across the earth and the sea, a supreme sovereign, she has cleared a track which she ceaselessly impregnates with the seeds of life, and, at her bidding, the world discovers how to procreate."

So Venus became nature itself; she became the sweetness of living and loving. It is highly probable that at this time, the end of the first century A.D., the ancient Venus of Hybla had taken on many traits of the nature gods of the Orient, and perhaps in particular of the Isis of the Alexandrine philosophers and mystics, who was to be lauded in Apuleius' novel, *The Golden Ass,* a half-century later.

Venus' influence increased daily over human souls in that Rome which extended to the borders of the known world. Love was not just a law of life. It was a promise, a guarantee of immortality. Tibullus promised himself Venus as a guide to the Realm of the Blessed. This could be dismissed as a poet's fantastic dream, if other evidence did not suggest to us that the belief in her efficacy was fairly widespread. Thus love's capacity to make us divine was not just an idea in an author's head; it was, for many unsophisticated persons, a deep conviction. Is it not natural, after all, to convince oneself that a goddess who can create and perpetuate can also accomplish the miracle of immortality for those who believe in her? The long and rigorous deprivations of Christian asceticism were necessary before the human Eros could be distinguished from the divine *agape!*

III

ROMAN MARRIAGE

HISTORIANS and poets assure us that marriage was for centuries one of the most stable and respected institutions of the Roman City-State. They praise the purity of the ancient customs and the times when a widow would never remarry. It was an age when, of course, divorce was even more unthinkable. On the other hand, they deplore the progressive weakening of a bond that became extremely tenuous during the Empire, whereas in the good old days respect for marriage was considered the surest guarantee of Roman greatness and the most certain indication of healthy moral standards. And many historians, even today, echo these lamentations, believing that one of the many reasons for Roman decadence was the abandonment of the old traditions that once influenced the sober-minded peasants of Latium.

Before asking ourselves why in the course of time Roman marriage became less stable, we should no doubt examine the institution by itself. It was one of those about which Roman jurists were particularly solicitous. They were careful to establish and define its legal application with marked attention to detail. The texts on the subject take up considerable space in legal compilations, indicating the importance attached to a legal observance expected to be permanent, and, perhaps even more, assuring the stability of the state.

But it must be admitted that the Roman concept of marriage, even in "the good old days," has a bad reputation, in spite of the plaudits of the moralists and the nostalgia of the historians. It is often criticized for having restricted woman's independence. Husbands went out of their way to keep wives in total slavery, denied them any autonomy whatever, deprived them of any life outside the home, and forbade them to manage or even possess any funds of their own, disdainfully relegating them to household cares. But if one is not satisfied with this oversimplified view, it can be seen that the truth was quite different. From very early times Roman marriage can be painted in much brighter colors. It then emerges as one of the most subtle, flexible, and humane institutions created by jurists.

The legal situation *in manu,* that is to say, in a state of dependence before the law, deprived of any autonomous civil personality, did not apply to married women alone. The son of the house had the same status. It could hardly be otherwise, since in the earliest days of the city of the patricians, whose customs strongly affected Roman institutions in the Classic era, authority was in the hands of a few heads of families, veritable chiefs of clans, which they represented at the "Council of Fathers." In patrician days the City-State recognized only these particular "Fathers." No one else had a personality before the law, which could not acknowledge the wife's position in the family. This was a domain considered to be outside legal jurisdiction. Surprisingly enough, however, the law succeeded little by little in penetrating the interior of the clan. Eventually it managed to mitigate the consequences of the wife's original legal status. Certainly this development would not have taken place if public opinion and custom had not demanded it.

Roman legends had already foretold this evolution. The idea they give us of the wife's position and role is much less gloomy than that furnished, apparently, by the law. At least in the ideal world the legends depict, the wife was apparently respected, even venerated; spared menial chores, and was virtually the absolute mistress of the home. Furthermore, even a cursory study of beliefs and rites relating to love and sex show that the Romans always tried to protect their spouses from illicit passion, and to guard them from evil spirits that might threaten the stability of the family. This could perhaps be attributed to caution on the part of the husbands—but why not also to an ever-vigilant respect for an ideal, and reluctance to see the relationship brought down to the level of mere sexual satisfaction? It would seem that Roman religion, open to the influence of the laws of human existence, wanted married couples to have the blessing of divinities influencing fertility and at the same time protect them from the lawless whims to which these daemons often gave way.

There was, in Rome, a goddess who acted as the protectress of legitimate marriage. This was the province of Juno, who in such a capacity was addressed as *Juno Juga*. It is worthy of notice that a goddess was chosen for the role, rather than a god. In view of the sacred, inviolable nature of the Roman marriage bond in the ancient City-State, one might think that the pious sons of Romulus would have preferred to entrust the task to other patrons: those whose duty it was to make sure vows were kept, such as Dius Fidius, or Jupiter himself. But Juno was chosen instead of these stern deities, probably because it was believed that the more important role in the union between husband and wife belonged to the woman, that it was she who bound herself more fully, and that the success or failure of the marriage depended mainly on what she could contribute.

This predominance of the woman appears even in the word for marriage: the term *matrimonium*, based on the word for mother, *mater*, implying that marrying a woman meant asking her to become a mother. And this appellation belonged to her before she had brought children into the world. Similarly, the husband received the name of father, *pater*, as soon as he was legitimately united to her. *Pater* and *mater* were names used as well in honoring powerful gods, some of whom, according to legend, had neither children nor mates. The newly wedded wife shared the name of *mater* with Minerva, Diana, or Vesta, the virgin goddesses. Would it have been bestowed on her if she had been no more than a subservient slave in the home?

When they were obliged to define marriage, the jurists elaborated a formula that did justice to its place in society. This can be found in the *Digest,* attributed to Modestinus, a writer living in the third century A.D. "Marriage," he wrote, "is the joining together of divine and human law," adding that "it is the total union of whole lives." Actually the first definition seems more accurate than the second, since marriages continued in force even if husband and wife were separated for unusual reasons. Ulpian, Modestinus' master, had foreseen such a situation:

"If a husband and wife live away from each other for a long time, but continue to hold their marriage in respect—as we know sometimes happens even between persons of consular rank—I consider that the marriage ties have not been broken. It is not the bond of flesh that constitutes the marriage, but conjugal sentiment."

Thus, if we are to believe the jurists, who appear to have reflected the attitude of the public faithfully, marriage was a total alliance, entered into by two human beings, on both the divine and human level. For the marriage to be valid, husband and wife must have the same status, the same value as persons in the eyes of God and man. The physical union required of them by the City-State, since marriage was undertaken in order to beget children—as the censors reminded the people each time the census was taken—did not in itself constitute a marriage. Procreation was only an adjunct to total mutual communion. The integral essence of the marriage relationship is to be found elsewhere than in physical possession.

A well-known phrase uttered by the bride during the wedding ceremony seems to have implied this: "Where you will be Gaius," said the young woman, "I will be Gaia." It was a ritual expression whose primitive meaning is not known to us; in fact it was already not clear to the Romans of the Classical period. But those who spoke it had the impression that they were binding themselves to a husband who would be not their master but their equal, their double; they would constitute two halves of the same being. And the synthesis which produced a new entity was not, as in that strange myth in Plato's Banquet, a symbol of carnal union, nor even of a communion between hearts. It was an essentially new creation. With marriage there began a *societas,* a union which was greater than either partner not only in its results but in its very character. Just as the City-State was a reality of a higher order than the citizens that made it up, the married couple formed a new being.

The nature of Roman marriage, then, which regarded the married couple as an entity, in a way transcendental, could be seen clearly in the rites performed during the union of the *flamen* and *flaminica.* The calling of *flamen,* a very old priestly order, could be assumed only by a married patrician. Whatever may have been the origin of the observance, which may go back to the Aryan component of the Roman City-State, it evidently retained a truly archaic flavor. Hemmed in by many restrictions, the *flamen* was obliged to remain absolutely pure. He could not take a vow, for instance, nor have any tie that could curb the magic force within him. And his wife was obliged to remain perfectly spotless as well. If she died, her husband had to give up the performance of his ritual duties forthwith. Plutarch, who reported the fact, wondered what reasons lay behind the law. To assume that the visit of death to that holy house was enough to soil it irreparably would be too easy. In truth, it was permanence in marriage that was the prime requisite for priesthood, and the *flamen* did not have the right to divorce. No exceptions were allowed until the time of Domitian, when the Emperor permitted the divorce of a *flaminica.* But it was necessary to expiate the dissolution of this holy union by rites exhumed from early days, which Plutarch called "horrible, strange, and murky." They were considered necessary in view of the religious scandal caused by the voluntary separation of a couple regarded as mediators between the City-State and its god.

The marriage of a *flamen* and a *flaminica* was an exemplary one, a "happy" one, having the force of a good omen for the City-State. Other marriages were modeled on it. It is significant that Jupiter's *flamen* presided at the rites of the *confarreatio,* apparently the oldest and in any case the most serious form of patrician marriage. It is also noteworthy that marriage was not solemnized during the month of May, when, in fact, the *flaminicae,* wearing mourning, and with their hair disheveled, took part in the procession of the Argei which consisted in immersing the little dolls that bore that mysterious name in the waters of the Tiber.

Marriage between a patrician and a plebeian family was forbidden during the first three centuries of Rome. The reason is obvious. It is not to be found in caste pride, no doubt, but in the true nature of marriage and in the feeling that since patricians and plebeians were not equal before the gods, two beings belonging to different castes could not—in the eyes of the jurists—make a harmonious couple, nor share a status rendered irreconcilable by their inequality. For a woman did not acquire her husband's standing before the law through marriage—and the principle remained in force during the Classical era. She kept her individual status. Her personality was in no way assimilated by that of her husband. This is proved by the fact that she did not take the gens name of her new family, but kept the one she was born with. In this respect she was more independent than the wife of today.

It is strange to observe—and this can be reckoned as one of the paradoxes of Roman marriage—that there was no religious ceremony to put equality before the law into effect, as set forth by lawmakers, similar to the process of authenticating adoption into a family, which was known as *adlectio.* Doubtless nothing can be stated definitely with regard to the early days, since our knowledge is so fragmentary and imperfect. But in the Classical period, even if the gods "witnessed" and approved a marriage, they had not called it into being. It was based on a freely affirmed mutual desire on the part of a man and a woman to share their destiny. And this would seem to have been its basis since the beginning of Rome.

There is no doubt that marriage was a religious observance. It could not have been otherwise for a people who preferred to act in harmony with the gods, and who sought to ascertain the divine will as a preliminary to even the most insignificant of life's undertakings. The search for portents, however, was no different before a marriage than before any decision, any initiative, taken in public as well as in private life. And later, under the Empire, the interpreters of omens were usually to be found among the persons gathered together to celebrate a marriage. But it was a vestige of the old days; they were no longer formally asked to explain the signs.

This did not prevent young girls and their close relations from trying in every way to discover the secrets the future held in store. Personal piety, or possibly superstition on the part of the engaged couple, was more exacting and made them perhaps less cautious than was called for by the official rites. Private attempts at divination just before the wedding ceremony were anything but rare. Naturally we do not have much information about what went on in these circumstances, but a few accounts have come down to us. For instance, we learn that Caecilia, Metellus' wife (at the end of the second century B.C.) was trying to ascertain the will of the gods one night in regard to her niece, a quite young girl, who was thinking of getting married. The two of them kept watch in a temple, but the gods remained silent. They waited so long that the girl, tired of standing up, asked the aunt to make room beside her so that she could sit down. And Caecilia graciously replied: "With pleasure, my dear, you may have my place." The innocent words, alas, turned out to be prophetic. Caecilia died suddenly, and Metellus married the young niece. This is the kind of story that circulated among the women when marriage was the topic of conversation.

The marriage ceremony has often been described. It had many picturesque aspects. Some of the rites had clearly retained their magic import, while others were a little-understood survival from a distant past. The object of most of them was to "protect" the bride at a particularly serious moment in her life.

The day of the ceremony was the "great day," but the observances began the day before. In the evening, the young girl doffed once for all her garments of an adolescent, the *toga praetexta,* with its purple border, which boys renounced in the course of a solemn ceremony usually long before marriage, when they were about to enter public life. But a young girl, who would never participate in it, ceased to be a child only when she became a wife.

The day before the wedding she was arrayed in a white tunic called—and the meaning is obscure—*tunica recta,* or "straight tunic." No doubt it was made out of a single piece of woven cloth, on an old-style loom by a weaver who stood up to work. For a ceremony as important as a wedding, only the old procedures would do. Anything newfangled might bring bad luck.

The belt that usually held in the tunic around the waist was tied in a special knot: "the knot of Hercules," which the young husband would undo for the first time the following day. The bride's hair was combed in a style that never changed. A woman parted it with the help of an esoteric instrument called a *hasta caelibaris,* which was a veritable weapon, a lance with a short iron shaft, and having a sharp edge. Even the men of those far-off days were puzzled by the custom. Plutarch wondered whether it could be explained by the fact that Juno, patron saint of marriage, was sometimes considered a warlike goddess.

The coiffure of the bride-to-be was also unchanging. The hair was woven into six tresses, held in place by a band around the forehead. During the ceremony, the hairdo was concealed beneath an orange-colored veil, the *flammeum,* which fell to her shoulders, framing her face. This color, the color of dawn, was considered propitious.

When morning came all the guests gathered in the house of the bride, and made an offering to the gods. The seers (*auspices*) examined the entrails of the animals sacrificed—at least in olden times—but, as has been stated, there was a growing tendency to do without their help. When the sacrifice was over, the wedding proper took place—that is to say, a declaration in front of witnesses that the couple consented. At the same time a woman called the *pronuba,* who led the nuptial procession and was in a way a model for the bride, and was also her guarantor, solemnly joined their hands together. This action, known as the *dextrarum junctio,* was the high point of the ceremony. It made manifest and symbolized the union of bride and groom, the mutual covenant which from that time on transformed them into a single being.

The gods were then called upon to bless the couple. Five of them —probably—were asked to take the bride and groom under their protection: four goddesses and only one god. If Plutarch is to be believed, they were Jupiter, Juno, Venus, Fides, and Diana. But maybe Plutarch was thinking less of the gods who really took the marriages of the Romans under their protection than of their Greek counterparts. Nevertheless, it is remarkable that goddesses predominated, and that it was the woman who benefited from their divine solicitude.

The couple then offered up another sacrifice, and everyone gathered at a banquet until nightfall. Until then the bride-to-be had not left her own family's house. The appearance in the sky of Vesper, the evening star, was the signal for her departure. Pretending that the separation from her parents was a heartrending affair, she took refuge in her mother's arms, but her attendants tore her away in spite of her protests, and, in a joyous procession, led her to the home of the groom. On the way traditional refrains were sung, studded with coarse pleasantries, like those uttered by the persons taking part in triumphal parades. The aim was probably to ward off the evil eye by the counteracting power of the obscene words, and at the same time to stimulate the couple's fertility. Nuts were thrown to those taking part—doubtless still another symbol of fecundity. The bride was accompanied by three young boys, all of whom still had both parents. One of these "ushers" held aloft a hawthorn torch, and the torches of other persons lit up the scene. Portents were determined from the light diffused by the torches: a bright light meant good luck; a smoky, flickering light was a bad omen.

The young woman was also accompanied by two servants holding a distaff and a spindle. Of course the new chatelaine would never have to use them herself if she belonged to the powerful Roman aristocracy that had innumerable slaves at its disposal. But the spinning of wool was a symbol of domestic virtue. It was the only task a freeborn woman could be required to perform. She would never, for instance, be obliged to grind corn or to knead dough. In the house of the Emperor Augustus, notwithstanding, princesses still made with their own hands the tunics worn by the master—a concession to ancestral custom.

Finally the procession reached the door of the house in which the wedding was to take place. The bride stopped to offer up a few prayers to the god who guarded the threshold. She anointed the pillars with oil, and tied strips of wool around them. Then, lifted by the strong hands of the young people in the procession, she was carried over the threshold without risk of stumbling, which would have been a lamentable omen. Now she was presented to the gods presiding over her new household. The bridegroom waited in the *atrium,* and gave her water and fire, the two elements essential to human existence, and to the performance of sacred rites. And the young woman, after uttering the ritual phrase mentioned earlier: *"Ubi tu Gaius, ego Gaia"* ("Where thou art Gaius, I am Gaia"), began her new life by making an offering of three coins, one to her husband, one to the gods of the hearth, and the third to the lares watching over the nearest crossroads.

There were several types of marriage. Literary and legal texts mention the *confarreatio,* the *coemptio,* and the *usucapio.* Actually it was less a question of three different "marriages," than of three equivalent legal ceremonies, whose object was to put the young married woman *in manum mariti* (in her husband's hands), to make her, it might almost be said, the "ward" of her husband. The variations in these observances suggest that marriage was never really confined to one particular ritual, but that the institution existed on its own, entered into and accepted by the two contracting parties of their own free will. The different juridical forms went no further than witnessing and legalizing these agreements.

The official confirmation was different, naturally, in different epochs. It varied also according to the class to which the young people belonged. The *confarreatio* was characteristic of the old patrician social group. It was solemnized in the presence of the grand pontiff, head of the national religion, and of Jupiter's *flamen*. In addition, ten witnesses were required, no doubt representing the ten *curiae* of the tribal unit. The offerings to the gods after the *dextrarum junctio* were particularly archaic in type, since they included a cake made from *far,* a kind of coarse, primitive wheat originating in the north that was for a long time the only cereal plant cultivated in Latium. A sacrifice was also offered up to Tellus, the fertile earth, and to Ceres.

Scholars who try to determine the significance of this double offering recall Servius' phrase: "Among the ancients, taking a wife or plowing a field was not permitted without first proffering an oblation." It was natural that Ceres, the creatress of mankind, should preside over human fecundation. The *confarreatio* takes us back to a world on which the rustic way of life left a deep imprint. Human actions were performed in sympathy with the mysterious forces of the earth, the sky, and nature.

Like the marriage bond between the *flamen* and the *flaminica,* that of the *confarreatio* seems to have been indissoluble, at least at the beginning. But later, under the pressure of tradition, it became necessary to make the rule more pliable. In order to rescind the union, a ceremony was invented which was just the reverse of the former. Named *diffareatio,* its aim was the dissolution of the *confarreatio.*

But that was only an expedient. For a long time before that, the Romans preferred other forms of marriage, existing side by side with the *confarreatio*. Only a few families kept up the old customs, and it was from them that the *flaminicae* were recruited, since to become a *flaminica* it was necessary to have been born of the union solemnized as a *confarreatio*. In Tiberius' day, candidates fulfilling this condition were not easy to find.

Two other forms of marriage had been practiced for a long time, no doubt concurrently. One was based on the custom of "purchase," the *coemptio;* the other, on a ~~de facto~~ situation, the *usus*.

These two types were not really lesser than the *confarreatio*, but simply two ways of legalizing the bond between the partners, with the aim of giving a legal basis to the social unit constituted by the couple. *Coemptio* and *usus* were to be found in another domain than marriage. They were essentially two kinds of legal acquisition, two ways of bringing complete ownership into being. It can be assumed that as applied to marriage they were no more than legal fictions, the products of the fertile imaginations of practitioners of civil law.

The *coemptio* took place in the presence of five witnesses, all possessing their full rights as citizens, presided over by still another citizen, known as a "weigher," or *libripens*. As in a sale, the buyer (in this instance the husband) uttered a ritual phrase in which he declared that he was acquiring the fiancée with marriage in view, not slavery. This was a necessary precaution, since the simple formality of purchase was the same in either case. According to circumstances, the seller was either the father or guardian of the woman, or it might be the fiancée herself if she was of the "emancipated" type.

The transaction was authenticated by handing over a coin in payment, which obviously could have only a symbolic value. Modern historians asserted for a long time that this "purchase" of the bride-to-be by her future husband was a survival from a very ancient past, and that it had replaced an even cruder custom, that of rape, no less. But one can no longer find supporters of this hypothesis. It has also been asserted that *coemptio* was the form of marriage characteristic of a given social group, but that is not certain either, since *coemptio* is not a nuptial rite but a kind of legal cession. Moreover, it had fallen into disuse by the end of the Republic, and Cicero assures us that in his day lawyers did not even know the exact nature of the observance.

De facto marriage, or marriage *per usum,* was a good deal like *coemptio* in character, and can also be explained by analogy with a kind of transfer of property. A person who had enjoyed the uncontested and public use of some property—during a time that varied according to its nature—was in effect considered to be its owner.

In the same way, if the union of a man and a woman lasted more than a year, the marriage became legitimate. The husband acquired the *manus* with all its privileges, just as if the bond had been legalized by *confarreatio* or *coemptio*. However, if during the year the woman had spent three consecutive nights away from her husband's home, she was no longer subject to her companion's *manus*.

The origin of this strange regulation has often been the subject of speculation. Perhaps this was still another legal fiction, invented in order to bring into being a marriage without *manus,* in which the wife would not become the ward of her husband but would keep her original legal status. The prescriptive period of three days and nights away from home may have been borrowed from an old convention, traces of which can be found in one of the taboos affecting the marriage of a *flamen* and a *flaminica*. The latter, in effect, did not have the right to spend two successive nights away from her husband, as if the ideal and exemplary marriage of a priestly couple required virtually absolute continuity in order to last. By means of this unusual device, the jurists managed to modify profoundly the essential character of the social reality represented by Roman marriage.

This invention of a marriage without *manus,* so significant in the development of Roman customs, is traditionally attributed to the *decemviri,* who toward the middle of the fifth century B.C. drew up the Twelve Tables of Laws. It may even be older still; perhaps the *decemviri* merely put into their statutes what already existed in fact. Probably this arrangement was worked out to take care of situations in which it was hard to maintain the full force of marital authority. It may be surmised that the authorization to contract marriages between patricians and plebeians, officially sanctioned by the *Lex Canuleia* in 445 B.C., is connected with mitigating the severity of the old patrician system of marriage. Conceivably the father of a young patrician girl would find it distasteful to hand over his authority to the plebeian she expected to take for a husband, and who was not her equal, at least in the eyes of the gods.

A wife who did not come under the *manus* of the husband remained in essence under that of her father. She continued to take part in the religious observances of the home in which she was born. This has still another effect: by virtue of his traditional authority, the father of the young woman kept the right to dissolve his daughter's marriage when he himself so desired, without the couple's consent. This privilege, which seems extreme to us, remained in force until the second century A.D.; it was not permanently revoked until the Antonines. A long time before that, however, no one had thought of taking advantage of it. It was simply an archaic survival. But the fact that it existed suffices to enable us to discern the real reasons for the development of a marriage without *manus*. Far from being motivated by a liberal attitude and a desire to give woman her legal independence, this innovation of lawyers of the fifth century B.C. testifies to their reluctance to diminish the prerogatives of the paterfamilias and to their ingenuity in trying to preserve the autonomy of the patrician household.

But in effect this brought about a veritable revolution, which, on a long-range basis, had the effect in practice of emancipating married women. We observe, for example, that at the time of the Second Punic War—a little more than two centuries after the Twelve Tables of Laws—the great majority of women were no longer subject to the legal guardianship of their husbands or their fathers. No doubt the wife, considered a "perpetual minor," came under the authority of a tutor in theory. But this tutor was not her father as a general rule. The latter usually selected a friend to play this role, even during his lifetime. If the "ward" disliked the tutor, she could ask the *praetor* to assign her another one, which he was usually willing to do. Guardianship, in fact, had almost disappeared by the end of the Republic. It was considered nothing more than a formality which could not seriously restrict the financial independence of women.

And even Augustus, wishing to encourage Roman women to bear children, permitted the mother of three to dispense with a tutor. Later, at the Emperor's discretion, the privilege was extended to wives who had even fewer children.

A "free" marriage, that is to say one in which the wife was not under the legal guardianship of her husband but under that of a tutor whose authority was only a legal fiction, soon became habitual. At the end of the Republic, it was the usual arrangement, except for a few great patrician families who continued to practice *confarreatio*. By then, as has already been stated, *coemptio* had completely disappeared, and marriage *per usum* was no more than a legal curiosity. The marriage bond was simply a private institution whose legal consequences, however, were clearly specified and were very limited. The husband, for example, could not make a donation to his wife. But she on her part could own property that was automatically free of his control. In practice women often preferred to leave the care of their fortunes to their husbands, but this was no more than a form of indulgence based on affection.

The dowry actually stipulated in a marriage came under the marital provisions for managing possessions, but in principle only the income was to be used, for the common good. Though there was no legal means to prevent an unscrupulous husband from dissipating these funds, nevertheless if the marriage was dissolved, the dowry was supposed in most cases to be restored to the wife, who was also getting back her freedom. Husband and wife made separate wills, and were not automatically regarded as each other's natural heir. It would be hard to imagine a legal arrangement that accorded more dignity to the woman and gave her greater material and moral independence. It did not go back to the primitive days of the Roman City-State; it evolved gradually. We have tried to show its growth in operation. It would seem that all forces conspired to make Roman marriage more humane, to insert in the legal code what was originally only a tendency among marriage customs, symbolized in legends.

It would be a mistake to believe, on the authority of rhetoricians, and of Juvenal in particular, that this change came about because of the loosening of morals, because of the progressive degradation of something that was originally pure. On the contrary, the Romans apparently recognized the moral nobility of their spouses, and granted them greater and greater confidence from one generation to another. And if they wanted them to be freer still, the reason was that they were learning to respect them even more.

Nevertheless, moderns continue to think of the Romans as a people who authorized divorce, and at certain times abused the privilege to such an extent that it grew into license. But in reality, the freedom divorce represented was the necessary result of the Roman conception of marriage. Since it was essentially a partnership, its continuance depended on the free option of the partners. If their choice changed, how could it be confined within its original limits? In the name of what principle?

The first divorce that tradition records goes back no farther than the year 231 B.C., when Spurius Carvilius Ruga separated from his wife because she was sterile. Nevertheless we are told that he loved her dearly, and that she was worthy of his love. But he had taken the customary oath before the censors that he married "in order to have children." He did not want his love for a woman who, he knew, could not give him descendants, to cause him to break his vow. Carvilius' motive was an honorable one, but this did not prevent public opinion from blaming him severely.

It was felt that *fides,* that is to say loyalty toward his wife, should come ahead of the civic oath. Marriage was viewed in the same light as other contracts: except in the case of strong reasons, of compulsion of some kind, they must be observed no matter what transpired. There existed in regard to marriage a "royal law" attributed to Romulus himself, that stipulated the conditions in which it could be dissolved. But as was generally the case with royal laws, its authenticity is highly doubtful. And its interpretation is dubious, moreover. Here is how Plutarch gives it:

"Romulus also enacted a few laws, among which is one that is extremely severe: a woman is not allowed to leave her husband, but a husband may separate from his wife if she has poisoned their children, if she has taken the keys of their home, or if she has committed adultery. The law requires that if he has put away his wife for any other reason, half his fortune should belong to her, and the other half should be offered to Demeter. He who has parted from his wife must also offer a sacrifice to the gods of Hades."

This very cloudy text surely reflected an early stage of society, doubtless not long after its patriarchal origins. The precepts it contains can be explained only as a result of the power of the paterfamilias, which at first was absolute, in principle, at least on the purely legal level.

But, no matter how paradoxical it may seem, the jurists ended by restricting the exercise of that power, since they limited the right of dissolution to certain very specific situations in which the wife had been guilty of particularly serious wrongdoing. If she was not guilty, it was still possible for the husband to separate from her, in theory. But he would have to pay dearly for the privilege of following his whim. Deprived of all his worldly good, he would get back his freedom. But at what a price!

The reasons that made divorce legitimate, according to the laws cited above, have long aroused the curiosity of legal historians, who believed they had the right arbitrarily to emend the texts, in order to eliminate what offended them. Considering it absurd that the "sequestration of keys" could have such serious consequences, they figured that Plutarch must have meant "exchange of children," that is, substituting one child for another.

There is really no reason to change the text. P. Noailles has shown that each one of the contingencies envisaged constituted in fact a violation of the most characteristic taboos of Roman marriage in primitive times. "The poisoning of children" referred to a kind of abortion brought on by the use of magic drugs. Adultery, a crime against the purity of blood lines, was obviously the greatest sin, and could not be expiated. It would undoubtedly remain so throughout the existence of the Roman City-State.

All that is left is "the use of false keys." But even here, the meaning of the ban is clear, when one recalls that Roman women, for a long time, were forbidden to drink wine without incurring the severest penalties. They were allowed to have all the keys of the household in their possession except the keys of the wine cellar. The historian Fabius Pictor, writing at the end of the third century B.C., recounts an anecdote which was perpetuated by Pliny, according to which a Roman lady one day forced open the chest containing the keys of the wine cellar. Convicted of this crime, she was condemned by a family council to die by starvation. Unfortunately we do not know at what period this tragedy took place. We can assume that by the time of Fabius Pictor it was already far in the past.

At the beginning of the second century B.C., a woman who had drunk some wine ran the risk of being divorced, but not put to death.

In the early patriarchal family, it would seem that the marriage bond could be dissolved only if the wife were condemned to death by the paterfamilias, acting in the capacity of judge. The sins that brought on such a frightful verdict were crimes against religion.

The true significance of the ban on wine has puzzled many writers. On the one hand, according to P. Noailles, wine, a sacrificial fluid, and a substitute for blood, was considered to contain the mysterious primordial life element. In drinking it, the wife submitted to an alien, and therefore hostile, life element. By ingesting this component, by taking it into the blood, which was that of the family blood line, she tainted the latter's purity. This represented a kind of "defilement by blood."

On the other hand, and this hypothesis has recently been put forward—we are reminded that in ancient medicine wine was believed to have contraceptive and abortive potentialities, and that as a result its use could be judged as equivalent to an attempt at an abortion, like those proscribed by Romulus' law. It has already been mentioned that wine was dedicated to the goddess Venus, and that its use could rightly be regarded as dangerous by mothers. This does not in any way contradict the two preceding hypotheses, which are themselves mutually quite compatible, although originating on different planes. But it must not be forgotten either that apparently only the matrons, that is to say ladies coming from "honorable" families, were subject to this restriction. At least this is brought out by another custom, a very strange one, and even more surprising in a society as Puritan in certain respects as that of early Rome. For a long time, indeed, ladies of good family were accustomed to receiving kisses on the lips from their blood relatives or connections. This was called the *jus osculi,* the right to kiss. This surprising privilege, which was not accorded to the women of the common people, can be explained only by the taboo against wine, and that was how the ancients understood it. In this way the relatives of a noble lady confirmed that her breath did not smell of wine. They were the ones who, if the rule was broken, would serve as the counsellors of the family tribunal, and would decide the fate of the offender.

One must be careful to distinguish between the condemnation of a matron by the family council, and the pure and simple dissolution of a marriage. And, in the face of the accounts of the early historians, one must determine whether they refer to patrician unions, in which religious considerations and the traditions of the clan continued for a long time to play an important role, or whether they apply to common people, for whom the stability of the marriage bond was less important. It will then become clear that most of the anecdotes and facts of all kinds that have come down to us are concerned with aristocratic families. And it is more than likely that the picture would be quite different if we had documents bearing on other social classes, those for whom the primary object of marriage was not to perpetuate the cult of gentility, and for whom it remained a much more personal affair. And then there were also those who did not have the right to marry, that *jus connubii* which was one of the prerogatives of citizens in full possession of their privileges; that is to say plebeians, for a long time, and then, after the *Lex Canuleia* of 445 B.C., the bulk of the freedmen, who could not legally marry persons of free birth (at least, apparently, until the last century of the Republic). All these unions, since they were not legitimate marriages, were certainly less stable than those contracted between freeborn persons. As social distinctions gradually disappeared, how could legitimate marriage escape contamination?

If it is true that the *manus* of the husband, an inheritance from patriarchal society, constituted the only legal guarantee of a stable marriage by making it impossible for a woman to leave her spouse just because she wanted to, once the principle of marriage without *manus* was admitted, there was nothing to ensure the durability of the union. But it is quite remarkable that divorce made its appearance in aristocratic families—the only ones about which we have information—only two centuries or so after the establishment and diffusion of marriage *per usum*. This shows the strength of tradition, and how difficult it was for aspirations toward individual liberty finally to see the light of day. Moreover, social restrictions were also effectively enforced by the censorship, the legal body that every five years entrusted two persons who were essentially investigators into customs, with the task of determining whether each citizen was worthy of the status he held in the City-State. And the censors did not hesitate to blame anyone, even going as far as to strike off the list the name of a senator who had divorced his wife on some trifling pretext. The lower one went in the social scale, the less strong the threat became. Doubtless the censors kept their severest penalties for the most conspicuous personages.

But for a long time, as a general thing, divorce was decidedly repugnant even when official restrictions did not apply. When a wife quarreled with her husband, it sometimes happened that she brought him into an audience with a reconciliation in view, before a judge of a most unusual kind. This was a divinity named Viriplaca, that is to say, "She who appeases husbands," whose temple was on the Palatine Hill.

Before taking extreme measures, husbands and wives went there, and, under the protection of the goddess, unburdened their hearts at leisure. By talking it out, they regained their peace of mind; the storm subsided, and, thanks to Viriplaca, the couple returned home as firmly united as they had ever been.

Nevertheless, at the end of the Republic, Viriplaca lost much of her vigor, and divorces became quite frequent. It was not just the husbands who repudiated their wives, using the hallowed formula: "Take your things and go!" But the women too left their connubial domiciles, and went back to the house in which they had passed their childhood. If there had been no *manus* in the marriage, that was enough of a formality; if there had been a *manus*, it was removed by a suitable legal observance in which the one who was divorcing the other was obliged to take part. The ease with which a divorce could be obtained certainly helped to spread the practice. But this facility was less the cause than the result of a complicated situation: divorces were easy because they appeared to be necessary, because marriage no longer seemed in itself a valuable institution, to which one's personal life should be subordinated as to an unconditional, absolute rule. The legal status of legitimate unions evolved, as did all other institutions in the Roman City-State. It would have been strange, almost shocking, if in the course of a transformation that made Rome into the capital of the world, the only unchanged concept was that of the family, suitable, in principle, to the most archaic type of patriarchal society. Moralists might deplore this evolution; historians could use the word "decadence," as long as they did not forget that everything that lives, by the very fact of its duration, advances toward death. Roman marriage was not beyond the reach of this law. Let us not think that perverse vagaries or widespread corruption were responsible for what is called the degradation of the marriage tie. Let us rather ask what the legal institution whose outline has been sketched out in these pages really was; how it existed in various epochs; what its intrinsic place was in individual lives—and perhaps, to the extent that we give up judging, we will begin to understand.

IV

MARRIAGE IN THE GOLDEN AGE

It is impossible, naturally, to gain a clear idea of what the day-to-day actualities of married life were in early Roman days. Reliable accounts do not shed any light on this question, any more than any other, until the third century B.C. And even then they usually are concerned only with aristocratic families. The situation must have differed considerably according to class, and in situations where the patriarchal tradition did not come into play. But since the City-State became united, with patricians and plebeians enjoying virtually the same privileges, patrician traditions seem to have exercised a kind of attraction over plebeian family customs. And, from the third century on, it would appear that the principal differences were more a function of the wealth and political responsibilities of the persons involved than any other factor. At that time the City-State was ruled by a strictly oligarchical regime. There were the families whose men sat in the senate, taking over the great state executive positions at regular intervals, and there was the great mass of citizens who never came to the assemblies except to ratify decisions drawn up by the senators, to elect candidates that were presented to them, and that they chose according to the standing of the men who backed them. The rest of the time they were the "clients" of the great seigneurs.

Obviously marriage did not have the same significance for one group as for the other. We have little information as to how marriages were arranged among the proletariat. When it comes to the others, we have a bit more. And from the beginning, one characteristic is obvious as far back as we can go: the union of two young persons, although legally based on their free consent, was in no way the result of personal choice. Since they were destined to continue a family, their marriage could not be left to their own individual fancy. The paterfamilias, who, in primitive times, had the power of life and death over his son, and could sell him as a slave, considered it his right and even more his duty to choose a wife for the good of the house of which he was the responsible chief. A marriage was above all the means of concluding alliances between families, of establishing or consolidating friendships, of making sure of the backing of one's fellow citizens in the City-State.

Monetary considerations, without a doubt, entered into the choice fathers made of a son or daughter-in-law. But it was far from being the primary consideration. Dowries were rather meager more often than not, in those faraway times when goods and chattels were rare, when the patrimony consisted of lands that could not be transferred, in conformity with patriarchal tradition. Valerius Maximus tells us how, at the beginning of the second century B.C., the tribal group Aelia, one of the most illustrious in Rome, owned only a small piece of property on which sixteen persons were supposed to live. Nevertheless Aemilius Paulus, future conqueror of Persia, did not hesitate to give his daughter in marriage to one of the young men of the Aelia family: Q. Aelius Tubero, and after his victory over the King of Macedonia, he presented his son-in-law with five pounds in silver, taken from the booty, an amount which half a century later would have seemed ridiculously small.

Two generations before Aemilius Paulus, C. Scipio, who was in Spain facing the Carthaginian troops, asked to be relieved of his command on the ground that his daughter had reached marriageable age, and that his presence was necessary to amass a dowry, without which he would never find her a husband. The senate, which appreciated his services and considered him irreplaceable at this time, decided to act as a proxy in the matter, and after consulting the young girl's mother and her near relations, took the amount agreed on out of the public treasury. The sum totaled 40,000 pounds in bronze. Valerius Maximus adds that this not only shows how solicitous the senators could be, but how modest fortunes were in those days.

At that time dowries did not represent an increase in the wealth of the husband. They were merely a compensation for the extra expense outlay necessitated by the arrival in his house of a young woman, accompanied by several servants who, as required by custom, took over all menial tasks. It should not be forgotten either that this often minimal dowry could not be spent, but must be invested, usually in the purchase of land, and that only its income could be used to defray the couple's living expenses. This explains why the amount of the dowry was not the primary consideration when a father had to select a daughter-in-law. Other factors were the basis for the importance of the marriage.

The senate, in fact, where matters of consequence were dealt with and political careers made or broken, was divided into several competing groups. The principles or precepts of the government were not what caused these differences, but, more often, personal rivalry or that of the clans. Each great personage drew into his orbit a number of lesser nobles who paid court to him, counted on his help to influence the magistrates, took advantage of his prestige in the eyes of the public, and grew in status beneath the sheltering wings of his glory.

Inversely, the power of the chiefs of these clans was measured by the number of friends following in their train in the Forum, on the Plain of Mars, and at private ceremonies.

And family alliances were the chief tie inside the clan. Moreover, from earliest times and even during the days when morals were at their purest, marriage was primarily a political measure, since it served to establish a kind of unwritten contract between families, a mutual assistance pact in public and private life. For a young man to be welcomed into a noble family as a son-in-law was a guarantee that he would be backed up and appointed to remunerative positions of distinction. For a father to give his

MARRIAGE IN THE GOLDEN AGE

daughter in marriage to a talented young man meant that the clan was assured of a new ally whose prestige might one day weight the scales decisively in its favor.

Fathers of families competed with one another with slow tactical approaches and subtle maneuvering. Mothers followed the advances from their hearths, and sometimes made the decisions themselves. Plutarch has described the engagement of Tiberius Gracchus, whose nobility and especially his talents put him in the top rank of "good catches." This happened at a ritual repast of the augurs. There, amid a pervasive atmosphere of well-being, Appius Claudius, a highly important personage, took the youthful Tiberius aside and made much of him—something Appius Claudius was not in the habit of doing. Then, coming to the point, he offered him his daughter's hand. Tiberius accepted on the spot. Even for a member of the *gens Sempronia,* with its illustrious past, an alliance with the Claudii, whose caste pride was proverbial, was a stroke of good fortune that should not be underestimated. The preliminary pledges were immediately exchanged. Then Claudius hurried home. He had hardly reached the threshold when he began to call loudly to his wife: "Antistia! I've just succeeded in getting Claudia engaged!" Antistia, a little irritated by this outburst, answered: "What's all the hurry? What's so urgent? Imagine how you'd feel if you had gotten her engaged to Tiberius Gracchus!" Such was the meaningful reply of a mother who had already reviewed all possible candidates, and who knew fully as much as her husband about the respective merits of all young persons of marriageable age!

One may suppose that young Claudia herself, brought up by such a mother, could think of no greater happiness than to be married to a young man everyone admired, who was handsome, who was considered worthy, and who by far outshone the others. How could her vanity not be satisfied—if not her heart? (But at the age when young people then got engaged, what could she know about that?)

This was marriage at that time: one of the instruments employed to gain or preserve power. When we see how the great personages of the end of the Republic concluded or broke engagements according to the requirements of their career, let us not be in a hurry to take that as a sign of decadence and immorality. Let us not forget that the Romans were acting in conformity with a tradition going back to the happiest period of the City-State. The only difference was that Caesar and Pompey chose their wives themselves according to the exigencies of the moment, while in past centuries it was the paterfamilias who imposed on his sons or daughters the alliances that best served the clan's interests.

The solemnity of the engagement ceremonies, no doubt in accordance with patriarchal tradition, had long been authenticated by means of a whole legal apparatus that tended to make the contract almost as binding as marriage itself. Servius Sulpicius, the legal expert, has described the function, commenting that it was in keeping with Latin customs. But it is probable that the little cities of Latium and the surrounding countryside had held to the ancient usages formerly observed by the old Roman patrician families. The fiancé, Sulpicius explains, asked the person who promised him a wife to pledge his word in accord with the conventions of the *stipulatio,* in terms of the ritual. On his side, the future husband, after receiving the promise, bound himself in the same way. If, after the engagement had been entered into, one or the other of the contracting parties broke the vow, legal proceedings were begun. The judge, after conducting an inquiry into the reasons for the rupture, estimated the amount of the damages that the one responsible for the breach was required to pay.

The young girl who had plighted her troth was required to observe all the rules of conduct imposed on married women. When two persons became engaged, rings were exchanged, symbols of the projected alliance. It was then, too, that the contract regarding the dowry and the disposition of worldly goods was signed. The dowry was either handed over then and there, or at the time of the marriage.

The legal texts provide an opportunity to ascertain the moral conditions in which the engagement was concluded. Most of the accounts are concerned with the Imperial period, but conditions during the second and third centuries A.D. were often analogous to those of earlier times, or at least had retained vestiges of them. For morals do not evolve in a monolithic manner, and customs, especially those having to do with marriage, are maintained unchanged voluntarily from one generation to another. Innovations brought about by jurists themselves, and their attempts to make certain restrictions imposed by tradition conform to the dictates of reason, also provide documentary evidence of disappearing mores.

The legal texts do not admit of contradiction. What was true of marriages held good for engagements. Neither were valid without the consent of the two young persons. In the days of the Empire, at least, this accord was the only requirement—both necessary and sufficient—to render them valid. Whatever might be the form in which they were executed, whether they were solemnly celebrated before the engaged couple, or whether they were the result of a simple exchange of letters, or even if the fiancés, instead of being present, simply had third parties subscribe to the undertaking in their name—we are told that this happened every day—it was necessary (and sufficient) for the future husband and wife to know what was in the agreement, and to indicate that they were in accord. This was true even if it was carried out after the ceremony. Such an understanding was axiomatic in the second century A.D. What was the situation during the Republic? This theoretically liberal approach, this respect accorded the wishes of the engaged couple, and, in particular the fiancée, were in practice somewhat limited. The same author who insisted that the young girl must consent, included a highly revelatory stipulation: "A young girl who does not specifically defy her father's will is considered as giving her consent. And she is not permitted to differ from her father unless the latter chooses an unworthy or culpable man."

It would be nice to know at what period the last clause was incorporated. There is nothing to show for certain that this took place very late in the day. As is well known, in such matters, when the family honor was at stake, the Council of Fathers and of friends was prevailed upon to give its opinion—a necessary protection against abuse of authority by a tyrannical father. And this council makes its appearance very early. Surely, therefore, it was not necessary to await the end of the Republic to endow the fiancée, at least in practice, with a veritable power of veto. Maybe at the beginning it consisted in a kind of appeal to the family tribunal. But that is only a hypothesis, which may nevertheless be borne out by the legal decrees.

In any case it is clear that the young girl, in a majority of cases, could only acquiesce. Until the Empire, her sole freedom of choice lay in a refusal. But here it is necessary to make an important distinction. The legal writings speak almost entirely of young women of good family, and particularly of those still under the *manus* of their father. It is not just because they were women, not just on account of their sex, that their choice was limited. It was for another and much more legitimate reason: the natural subjection in which they found themselves. Emancipated girls, no longer subject to paternal authority, and "freedwomen," who enjoyed still greater liberty—no one would think of contravening their desires. The guardian of a girl or young woman no longer under the *manus* did not have to concern himself with her marriage. His function, we are told, was to administer her own individual fortune, and did not give him the right to interfere in her private life. As for a freedwoman, her employer could neither force her to marry against her will nor impose a husband he had chosen, unless this was expressly stipulated in the terms of the agreement which gave her her liberty. The general tendency was perfectly clear: except in the case of girls of good family, women were accorded the right to choose their husbands, or at least the privilege of accepting or rejecting the men chosen by someone else. A liberal approach was emphasized whenever it did not con-

MARRIAGE IN THE GOLDEN AGE

flict with the principle always threatened and always very vigorous, of paternal authority.

Respect for such, in the case of young women of good family, was all the more necessary since they so often became engaged when still very young, before they were old enough to make up their own minds. Because—and this is a fact that for a long time remained unnoticed, but which has recently been unearthed on incontrovertible evidence—Romans voluntarily practiced "child marriage." Whatever repugnance persons with modern ideas of morality may feel in regard to such a custom, which is nevertheless widespread today "from Morocco to Cambodia," there are undeniable proofs that young Roman girls were turned over to their husbands very young, and also that legal experts tried to curb a custom which, if it did not always cause physiological catastrophes, was certain to result in serious psychological traumas, or, at least, tended to bring about a dangerous deviation in the growth of the feminine psyche.

According to the jurists, males were required to be fourteen before they could marry; females, only twelve. But girls *could* become engaged much earlier. Legal experts admitted that there was no downward limit before the law. In fact families found it necessary for the reasons cited earlier—because these furthered their political aims and alliances—to bring about the engagement of babies in the cradle.

But while this practice was quite admissible as long as paternal authority was all-powerful, it ceased to be so when the idea that the fiancée should be in agreement began to take effect. That is why Modestinus, basing his argument on certain earlier texts, evinced the desire that an engagement should not be concluded before the bride-to-be had reached her seventh year. After Augustus' legislation regarding marriage and the *Julia et Papia* law, a further reason came into being. The custom of early engagements tended in effect to become even more widespread, since it was often a stratagem for postponing marriages without being exposed to the rigors of the law. A man engaged to a baby in the cradle had a right to consider himself outside the reach of the penalties imposed on bachelors. And it was no doubt to prevent this maneuver that a limit was set below which there could be no engagement in the legal sense. The two motives—respect for the will of the fiancée and the desire to put an end to an abuse—were certainly strong. Nevertheless custom had to be taken into account, and if the boundary line was set as low as it was (actually the lowest conceivable limit), this was because the moral code had become much less rigorous. And research shows that a fiancée seven years old was not always left in the bosom of her family to await the moment when she would be handed over to her husband.

The minimum age of twelve fixed by the jurists for marriage should not lead us to make any false assumptions: this was merely the age at which the marriage acquired the totality of its legal implications. Actually, Ulpian wrote in his commentary on the Praetor's edict: "The question came up whether an engagement was valid when the marriage was solemnized before the twelfth year, and I have always agreed with Labeo's advice, according to which the engagement continued in force even though the young girl had begun to live in her husband's home with the appellation of wife."

The legal device is evident. From seven to twelve there could be no marriage in the eyes of the law; there could at most be an engagement. Legal marriage could not take place before twelve, even if the consummation of marriage and life in common had begun earlier. Would all the precautions of the jurists make sense if it had not been the custom to marry off girls at a still tenderer age than twelve, long before puberty? The latter, moreover, was not considered a prerequisite for marriage by the jurists themselves. It was recognized, in effect, that it could take place at fourteen—which has been confirmed by the researches of modern medical men. But in spite of that, the minimum legal age had been wittingly lowered by another two years. This is made abun-

MARRIAGE IN THE GOLDEN AGE

dantly clear by a curious passage from Macrobius, which M. Durry brings forward to back up his conclusions.

"After twice seven years," writes Macrobius, "puberty is attained with all life's vigor; at that time the power to reproduce begins in boys and menstruation begins in girls. That is why boys, who from then on are men, are freed from the tutelage that is brought to bear on children, from which girls, on the other hand, are legally liberated two years earlier on account of the imperiousness of their desire."

To describe a young girl who was too young to be legally married but who was already in the physical sense a wife, lawyers used such circumlocutions as *in domum deducta*—she who has been brought into the house, or *loco nuptiae*—she who has the rank and functions of a wife. Thus a major edict, formerly inexplicable, is from now on perfectly clear: "If a girl less than twelve years old, brought into the house, commits adultery. . . ." And it must not be thought that this referred to exceptional cases or figments of jurists' imagination. Ulpian, among others, cites it, included in the list of all those cases in which the crime of adultery, if it has really been committed, might escape the rigors of the law. Ulpian answers this in the affirmative. A young girl who has committed adultery before twelve, cannot be accused of it since there has been no legal marriage, but she shall be treated the same as a fiancée, whose adultery is punishable according to a dictate of Septimius Severus.

One final piece of evidence is taken not from the jurists but from a philosopher who knew Roman mores well. Plutarch, in his "Life of Numa," praises his hero for having authorized the Romans to marry girls of twelve and even less. "Thus," he says, "the fiancée brings the greatest possible purity both of body and character to the union—a solution which makes it possible to achieve the greatest harmony in the couple's married life together."

Thus we arrive at a better way of getting an idea of what Roman marriage was like, at least for the aristocracy—that Roman marriage "in the old style," which moralists have so greatly regretted. For we do not have the right to assume that child marriages were the noxious expedients of a decadent society.

Everything in the accounts of jurists indicates, on the contrary, that morals evolved in the opposite direction. The pertinent laws represented an attempt to correct early malpractices.

To tell the truth, the inscriptions on tombs that remain to us, epitaphs that in general tell us the age of the deceased and the number of years that she was married, date only from the Empire, and consequently cannot provide information on the state of things during the splendid times of the Republic. And if it can be ascertained that many women in all the provinces of the Empire married at ten, this does not prove that things were the same three or four centuries earlier. But one would be wrong in thinking that between the two epochs morals underwent a radical transformation. The most that can be said is that they evolved in the direction of greater humaneness and respect for childhood. Otherwise, why would Plutarch commend the ancient King Numa for having instituted a custom whose happy effect on conjugal life drew his plaudits? Why, if this practice was not only new but also depraved?

What led the Romans to marry their daughters off so early? The answer had best be left to the sociologists. But we can guess that this observance bears a direct relationship to the organization of society at the time it made its appearance—that is to say, without doubt, long before Rome was founded. Does it stem from the patriarchal system and that of the gentes? Are we to think that each clan felt a pressing need to ally itself with another clan as soon as possible? Or that these clans, in adopting these practices so early, wanted to integrate wives who were really intruders? Perhaps, too—but this argument belongs on a different level, and is especially for marriages that took place at fourteen, after puberty had been verified—shouldn't we be careful to remember that human life was shorter, the aging process more rapid, and that families, in their desire to perpetuate themselves, meant to stretch the duration of these alliances as long as possible? The social habit of marrying young Roman boys and girls at an age when, today, young people are far from being called upon to bear such responsibilities, strikes us as an inheritance from ancient times, one of the traditions of the *mos maiorum,* an ancestral usage which it would have been dastardly even to think of changing.

And what was doubtless originally a social necessity became an institution that was hard to justify, a *de facto* situation which for centuries determined the nature of the relationship between married couples.

As a general rule, at least under the Republic, men married much later than girls; at the end of their adolescence, in fact, even if they were legally permitted to do it as soon as they reached their fourteenth year. So there was a considerable difference in age between husband and wife, and an even greater one in maturity. The husband's intention was naturally to form the character of the person who was to be the lady of the house, in accordance with his own desires. For him it was not enough to have her come into his home innocent and undefiled. He wanted someone who had not been exposed to any moral influence before his. Was this a precaution stemming from jealousy, from a conscious wish to establish his supremacy as a husband more easily? Or, simply, the inevitable effect of ancestral tradition? We may assume that it was one young people accepted without enthusiasm, at an age when they were eager to get more out of love than complete docility or the passivity of a little girl.

These marriages—so different from ours—were they happy? It does not appear that girls who married at such a tender age felt any particular aversion toward their husbands for that reason. There is no doubt that Roman marriage was often the butt of facile pleasantries. People enjoyed giving currency to anecdotes and witticisms in which it was lampooned. But this does not imply that the majority of these couples were not happy.

From the end of the fifth century B.C., in 403, to be exact, Camillus and Postumius, when they were censors, decided to levy a special tax on men who reached an advanced age without having taken wives. Nature, they asseverated, imposes a double law: to be born and to produce offspring. The very fact that your parents brought you up creates an obligation on your part to raise children. So do not be astonished at having to make a contribution for those who bear the responsibility of a numerous progeny. This "special tax" was in fact no more than a disguised fine. It was the only possible answer, since no one could be forced to get married or make any kind of agreement to do so.

But there are grounds for thinking that even very far back, men who were comfortably off tended to be repelled by the idea of getting married. The tendencies that Augustan legislation would try to curb without much success some three and a half centuries later had already made their appearance.

Every five years each censor in turn admonished the citizens to marry. Sometimes he would introduce a note of humor into his exhortation. A passage from a speech of Metellus Numidicus, who defeated Jugurtha, has come down to us from when he was Censor: "If we could stand being wifeless, citizens, we would all do without such encumbrances. But since nature has so made us that we cannot get enough pleasure from living with them, and since we cannot get along at all without them, we should sacrifice transitory enjoyment in favor of having a chance of survival in the long run."

Not all the censors were as genial as Metellus, and some had no intention of letting people make a joke of marriage. Thus one of them, during the taking of the oath of office, asked a senator, according to custom: "Do you—speaking truthfully and from the heart—have a wife?"

The man being questioned was, according to Aulus Gellius, a rather mediocre wag, always ready to turn everything into a joke. So he answered the Censor's question in a way that struck him as funny: "Yes, in truth I have a wife, but not the kind I would really like!"

His inopportune facetiousness was rewarded by exclusion from the senate and demotion to a lower rank of citizenship.

The theme of the henpecked husband seems to have been an inexhaustible one. In one of his Menippean satires which were a kind of half-serious, half-joking philosophic sermons, Marcus Terentius Varro, writing of the duties of a husband, said specifically: "The faults of one's wife must be suppressed or endured. If they are suppressed, one's wife is thereby rendered more agreeable. If they are endured, one becomes a better person." This skeptical philosophy epitomizes one whole aspect of married life as it presented itself to the Roman writer. According to Plutarch, Numa wished Varro to marry a girl so young he could form her personality the way he wanted! Apparently not all husbands succeeded, nor were all wives equally compliant.

To be sure, it was not the wives who had the unfortunate reputation of being dominating, not to say tyrannical, toward their spouses. For a long period they remained submissive. But their prestige grew after giving birth to several children, and after reaching maturity. One is led to believe that after they had been liberated from the jealous ascendancy of older relatives, they took a striking revenge. At that time husbands who had long ruled over them during their tender years were the chosen victims of a domestic revolt. And the victims were all the more vulnerable, since the age difference was no longer in their favor, and at the very time they were hoping to lead a restful existence, their spouses turned out to be insatiably vehement!

This will give us a clearer understanding of a number of anecdotes recounted by Roman historians in which one sees matrons suddenly seized by a veritable frenzy, ready to overturn not only their own homes but the whole Republic in their effort to keep their prerogatives. Marcus Porcius Cato, who was dissatisfied with the noble Roman ladies when the question of rescinding the

Oppian Law came up—a sumptuary law enacted during the darkest hours of Hannibal's war, and which, long after the victory, had continued to limit women's expenditure for jewels, toiletry, and retinues—gives a fairly clear picture of the ironical and disillusioned attitude of Roman men toward the fair sex. Here is what he recounted in a speech—the only part of it that has come down to us:

"It was formerly the custom in Rome for senators to come to the Curia accompanied by their sons who still wore the *toga praetextia*. Now one day an important matter had been discussed in the senate, and the deliberations had lasted so long that it was decided to carry them over to the following day. But they must be kept secret until the final decree was promulgated.

"That evening the mother of young Papirius, who had been to the assembly with his father, asked her son what the senators had discussed that day. The young man told her it was a secret, which he did not have the right to reveal. This made the lady even more anxious to learn what had been going on. The secrecy, the silence of her son, led her to ply him with questions. She pressed him further, and became almost violent. At this point the youth, still hoping to ward off his mother's importunities, took refuge in a pleasant and elegantly contrived fabrication. He told her that the senators had deliberated whether it would be more useful to the state and more in conformity with the state's interests for one man to have two wives or for one woman to have two husbands. The minute the lady heard this, she was quite upset. Greatly disturbed, she left the house and rushed to the homes of other matrons. And the next morning a crowd of married women could be seen converging on the senate. In tears, as supplicants, they implored the senate to give two husbands to one wife rather than two wives to one husband. The senators entering the chamber were stupefied; they asked one another what all this excitement and these entreaties might portend. Then young Papirius advanced to the center of the curia and told of his mother's adjurations and the answer he had given her. . . ."

The anecdote is certainly authentic. It was not the only time Roman ladies had indulged in such manifestations in public. In the course of the campaign waged against the notorious Oppian Law, which ran counter to their inclination towards finery, they blocked the streets leading to the Forum with their parades; they interrogated the magistrates, the senators, even the consuls!

On reaching the senate Cato complained: "I am not surprised by what has been told me about a certain island; how, in other days, a conspiracy organized by the women resulted in the complete extermination of the men." He himself was careful not to give his wife the slightest encouragement. He never kissed her in public, even in front of close relatives, except on some unusual occasion—for instance, if a storm threatened and she was afraid. The female sex was dangerous, he opined, and must be kept at a distance.

This puts one in mind of the reservations with which the restoration of the cult of Venus had been hedged about. Women were capable of being drawn into a kind of whirlpool of passion which could destroy one's composure, one's *auctoritas,* as well as one's *gravitas.* This potential harm had to be put up with, however, because without wives the state could not continue. Yet it remained a perpetual danger because harkening to them too much might lead the state along the road to destruction.

At times the women were capable of rising to heroic heights; they would donate their jewels to the state en masse, sometimes even their hair to be used in the operation of engines of war. Individually, they were willing to give up their children. But both the great surges of patriotic enthusiasm and the heartrending sacrifices were balanced by the relentlessness with which they resisted encroachments against their authority in the home—which the law did not recognize but which custom was unwilling to deny them.

This ambivalence on the part of the wife, sometimes an insignificant presence and sometimes a redoubtable tyrant, is reiterated, we find, in Roman comedies—at least in those of Plautus —the most typically Roman of all.

But just when we are on the point of adducing the testimony of the comic authors, a reservation presents itself. Everyone knows that Roman comedy (and there was never any pretense that the situation was different) was directly derived from the "new" Greek drama. So one can ask, with some reason, to what extent the conclusions we may draw really correspond to the true state of things in Rome. Yet though it is true that model and subject are Greek, the construction of the plots, the remarks of the characters, and their feelings all bear the Roman imprint. A continuous comparison with the comedies of Menander, which is now made possible by the all but miraculous discoveries of Egyptian papyrus manuscripts from the beginning of this century right up to the present, make it possible to confirm the fact that Plautus and Terence subtly transformed the Greek influence, and using it as a base, constructed works that were truly Roman. This was not always very hard. Athenian society in the Hellenistic period revived by Menander and other authors of the New Comedy, had many characteristics in common with Rome at the end of the third and in the middle of the second century B.C. In Rome as in Athens, you had the same juxtaposition of a traditional aristocracy and a cosmopolitan caste of plebeians; the same horde of common people which included merchants, soldiers, travelers, courtesans looking for a protector, and young persons of good family closely watched over by their fathers; the same swarm of flunkies made up of slaves ever ready to perpetrate some swindle, to further the amorous inclinations of their young masters or help them extract money from their fathers. All these resemblances made a continuous transposition plain sailing. The names of characters and places may be Greek but the souls are Roman! This allows us today to think of the works of Plautus and Terence as valid accounts of the mores and feelings of the men and women of their time.

Now Plautus and Terence give us two perceptibly different pictures of marriage. The differences alone are a guarantee that the authors did not slavishly follow Greek models.

Plautus considered marriage an unavoidable calamity. A father, provoked at a son who has committed too many inanities, can find no better punishment than to marry him off:

"THE FATHER: Look, if you want to be a man of parts—I've gotten you engaged to Callicles' daughter!

"THE SON (*in repentant mood*): I'll marry her, Father, and any others you want, too.

"THE FATHER (*moved by such heroism*): Although I'm angry with you, that would seem like punishment enough for one man!

"CALLICLES, THE FATHER-IN-LAW (*going him one better*): No, for him it's not enough. If he married a hundred women it would still not be enough!"

Plautus is no less of a woman-hater than his contemporary, Cato. Listen to the remarks he attributes to a courtesan who no doubt is speaking in her own name and as representative of her calling, but which give the poet's opinion of the whole female sex:

"When a woman wants to do something evil and does not succeed, she becomes listless and ill, misfortune and misery are her lot. If she starts to do some good, she tires of it before long. There are few women who grow fatigued when they have begun to do some harm, and few who persevere to the end when they have decided to do something beneficial."

One could cite many similar comments. A man announced that someone's wife had died, and by way of funeral oration he added: "It was the first time she gave her husband any pleasure." All such witticisms can doubtless be traced back to a tradition of malice, but what is significant is that the tradition existed.

The picture Plautus painted of family life—one that his public believed to some extent to be in conformity with the truth, and at which they laughed by way of taking a legitimate revenge—was just as pessimistic as that implied in the preceding quips. The wife was depicted as a tyrant, capable of unrestrained violence toward her husband, to the point of beating him. The husband, on his part, was afraid of her. There was no harsher curse than to say to a husband, "In the name of your old age, in the name of her whom you fear, that is to say, your wife, if you do not tell the truth about me, may Heaven cause your wife to survive you."

Wives, at least old ones, jealously watched over their husbands' conduct and also the household funds. They kept an eye on everything, and if the way matters were going did not please them, raised the roof. It often happened that they complained to the neighbors, and organized conspiracies to victimize those who were supposed to be their masters—to whom they denied even the most legitimate privileges.

When old Lysidamus tried to alleviate the ill humor of his Cleustrata in Plautus' play *Casina,* and started to caress her, she repelled him violently and made as if to go away. She knew, doubtless, that the old man was being hypocritical, and that what he really had on his mind was seducing some serving maid, but Cleustrata's conduct seemed so natural to Lysidamus that it did not evoke any qualms in his guilty conscience. It was his wife, to be sure, who spontaneously affirmed that "it is the husbands who usually cannot subject the wife to the exercise of their connubial rights."

But while in Plautus' plays, middle-aged married women are frequently portrayed, young wives do not appear at all. The poet took no interest in their feelings and their reaction to the new life that had been prepared for them. The explanation is often given that intimate family life could not be shown on the stage. That may be true, but more so, perhaps, of Greek than Roman comedy. The former, as we see, did not fail to make fun of the conduct of married women, and bring them directly onto the boards, but only in the case of matrons who had left their first youth behind. One can ask at what age respect for proprieties ceased to obtain. What would be shocking indeed would be to show a young wife in love with her husband. Roman morals were

MARRIAGE IN THE GOLDEN AGE

not in the least offended by the most lively love scenes, provided the loving one was not a respectable young woman but a courtesan. The taboo applied neither to the portrayal of love itself, nor to showing family life on the stage, but, specifically, to depicting conjugal love. On thinking it over, this seems surprising. French classical comedy, which owes so much to Roman comedy, is based on exactly the opposite social convention. Whether in Molière, Marivaux, or Regnart, love can be represented only if it leads to marriage; the notary always turns up in the final scene. And that is precisely what Plautus' public would have found shocking.

On this point, his plays reflect the mores of the times with absolute fidelity. This reluctance to show legitimate love on the stage conformed to Roman prudishness in regard to this aspect of conjugal life. It is certain that the love young Roman men felt for a mistress, outside the marriage bond, was not the same as the emotion that drove them on to perpetuate the race in the arms of their spouses.

In those days a young husband was not expected to *love* his wife in the way he loved—had the right to love—a courtesan, nor with the same ardor and the same sensual rapture. The difference will be the more readily understood if one remembers that the young bride was often married just as she outgrew childhood, if, indeed, she was not brought into it as a little girl. It would be natural for a husband—the best among them—to have a feeling of respect for her, or at least a confused recognition of some kind of responsibility. More than ever the husband's role was that of a guide who was expected to teach his spouse the quality of *pudicitia,* that reticence of body and soul considered to be a sign of virtue in women. A legitimate spouse should never know the full extent of Venus' power, and her husband would take care not to reveal it to her.

This was the somewhat hypocritical convention affecting the first stages of a Roman marriage at the end of the third century B.C. Of course it was no more than a convention; it was the ideal to which such bourgeois unions were supposed to conform. The young bride was brought into her husband's home still pure in body and spirit; her husband, treating her with respect but without passion, would make her gradually into the lady of the household, whose authority over it would be undisputed. This dominance would not be exercised without crises and storms. If the wife exceeded the limits imposed on her, and wore out her husband's patience, she ran the risk of hearing the fateful words: "Go away, woman! Take your things and leave." This was total repudiation on his part; total perdition on hers. But few husbands went so far as to make this dramatic pronouncement. Public opinion, as we saw, forbade them to do so lightly. And most of the women were clever enough to avoid provoking an open break, which, in the long run, would militate against them. In Rome as in many other places and in many other times, "bourgeois" marriage was not based on love. It was even thought desirable that it should be free of such a dangerous and unreasonable passion, which troubles men's hearts and throws women's into confusion. For marriage, a more peaceable emotion was preferred, firmly based on mutual esteem and respect. The latter sentiments were set forth in several customs that, at least at the beginning, exercised their sway over the daily relations between husband and wife.

Tradition required, for example, that when respectable women attended meals, they should not do so reclining on table-side divans, as the men did, but seated. The rule applied even to the "meals" of goddesses. Juno and Minerva, the two divinities of the Capitol, were offered an annual banquet that they shared with Jupiter. Each one had her stool, while a couch was made ready for the god. For a long time this usage was observed where goddesses were concerned. But the women had thrown it off long before the end of the Republic. They had finally gained the right to dine stretched out like men, as from earliest times courtesans and women unworthy of respect had also done.

A husband aware of his obligations when he returned from a voyage or even simply from his country house did not fail to send a messenger announcing his arrival. And Plutarch, who describes this custom, speculates on the reason behind it. Was it so that the lady of the house, notified in advance, could free herself from all the little chores that preoccupy the chatelaine, make the valets, serving wenches, and children stop their chatter in an effort to make the master's return as pleasant and desirable for him as for her? It is quite significant that Plutarch does not even think of the explanation that, in other times, would instantly spring to mind but that is certainly not the right one. A woman, in a house full of servants, her every step observed by her handmaidens, surrounded by a thousand prying eyes, could not, in the great days of Rome, compromise her honor at the risk of her life by indulging in some intrigue during her husband's absence. And it is even surer that if the husband suspected she was guilty he would not have himself announced sufficiently ahead of time to safeguard his peace of mind!

It is more sensible to think that the husband had enough respect for his wife to give her the time she needed to look her best, and to avoid finding her occupied with tasks or in a state of mind that would not be a good omen for their reunion.

Another question Plutarch brings up is no less persistent: why, he asks, on their wedding night, do husbands approach their wives only in the dark? And the author, with his sure insight into Roman feelings, explains that husbands were anxious to treat their wives with respect, to avoid ever offending their modesty, and that it would have been shocking to treat them as one would a courtesan. For, he says, "There is something shameful about legitimate love"; as if physical consummation tended to contravene the nature of the conjugal union, which was more moral than physical. Marriage, in those far-off days, was not the consecration by laws and rites of the attraction of two persons' hearts, nor the concord of their senses. It was the basis of an alliance that implied the sharing of two lives in common, and, it might be added, the harmony of the physical relations aimed at perpetuating that affiliation.

In such a venture, love might spring to life, and mutual enjoyment as well, but that was not essential. It was not even to be desired; a "good" marriage should be founded on more substantial sentiments.

But it can easily be imagined how in real life body and soul sometimes took their revenge. There were good marriages that could also be enchanting. It is in the writings of Plautus himself, despite his antagonism toward the fair sex, that we find the portrait of a woman who had the courage to love her husband with physical passion and still keep her feelings of respect for honor and duty.

Alkmene, the wife of Amphitryon, was the heroine of an exploit as famous as it is unbelievable. Her husband went off at the head of the army of Thebes, to fight the enemies of his adopted country. Their marriage was still quite new. According to Greek tradition, it had not even been consummated, since Alkmene had stipulated that she would not give herself to her husband unless he returned victorious. But Plautus did not think his audience would accept such an improbable situation. The submission required of a Roman wife on her wedding night made it unbelievable. No, Amphitryon, before going off to war, had entirely fulfilled his duties as a good citizen; he was aware that not long after his return Alkmene would bear a child. But, when the fleet was back in port, and the moment was approaching when Amphitryon would rejoin his wife, Jupiter, who was in love with Alkmene, took her husband's place and celebrated the false reunion with her. The god ordered the sun to spin out that night to twice the usual length. The following morning, before dawn, giving as his excuse the discharge of his duties, he took leave of Alkmene without revealing who he really was. Alkmene, during their good-bye scene, which took place before the front door of her house, poured out the promptings of her heart without restraint. On his part the bogus husband wanted to be natural and act as a spouse would who had been led to return by the pangs

MARRIAGE IN THE GOLDEN AGE

of love, and who was not entirely free of shame at this weakness. It is amusing to observe Roman *gravitas,* which could easily become pedantic, in conflict with the tender sentiments the "husband" only half dared to admit, even to himself:

"Farewell, Alkmene, keep well," said the husband who had just enjoyed her favors, "look after our house as you are doing, but also take care of yourself, I beg you, your confinement is reaching its term, as you see. As for me, I must go, but when the child is born, cherish it in my name."

This is a convincing picture of a Roman magistrate with heavy responsibilities but who nevertheless steals a moment to be with his wife, and who thinks tenderly of the fruit of their love. She whom he leaves behind at the family hearth is another part of himself; he delegates his rights as head of the family to her. It is she who will take the newborn child in her arms and, in place of her husband, lifting the little being before the whole household, will solemnly declare that it is legitimate.

Alkmene, who has no suspicion of the trick played on her, speaks as one in love. For the first time in these plays, we hear an extraordinary dialogue in which legitimate love is expressed without reticence. The more or less miraculous nature of the situation is what permits such a lapse from convention: thanks to this unusual "poetic license" we can really penetrate the intimate relationship of a young Roman couple, and we find feelings that modesty usually conceals from us.

Alkmene, sad at seeing the partner in her long night of love leave her side, pretends not to believe the tender, but rather awkward asseverations of her husband!

"I would rather have proofs of your tenderness," she told him, "than hear it expressed in speech. You are leaving me before the place in which you lay in the bed has been warmed again. You came yesterday during the night, and now you are going. Is that your idea of pleasure?"

And she disclosed her tearful visage: "I am weeping; it is your departure that makes your wife weep!"

"Oh, be quiet," answered the false Amphitryon. "Don't hurt your eyes. I'll come back right away."

"Right away—how long that is!"

And as if this dialogue was not enough to reveal what was in Alkmene's heart, Plautus has her recite a monologue a few scenes later, that is the most sincere portrayal we know of the feelings of wives whose husbands, enamored of glory, risked daily on the battlefields lives that their spouses wanted to keep for their very own:

"Surely we have little enough pleasure in our lives, during our whole existence, at the cost of so many troubles! That is the way of human life; the gods want every pleasure to be followed by pain—or rather, that still greater suffering and sorrow immediately ensue, as soon as one has experienced some satisfaction. Yes, I am now undergoing this experience myself, I realize it only too well. I had a moment of enjoyment myself, as long as I had the chance of seeing my husband—only one night, no more, and then he was gone, leaving me as soon as dawn came. How lonely I feel, now, since he is no longer there, the man I love above all others. But what makes me happy at least is that he defeated his enemies, and returned home covered with glory. That consoles me. Let him go far away, if only he brings glory when he comes back. I will bear his absence to the very end, I will endure with a vigorous and firm heart if I can be rewarded by hearing him called the victor; that will be enough for me, I feel. Valor is the finest recompense, it surely exceeds everything else: it protects and saves liberty, security, life, fortune, parents, country, and family. Valor contains everything; he who possesses it possesses all!"

In spite of the traditional scoldings and quips, it is here that Roman marriage is truly depicted. In this heroic and fervent declaration of faith, the wife, well aware of her husband's standing, shares his pride and his ideals.

It is true that she does not play an active role in affairs of state, but she has the same feelings as the men, and, modeling herself on them, is capable of overcoming her womanly instincts, of mastering herself so that impersonal and almost inhuman qualities come to the fore. Like that *virtus* whose name, derived from that of "man," *vir,* is a clear enough indication that it is not natural to her, but is an acquired ideal trait.

When, a while later, the real Amphitryon returned and learned from the lips of Alkmene "that he had already been there," and accused her of being unfaithful, she defended herself with simplicity and nobility:

"No, I do not think that my real dowry is what can be called by that name. My dowry is good behavior, restraint, control over my senses, awe of the gods, love for my parents, and good relations with our family; it is to obey you, to be generous with upright persons, and helpful to honest ones."

Such was the catechism of the perfect spouse at the beginning of the second century B.C.: a creed whose first article of faith is resistance to the power of the senses and of sensual love. Fundamentally, Roman love expected of the married woman, who was responsible for her *familia* before gods and men, a discipline similar to that required of men. But while the man had to put his instinct for domination, his ambition, and his taste for pleasure at the service of the collective interest, the woman had to keep from feeling in her heart and in her body the spontaneous impulse to love. When she acceded to her husband's desires, it was from obedience and respect—a severe apprenticeship which wellborn Roman women underwent for centuries, substituting for forbidden, dishonorable carnal appetites others that were tolerated: a preference for authority, even for intrigue; a code of honor that went as far as heroism if necessary; pride, and more often vanity; greed, and avarice, violent expressions of devotion; equally violent expressions of anger—everything was permitted except to be shamelessly amorous.

Women, in the works of Plautus—matrons, at least—accepted these ideals of conduct, and if sometimes, like Alkmene, a complaint burst from their hearts, they quickly brought their emotions under control.

But in the plays of Terence, a generation later, human nature was freer to speak out. The demands of the proprieties were less tyrannical, or they had evolved. No longer did convention prohibit depicting the beginnings of a couple's private life on the stage. The feelings of a young bride or a young husband could be expressed without constraint, and what is no doubt still more important, marriage was no longer regarded as a punishment. It began to figure more and more as the consecration and reward of love.

In plain fact, love as we think of it today hardly appeared at all in Plautus' comedies; neither in regard to the legitimate wife—and we have explained the scruples barring the way—nor toward the companion who is bought and paid for. With the latter, the only dramatic suspense in the man's courtship lay in whether or not he could pay the price she asked; and, for the courtesan, in whether she could extract the utmost from him in the way of payment. Nowhere does the dramatist show any interest in the awaking of feelings of love. For the man, it is only a question of crude desire as he seeks his pleasure. For the courtesan, it is only a question of fulfilling (resignedly or happily?—Plautus does not trouble to inquire) her professional duty. In the plays of Terence, on the other hand, the point of view is quite different, in spite of the resemblance between the plots, which are sometimes actually identical.

With Terence as with Plautus, a constantly recurring theme was that of a young girl who had been ravished, during an evening celebration, by an unknown young man. As a result of this deed of violence a child was born or was about to be. But the workings of fate required that at the end the seducer and his victim be brought face to face, without anyone knowing it, least of all themselves, through the efforts of their parents, so that both morality and love won out. But while in the plays of Plautus this ultimate marriage is merely a convenient convention, it is in Terence's

MARRIAGE IN THE GOLDEN AGE

comedies the happy resolution of a critical situation in which feelings and sentiment were engaged.

And this was of great import: it signified that the whole social and family structure was in a state of transformation. And that in real life as well as on the stage marriage was ceasing to be an impersonal institution and becoming the joining together of two hearts.

This development is made manifest in the works of Terence in several ways. It can be sensed in the remarks and the attitude of the young persons, which is understandable, but also in that of the fathers, who are sometimes remarkably indulgent and at other times conscientious in a way that Plautus' contemporaries would have thought quite uncalled for. Legally, young people continued to submit to paternal authority, but the latter was exercised without any violence. Chremes, one of the old men in *Andria,* was mainly concerned with the happiness of his daughter. He was unwilling to marry her off for reasons purely of family convenience and, in particular, to marry her to a man whose affections were elsewhere engaged. His crony, Simo, more of a conformist, less sensitive, insisted that the marriage be tried out. To which Chremes answered: "Such an experiment would be too serious a matter where my daughter is concerned!"

His obligation has a strangely modern sound and showed an unexpected regard for the rights of the human heart.

To be sure, such an attitude could be dangerous, and even the most indulgent fathers were quite aware of it. They would not agree to just any marriage—the ensuing scandal would have been too great. And Terence's audience would have protested violently in the name of the moral code. Just the same the playwright did not hesitate to go even further. He shows us young people who, in order to marry those they love, have recourse to subterfuges that until then had been, in the plays of Plautus, for admirers of courtesans, and who seek happiness not in ephemeral adventures but in marriage.

There is Antipho, for example, a young Athenian who remained in town alone, while his father left on a trip. One day, he saw a young girl in tears, overcome, beside the body of her mother, who had just died. Then and there he became enamored of her. But when he tried to see her, an elderly relative who lived with her as a chaperone absolutely refused to receive him. The young girl was freeborn, she was a citizen; if he wanted to marry her, it could perhaps be arranged, but otherwise, nothing doing! And young Antipho, ready for any sacrifice to gain the one he loved, took her to wife—an orphan, without a dowry, and apparently without any standing! Later, to justify this marriage that seemed improper in his father's eyes, he concocted a sort of legal comedy—in collusion with a shady old lawyer—a complicated rigmarole according to which a tribunal had ordered him to marry the young girl. (Athenian law permitted such orders in certain cases.) In the works of Plautus, it was the slaves who were guilty of such tricks, and then only to swindle money out of someone to buy the favors of a courtesan. Here, the matter is more serious: the paternal authority is made a game of; the very principle of the family is flouted. Just the same, it is obvious that the author's sympathy goes to the "unworthy" son, whose only excuse was that he was in love. It must be admitted that in the plays of Plautus, the conduct of lovers, who wanted nothing more than to buy enjoyment, was, so far as morals were concerned, if not praiseworthy, at least "natural" and pardonable.

The conduct of Terence's lovers, who involved their whole lives and their family's honor for what was perhaps only a whim, seems deeply immoral according to the same yardstick.

Terence did not pretend otherwise. When old Simo, in *Andria*, learned that a low-class girl was pregnant by his son, and, what was worse, that this same son intended to marry the person he had dishonored, he cried bitterly: "But why torment myself, why torture myself? Why ruin my old age with worry about his inanity? Let him keep her and good-bye! Let him live with her!"

And since Pamphilus, the guilty son, still felt respect and affection

MARRIAGE IN THE GOLDEN AGE

for his father in spite of all, he cried out to him: "Oh, my father!"

The old man replied: "How's that, 'Oh, my father?' As if you needed that father! House, wife, legitimate children—all this you found without your father. You brought persons here to pretend that she was a citizen. You are the winner!"

Love, the capricious yet all-powerful god, burst violently into literature and even life, and the whole existence of the family was disrupted. The young hero of *Hecyra,* who was also named Pamphilus, agreed, to please his father, to marry the daughter of a neighbor. But he was in love with Bacchis, a courtesan, and it appears that she returned his affection. Faced with martyrdom, he let himself be married off, but on his wedding night he was unable to do justice to his young wife. More nights passed, leaving poor Philumena intact! Meanwhile Pamphilus had thought things over. He realized that he could not treat as a wife a woman he had deep in his heart resolved not to keep by his side. But neither could he repudiate her openly, because she did not deserve such an insult. He could only hope that she would grow bored and break off the marriage of her own accord. Such feelings, which strike us as extremely considerate, would certainly shock a society used to more discipline and self-control.

Nevertheless Bacchis, who was jealous of his marriage, grew wayward and Pamphilus tired of her. At the same time the virtues of his young wife: her modesty, her reticence, the care she took to conceal her distress over the affront Pamphilus had given her, aroused first esteem, then tenderness, in his heart. Meanwhile, he was obliged to go on a trip, and, as custom demanded, he left his wife in his own home, to be looked after by his mother. He had hardly left when on a trifling pretext, Philumena went back to her father's house, refusing to join her in-laws. An embarrassing situation for the "old folks": Pamphilus' parents were astonished at the antipathy manifested toward them by a young woman whom they had showered with attention. Philumena's father, ignorant of the real reason that obliged her to stay with her mother, was reluctant to use coercion. But he felt culpable with regard to his old friend Laches, Pamphilus' father. Only his wife Myrrhina knew Philumena's secret: although Pamphilus had not touched her, she was about to bring a child into the world. This as the result of having been violated one night long before by an unknown young man. It is not hard to guess that this was none other than Pamphilus, but both were ignorant of the fact. The plot thickens. Everyone wants to know how the young woman at the center of it really feels. Pamphilus learned her secret, but since he loved her by now, refused to give it away. So he was torn between honor, which enjoined him to repudiate his unchaste wife, and his growing tenderness for her, which forbade his disgracing her by a divorce she did not deserve.

This then was the final scene of a "family drama": the two mothers only wanted their children to be happy. Each father believed that his own wife was responsible for Philumena's wayward conduct. And Pamphilus' mother, realizing how much young brides dislike living with their mothers-in-law, was thinking seriously of retiring to the country to leave the young couple to their own devices—up to the instant the truth was finally revealed. The father of the clandestine infant was Pamphilus! A wise Providence had worked out a climax that restored order everywhere.

A problem of conflicting sentiments such as this would hardly have been conceivable in the days of Plautus, some thirty years before. In any case, Terence had the greatest trouble getting his work a favorable hearing. The first performance was a resounding flop, and it was not until the third try that the play caught on. The slowness of the action, its static character, may well have been responsible for the initial failure. But all that would not have counted for much, except for the fact that the play's subject matter was extremely unsuitable (in Roman eyes) and almost outrageously "modern." Do you mean to say that a young woman's whim could upset her in-laws' existence: that a son could first refuse to play the role expected of him, then hesitate to protect his threatened honor, and all this for love? How wild, how unrestrained could young people be?

There is no use deceiving ourselves: the portrayal of all the refinements of the feeling of love, the search for a genuine love between husband and wife, everything that seems so natural to us today, was at first nothing more than a stroke of audacity, a gesture so bold as to be scandalous in Roman eyes.

V

FREE LOVE

EACH Roman had but one wife before the law. This tenet was never questioned. Confirmed from the very beginning, it remained valid down through the centuries. The discharge certificate, given to soldiers released from the army when their period of service was terminated, authorized them to convert into legitimate marriages the relationships (tolerated, but not officially recognized) that they might have entered into during their stay in the armed forces. But on one condition: that such marriages were confined to one per soldier! Nevertheless, neither law nor custom was ever concerned with restricting husbands where faithfulness was concerned nor inciting them to constancy. Passing affairs, whose bonds were tenuously tied and untied without benefit of ritual, were countenanced as long as they did not affect the honor of a married woman or that of a young woman of good family. As Cato plainly stated in one of his speeches:
"If you surprise your wife committing adultery, you may kill her without waiting for a legal verdict, and without fear of punishment. But if you are the one who commits adultery she would not dare touch you with the tip of her finger. What is more, she would not have the right to do so."
Let us not jump to the conclusion that these laws were "men's laws," drawn up by jealous, profligate husbands, anxious to preserve a freedom that they did not allow their spouses. It was not really a woman's license to love that they condemned in itself. There was a whole category of women who gave themselves freely: slaves, those whose situation, economically, did not keep them under their master's eye, but enabled them to "live their

life"; freedwomen, and, generally speaking, even women born free who habitually gave themselves over to prostitution or "dishonorable" callings, such as dancers, and who had thus lost any claim to being respectable. These were not considered worthy to become mothers, which robbed them of any interest as far as the legal and moral code was concerned. Since they could not contract legitimate unions, they obviously could not be guilty of adultery. But while widows or daughters of good family, whose transgressions did not involve adultery since they took place outside the marriage bond, could not misbehave without running the risk of being accused of *stuprum,* women "without honor" had nothing to fear. The *stuprum* was essentially the defilement, affected by illegitimate sexual relations, which was considered to taint the blood of the "passive" partner, willing or unwilling, in intercourse. An honorable woman who gave herself to a man outside of legitimate marriage could never become a wife or assume a wife's responsibilities. A woman "without honor," who was already subject to the same taboo, had no reason to restrict her liberty.

Here we find again that idea of the "blood taint," which seems so basic in Roman marriage, and on which rests, in the last analysis, the whole moral code of the day insofar as it related to love. A strange concept, no doubt, but its inevitable consequences affected all the sex life of the time. Normally, the man could not contract this taint, since in intercourse he is the "giver." In these conditions what was there to prevent his loving anyone he wished, just as long as he did not compromise a free, honorable woman, one whom the law protected and reserved for legitimate marriage? The restrictions imposed on the love life of a woman were simply the result of the situation in which nature had put her.

In truth, the man could also acquire the "blood taint," but that was when, giving up his manly prerogative, he yielded, like a woman, to another man's desire. This brings up the whole question of homosexuality, toward which the Roman moral code differed from the Greek in being very severe. But this strictness was not applied indiscriminately to all homosexual affairs. Even in very early times it would have occurred to no one to be shocked if a master conceived a passion for one of his male slaves—an infatuation that today would be considered reprehensible.

The following story provides an example. A Roman once had a favorite slave of this kind, and the young man, in the country with his master, wanted to eat some roast beef. Now in that village there was no roast beef to be bought. So the master had a steer slaughtered—one of those used for plowing—which was strictly forbidden by law. He had to appear before the tribunal, but no one reproached him for his unnatural attachment. The only accusation against him was that he had killed a beast of burden! But this tolerance was not present if the slave was of Roman blood. Thus it was that at the time of the Samnite wars a young man named Veturius, son of a magistrate who had lost all his fortune, had been forced to sell himself as a slave to pay the debts he owed to a certain Plotius. The latter, having fallen in love with him, made advances to him, and when Veturius demurred, had him whipped. The young man complained to the consuls, who referred the matter to the senate. The senate "Fathers" had Plotius thrown into prison, saying that the purity of Roman blood must be preserved, no matter what the status of the person threatened with contamination.

In the army the problem frequently arose. It was only natural that during long campaigns, in the course of several winters spent in isolated outposts under severe discipline, even friendships tended to give way to similar attachments. But since these endangered the purity of Roman blood, they were pitilessly repressed. Soldiers guilty of this crime were in principle condemned to death. No doubt this did not prevent such relationships, but they were kept secret; if the scandal became known, the perpetrators could expect no pity.

Plutarch tells how a nephew of Marius named Gaius Lusius, who served him in the capacity of staff officer, was killed as the result of just such an escapade.

He was not a bad fellow, as Plutarch tells it, but he invariably succumbed at the sight of a handsome youth. He could not restrain his concupiscence. And one of the soldiers in the same legion, a certain Trebonius, had unwittingly aroused a violent desire in him. But Trebonius refused to yield to his advances. One evening Lusius sent a subordinate ordering him to come to his tent. As a good soldier should, Trebonius obeyed. But when Gaius Lusius, unable to restrain himself, tried to assault him, Trebonius drew his sword and killed him. Marius was away at the time. When he returned, Trebonius was brought before him. While there were plenty of persons to accuse him before the Imperial Tribunal, no one could be found to defend a man who had killed the general's nephew! Then Trebonius spoke in his own defense. He called up witnesses, who were obliged to disclose how often Lusius had tried to seduce the young man, and the latter's dogged resistance. To make a long story short, Marius clearly discerned the truth, and instead of punishing the murderer, bestowed a crown on him, declaring that his action was an example that all should follow.

A number of similar accounts have come down to us. Sometimes they relate to young officers like Marius' nephew. Sometimes to veterans, centurions with decorations, whose careers ended shamefully. The more rank the guilty person had held, and the more authority that went with it, the more severe was the punishment, and they were made to understand that they should be the leaders, not the corrupters, of the youths entrusted to them.

Take the case of a centurion, M. Laetorius Mergus, whose colonel, the leader of the Cominius troops, brought him into court for having seduced a young ensign. And Laetorius did not even dare wait for the judgment to be passed, but went into voluntary exile, and shortly afterward committed suicide.

Or, again, take a *primpilus,* the oldest N.C.O. of his unit, C. Cornelius, who had had immoral relations with a young man of free birth. Thrown into prison, he appealed to the tribunes on the ground that his supposed "victim" was really a libertine engaged in prostitution. But the tribunes refused to listen to him, and let him die in prison. It was their opinion that the Roman people should not make a kind of pact with such persons and tolerate laxity, even if the guilty party had a fine service record.

Nevertheless, at least in the general staffs, during the Civil Wars, it would seem that "Greek customs" were frequently indulged in. But the objects of love were not soldiers, they were only young slaves, like those maintained in wealthy homes for the pleasure of the master. They were brought along on the campaigns together with the fine horses, the rugs, and purple-dyed tents—all the luxurious things a Roman of those days considered indispensable. Sulla had his favorites. There were also some in Sertorius' entourage, and a number of complicated intrigues resulted.

When Perperna plotted against Sertorius, he revealed his design to one of his friends named Manlius who was in love with a youth from whom he concealed nothing. This young man bestowed his favors not only on Manlius but also another officer, a certain Aufidius, who in turn was let in on the secret. Luckily for the conspirators, instead of making a clean breast of the matter to Sertorius, Aufidius was satisfied to warn Perperna, who, having been taught a lesson, immediately put his plan into execution.

And at this time, in spite of everything, sexual relations between two free men continued to be regarded as immoral. Plutarch, that goodly soul, who was accustomed in his homeland to a greater tolerance for sins regarded as venal, was astonished at the fuss made over what he considered trifling. Wondering why freeborn youths wore a gold ball around their necks until they assumed the *toga praetexta,* he pretended that he supposed the reason must lie in the aversion Romans felt for pederasty when the loved one was a freeborn child:

"Perhaps," said he, "the Romans of the early days, who were not loath to love male slaves in the flower of their youth, and who did not consider such an act unworthy of them—as can still be verified in the comedies of our day—but who strictly abstained from touching freeborn youths, had children wear the ball in order not to run the risk of violating them even when the latter were nude."

Plutarch knew perfectly well that this was not the right explanation but, since he was anxious to consider every possible hypothesis, he felt that he should not ignore an instinctive reaction on the part of Romans faced with opportunities for "love in the Greek style"—a direct consequence of the Roman idea of the nature of the sexual act.

The general attitude toward extramarital adventure followed the same lines as those provoked by homosexuality. The carnal act put its tainted mark on the blood of the receiving or submissive member of the couple. The crux of the problem lay in determining whether the defilement had been inflicted on someone legitimately entitled to receive it, or one who was supposed to remain untouched. In itself the act was neither good nor bad; it did not deserve to be qualified in a moral sense, since it was simply the satisfaction of a natural urge. But it was fraught with possible consequences quite apart from the desire or intention of the lovers. That is why the virtuous Lucretia, even though pardoned by her husband, believed after the rape that she had been defiled forever and her body rendered unworthy to be that of a mother. It would be a mistake to think that intercourse was considered a sin. It was simply, for the person who yielded to it, an irreparable action.

This aspect of love explains both the tolerance the Romans sometimes showed, and the ferocity with which, at other times, they repressed the slightest transgressions. Naturally adultery was severely punished. Usually, in the early days, the guilty person was put to death. But her accomplice, if caught in the act, was not dealt with any less severely—and this went on right up to the Classic epoch.

Tradition has preserved the recollection of some particularly horrifying punishments. One outraged husband had his rival whipped to death; another had him mutilated, thereby making sure that he would never again endanger a woman's honor; another rake was turned over to the servants, at whose hands he received the vilest ill-treatment—and we are told that these atrocious acts of revenge could be perpetrated with impunity.

In the *Metamorphoses,* Apuleius tells of a miller who, having surprised a young lover in bed with his wife, did not want to kill him, but forced him to spend a night beside him in the course of which he was "treated as a child," and the next morning, after a severe lashing, was sent home completely crestfallen.

In the Classic period, truth to tell, such instances had become the exception. Outraged husbands no longer thought of disclosing their dishonor to the public. They were satisfied to repudiate the wife, keeping her dowry, and the adulterer often got little out of it but a feeling of shame. If the husband pursued his revenge further, public opinion was by no means always in his favor.

Petronius, for instance, tells of the escapade of a woman whose husband surprised her "in the act" with his house steward. He did not dare attack her, because her father was an influential magistrate in the little town where they lived, and he might get himself into trouble. But the fornicator was thrown to wild beasts —for he was a man of servile degree. Then came the comments on his decision. Jealous types approved him, but they were in the minority. Young people, all those who enjoy love, declared that the slave, no doubt importuned by his mistress who had him completely in her power, was not in the least to blame, and that to punish him was eminently unjust. But everyone agreed that a husband who revenged himself in such a way—even if he was in the right—made himself utterly ridiculous by making everyone aware of what should have been kept secret. And it would seem that husbands in general were of the same opinion since Augustan laws obliged a husband to put away his wife or be classed as a pimp and branded as despicable.

Adultery, however, was not—at least in the old days—the only "sexual crime" to be punished severely. Custom was inexorable in regard to young freeborn girls.

One Publius Maenius had a young freedman of whom he was very fond, and who had the duty of giving lessons to his master's daughter. Well, one day the freedman forgot himself so far as to give his pupil a kiss. She was still young, having just reached marriageable age—perhaps twelve. No doubt the kiss was not a guilty one; the tutor wanted in all innocence to show his affection for his pupil. Nevertheless, the father had the imprudent teacher killed, because in his opinion his daughter should be turned over to her husband "not only virgin in body, but uncontaminated by any kiss."

Another father, for a graver offense, since the pedagogue had become the lover of the pupil, not only killed him but his own daughter as well.

These frightful examples of harshness in early times should not surprise us. In those days, there was a veritable religion, if not of honor as understood in other epochs, of blood purity—an absolute imperative, which could not even be discussed and which had its origin in religious beliefs buried in the racial unconscious.

This makes it possible to understand the fearsome heroism of Virginius who, in the middle of the fifth century B.C., strangled his own daughter with his bare hands in front of the assembled throng rather than hand her over as a slave to a man who had conceived an immoral passion for her and worked out this means for satisfying his fancy.

It must not be thought these tragedies indicate that Roman customs in ancient times were particularly austere. These same Romans, in fact, who were so ruthless when it was a question of protecting the purity of young freeborn girls, were entirely tolerant of what were known as "permissible amours." The elderly Cato's remarks on this point have become celebrated. One day the stern Censor, returning from the Forum, saw a young man leaving a nearby house of ill fame, hiding his face. The fact was that he had recognized Cato, and was filled with shame at being seen at such a juncture. But the dour Censor, instead of blaming him, cried out: "Courage, child, it is right that you should frequent harlots instead of going after honest women!" The story goes on to say that the next day the young man, proudly conscious of Cato's approval, left the same establishment at the same hour, but openly this time. Cato saw him, as he had the day before, but instead of complimenting him, he said: "It is true that I praised you for going to the whores, but you don't have to live with them!"

To have relations with women who were professionals was quite permissible. Danger threatened only if they became habitual, giving rise perhaps to affection, maybe even love. Was Cato not in the habit of saying that a man in love "allowed his soul to live inside another's body"? The wise thing was to flee from this ruinous passion that devoured the patrimony and, what was worse, the willpower of the young. But how could one escape from nature's demands? How—except by tolerating such satisfactions as appease the natural instincts and mitigate their virulence? The ancient Romans believed, rightly or wrongly, that a lover who satisfied his body's demands protected his heart from wrongful desires.

In ancient times a father (whose name we do not know) had a son who became enamoured of a forbidden "love object" with an incurable passion. Instead of using duress, his father—a man of sense—agreed to let him try to satisfy his guilty concupiscence, but on condition that before arriving at his fair one's dwelling, he make a detour and spend some time in the company of courtesans. The young man agreed, only too glad to have gained his father's permission. But as soon as he had satisfied his bodily cravings, his eagerness to confront the dangers in the way of his trying to win the other lady diminished considerably. The same treatment, after several applications, cured him completely. Horace, in one of his *Satires,* sings the same tune, backing up the moral with examples borrowed from the Cynic philosophers and from popular preachers:

"The idea!" he exclaimed. "Is the body of a princess prettier and more desirable than that of a courtesan? What use is it to risk a frightful punishment by pursuing ladies whose charms are veiled by the long dresses worn by matrons? When the great of this world buy a horse they pay no attention to its harness; one should not be taken in by the fine trappings that conceal it from view. And it is the same with women shielded from our gaze by elaborate, studied finery. How much more satisfying it is, and how much less dangerous for one's patrimony and one's honor, to take one's chance in the byways where beauties who are not in the least shy offer charms that everyone can see, to all comers! All the rest is only an illusion, the caprice of a disordered imagination, which does not take into account nature's exigencies, and dangerously complicates the conditions required for it to be happy."

Such dicta, borrowed for the most part from the Hellenistic "philosophers," repeated theses dear to the sagacious early Romans, and Horace knew it. Speaking as he did, he specifically wanted to show that the Epicureanism and even the cynicism of the professional philosophers were remarkably close to the national tradition. And as a matter of fact, young Romans had always satisfied their sensual yearnings outside marriage. It could not be otherwise in a society based on slavery. Long before the growth of Roman power had brought them into contact with peoples who practiced prostitution, the "virtuous" Romans did not consider it blameworthy to have one or more concubines in addition to their legitimate wives. Legal monogamy was mitigated by *de facto* polygamy, which was tolerated to the degree that it did not threaten the religious and legal integrity of the family.

However surprised and shocked one may be to catch the early Romans flagrantly engaging in such libidinous practices, the accounts in numerous and precise texts cannot be doubted. That concubines existed and were at the same time recognized is attested by a well-known fragment from a law attributed to King Numa: "Let not the *paelex* touch Juno's altar: if she touches it she must unloose her hair and sacrifice a little lamb to the goddess."

This "royal law" surely does not go back as far as the eighth century B.C. Nevertheless, it is very ancient. The curious compensatory rite it prescribes, the concept implied in it of defilement transmitted by contact alone—all this has an archaic flavor, and is an indication that the custom of keeping a mistress goes far back in time. The term *paelex* is used to designate a woman who habitually has relations with a man who is legally married. Truth to tell, the word is highly obscure; if we knew its etymology, we would be better informed on the character of what seems—at the time the law we are concerned with was drawn up—a veritable social institution. But possible analogies with Greek and Hebrew teach us little. At the most we can suppose that it was borrowed by the Latin tongue from a Mediterranean language, and accept the fact that the *paelex* was originally a "foreigner," a captive, a slave whom the master deigned to harbor and protect. For this reason her position within the home was ambiguous; her body and her blood were considered "impure" because of her sexual relations with the master of the house. It would have been blasphemy to allow her to take part in the family rites; her presence would have desecrated them. It would have been a still greater profanation if her person had come into contact, even accidentally, with the altar of the goddess of "legitimate marriage." But while similar sacrileges in other fields resulted in the death of the guilty person, according to the dread pronouncement *sacer esto*—"let him belong to the gods"—here Roman casuistry had conceived of a means of expiation—the sacrifice of a lamb—that would preserve the purity of the altar while keeping by the master's side the person under his protection and whom he perhaps loved.

Of course we are rather poorly informed as to the lot of a concubine in early times. We can suppose that it resembled that of the "captives" with which the heroes of the Homeric epic surrounded themselves. Without legal or religious protection, it can be assumed that the concubine was nothing more than the servant of the master, watched over hawk-eyed by the lady of the house, who as soon as the *dominus* had ceased to honor her with his caresses, repaid the concubine in full for her complaisance by humiliating her. Literary texts have not preserved any recollection of these domestic dramas, which were a part of daily life, totally lacking in any element of nobility or grandeur. Nevertheless there are a few sparse accounts that allude to them.

We know, for example, that the great Scipio, the leader in Africa, had in his old age a soft spot in his heart for a young serving maid. His wife, the grandmother of the Gracchi, was aware of it, but, as long as her husband lived, she feigned not to see what was going on. When the great man died in exile in his villa at Liternum she was high-minded enough not to wreak revenge: she gave the "guilty" girl her liberty, and even married her off to one of her freedmen.

A few years later Cato, Scipio's opponent, did not behave any better. In his old age, he had lost his wife and one of his children, but he remained vigorous, and still felt the promptings of nature. The widower lived with his second son and his daughter-in-law. At night a young girl of the household came often to stay with him, in secret—or so he thought. But in such a small house as his, presided over by a daughter-in-law, nothing could be concealed. It was not long before his children knew about the old man's affair. His son said nothing, but assumed such an aggrieved air that his father could no longer deceive himself that the secret was being kept. So Cato decided to put a good face on the matter and "legitimize" the relationship by making the *paelex* his legal wife, no doubt to humiliate and punish his son. The young girl's father was one of Cato's secretaries who depended on him for his living. At the Forum one day, the old man announced to the father that he had found a quite suitable husband for his daughter, a man who was rather old, but rich and of good family. The father answered that he agreed to the marriage in advance. Then Cato told him that he was himself the prospective husband, and the engagement was concluded forthwith. The marriage took place, and in due course a son was born, the last child of the illustrious Censor.

Such ancillary marriages, whether or not they were eventually legalized by a marriage in due form, appear to have been quite frequent. The noble Romans, who often had an uncontrollable aversion to taking a wife of their own rank, preferred to take some slave as a concubine, and, once they had made a habit of the relationship, set her free. And the juridical experts fully approved of the procedure. They had worked out a complete legal ordinance regulating the status of a freedwoman who was the concubine of her master, and were shocked only when the senators scorned public opinion to such an extent that they legally married such women. At the beginning of the Empire, the laws of Augustus to some extent restricted this freedom that was gradually diminishing the number of noble families, and exhausting the regular supply of senators, since the children born of these alliances could not be legitimate. But this legislation applied only to persons of senatorial rank. The other citizens were free to live with the woman of their choice.

Nevertheless, even a legally married senator kept the right to maintain as many concubines in his home as he desired, and even the Emperors were not above availing themselves of the privilege. Suetonius informs us that in Augustus' household, the master's legal wife chose young servant girls for him who ministered to his pleasure. As for Domitian, he had a special apartment fitted out in his palace which was reserved for concubines. Ancient and modern historians, to be sure, have painted Domitian in the blackest possible colors, but this is not because of his licentiousness, which was considered perfectly normal at the time—Pliny the Younger, in a letter telling of the horrible death of a senator at the hands of his slaves, alludes in the most natural way, and without any show of indignation, to the presence of concubines in the victim's house. The rank and wealth of the Emperor permitted him to make fuller use of a privilege accorded to all. This brings to mind the fact that Commodus, who enjoyed imitating the feats of Hercules in the arena, had a veritable harem in which lived three hundred young men and three hundred young women, all there to minister to his wants. One of these women, Marcia, who had formerly been the concubine of Ummidius Quadratus, succeeded in becoming the Emperor's favorite, and, as is well known, soon came to rule over his heart and his senses to the exclusion of anyone else.

The "good" Emperors, if they were more discreet, also had their concubines. Antonius Pius loved a certain Lysistrata, a freedwoman of the imperial household, who had the appellation of "the prince's concubine." It was bruited about that she was all-powerful at the palace; that the Prefect of the judgment hall owed his advancement to her. Marcus Aurelius himself, the Emperor-philosopher, whom modern historians praise to the skies, and who was, at the very least, an honorable man, took a companion after his wife's death who was the daughter of her steward. This young woman, whose name was Fabia, would have liked nothing better than to have the Emperor marry her. But the Emperor always refused, out of consideration for the children he had by Faustina.

At no period in Roman history was the presence of a concubine in the house considered discreditable. The laws did not protect her in any way; she had to rely entirely on the goodwill of her "friend." This guaranteed that she would prove accommodating—an important point when one recalls the reputation that had been acquired by the "matrons." Plautus had already emphasized the unfortunate situation of a husband who had to subject himself to the domination of a rich and well-born wife. Pity the man who had been weak enough to let himself be tempted by a dowry, and contracted a marriage of this sort. Unwilling or incapable of returning the dowry, he could not think of getting a divorce, and had to submit to his wife's tyranny. Whereas, if he had been satisfied to take a concubine, he could look forward to a succession of happy days.

In the course of time the institution of concubinage became a sort of "unofficial" marriage, to which some of the rules governing legal marriage applied. It could not be recognized as valid, for example, if the female companion was less than twelve years old. The appellation of concubine was conferred on all women for whom marriage was either dishonorable or impossible under the law. As a usage with legal backing, it represented the last stage in the evolution of marriage—when it finally became human. A *de facto* union, motivated by tender feelings only, its aim was less to legitimize debauchery than to provide a substitute for a nonviable marriage. This was especially true in the case of slaves, whose unions posed serious problems for the legislators—and for public morals—that could not be solved in any other way.

Slaves, to be sure, could not be legally married, since they had no personality or self in the eyes of the law. In the early days, sexual relations between slaves were regarded in the same light as those of farm animals: as a way for the master to increase his wealth thanks to their productivity. But they could not be controlled as easily as the animals in the barn. One can easily picture how ticklish the problem could become, in the farms as well as in town houses. It was not enough to shut the domestics up at night in separate parts of the house. Lovers could find a thousand dodges, and few guardians of either sex were above accepting bribes. A jug of wine pilfered from the master's cellar, some delicate morsel of food, could win over the most vigilant old woman. Roman comedies are full of these housekeepers, old wet nurses without any consolation in their old age except the pleasures of the bottle, who knew how to look the other way if this desire was gratified.

Old Cato, who was methodically minded and careful to regulate the slightest household details to his advantage, had found a practical solution to the problem. He had conceived the notion of authorizing sexual relations between slaves provided they paid him a stipulated fee. In this way, at the cost of a few coins taken from their savings, slaves could satisfy nature's promptings without the risk of being punished.

Whatever one thinks of Cato's stratagem, the inhuman restriction that systematically denied slaves the right to love and to perpetuate their own kind could not be enforced indefinitely. It ran counter to natural feelings, and in the long run its observance proved ruinous. Slaves born in the home, for instance, known as *vernae,* grew up with the master's children, joined in their games, and when they were adult were given responsible posts. How could they be considered purely as "things," or, worse, solely as livestock? It was inevitable that, little by little, slaves should acquire a *de facto* right to be considered as persons "of a sort," a quasi-human status, and what amounted almost to the right to live their own lives.

A joke of Plautus in *Casina* has led a few historians to think that real marriages of slaves had existed as part of the legal Roman system. But this was not so. The idea is actually a fantastic one although the mere fact that it was proclaimed, during the Punic Wars, brought joy to the Roman populace. But if there were not, and could not be, legitimate marriages between slaves, custom tolerated lasting *de facto* alliances between persons of servile condition. Theoretically the continuity of these unions was precarious, depending as it did on the master's pleasure. But in the great majority of cases this "concubinage," or as it was more often called, "cohabitation" (*contubernium*), could go on without interruption. It was looked on as a true marriage. The husband and his mate lived together; no one even thought of separating them. The children were legally the master's property, but there was no advantage to the latter in breaking up this family unit within the confines of the domain that contributed to its prosperity.

In the country, especially, where a steady supply of workers guaranteed the productivity of the land, it was quite natural that slaves should become "serfs," whose legal status did not condemn them to uncertainty as to what the future might hold.

But this phenomenon was not characteristic of country estates alone. In the city as well, in the great households full of slaves, which grew in number at the end of the Republic and under the Empire, many lasting stable alliances could be found among those of menial status. The environs of Rome are thickly studded with huge commemorative monuments whose epitaphs indicate that these extralegal couples, whose union was approved only as a matter of usage, stayed together until they died.

Can the "humanizing" of the status of slaves be attributed to the laxity of morals? Are we to think that the excessive increase in domesticity among the noble families tended to protect slaves from their masters' caprices by conferring on them a kind of anonymity? Each of us can choose the answer that satisfies him according to his preferences and to his opinion of Roman society. Perhaps the prudent course is not to come to any overgeneralized conclusion: the compassion or the insensibility shown by different masters, in different households, may have had the same ultimate effects. One thing is certain: in this domain, ruled by discretionary laws, habits ultimately crystallized; little by little "families" of slaves could be seen to prosper, and enter into "marriages" that were in no way different from those of free men. And it is the institution of "concubinage" that brought about the rapprochement between the two social conventions.

How strong really were these allegiances when the capricious forces of passion came into play? Petronius' *Satyricon,* so rich in "true" details, reveals to us some of the romances and dramas that were acted out in the households of the great. The hero of the best known of these episodes that has come down to us, Trimalchio was a slave brought from Asia when he was still young. His long hair falling about his neck in curls, his lively manner, and his intelligence had quickly captivated his master, who made the child his dearest companion. At first Trimalchio was but one of those *pueri delicati* (delicate youths) maintained in idleness, decked out in elegant raiment and jewels, whose chief attraction lay in their beauty and in their utter complaisance. Little by little he became the master's favorite. Now it happened that the mistress of the household, on her part, did not remain indifferent to the charms of the youthful Oriental. But, Trimalchio himself said, when in drunken moments he recalled far-distant memories: "Be silent, my tongue, I will give you some bread." The pleasure with which he gratified the master openly, and without shame (for, said he: "How could I not obey the master's orders?") and, secretly, the lady of the house, ultimately made his fortune. The master, to be sure, was not entirely certain that his wife was faithful to him. He banished Trimalchio for a while, but in his will gave the slave his freedom. Made wealthy by the presents which his talents had won him, Trimalchio in turn was able, once he was free, to organize some profitable business deals and taste the power that money brings. He had taken a mate, Fortunata, who had stuck by him when the going was hard. Fortunata was an old-time "lady of leisure" who, according to malicious gossips, was so stingy you wouldn't dare share a crust of bread with her. No one was more economical than she—and besides, she and her husband had so many common memories! The richest heiresses in town wooed Trimalchio in vain, for he turned a deaf ear to their blandishments. He wanted to keep Fortunata— "an old love," he said, but according to others, "an old canker!" The quarrels between them delighted the household; they tried separate bedrooms but this did not keep them apart after all; their tempestuous and jaded love for each other followed them to their final resting-place, where, despite what Trimalchio used to say when he was angry, their statues faced the passersby side by side. Moreover, Fortunata had proved to be such a good housekeeper: nothing escaped her watchful eye, she counted the silver, and kept hold of the purse strings—which does not displease any master, no matter how rich.

The adventures of Trimalchio, who was the delight of both his master and his mistress, are to be found in the romance of Perinthus and Sulpicia which contains an account of some of those forbidden amours that could not but arise inside the great homes. One of these is told, not without a certain constraint, in a few verses attached to the *Elegies* of Tibullus. It concerns Sulpicia, a young girl, niece of the noble Valerius Mesalla, who tells of her passion for young Cerinthus, who was no doubt a slave, or perhaps a freedman of the family. It was an ardent but guilty love that flowered in the shadow of secrecy. Sulpicia well knew that she could not belong openly to the man she loved, but she gave herself to him, and learned, loving him, "she was worthy of him, and he was worthy of her." The thought that he might be in the arms of some female slave—the inevitable concomitant of his low degree—made her suffer. She awaited him one night when she had been obliged to leave Rome and to go to the country; secretly, she celebrated his birthday. He aroused in her all the most delicate feelings, all the ardor she would have felt for a man not separated from her by so many conventions and insurmountable obstacles. We are not told how the idyll ended, the few separate sheets that have been preserved stop before the end. Maybe Sulpicia, her sense of duty restored, accepted the offer of one of her noble young suitors. Perhaps Cerinthus was the first to grow tired of a dangerous entanglement that could lead nowhere in the future. In any case we can assume that there were many such affairs in the great Roman households, which remain forever concealed from us since the hero and heroine were not poets who could tell the story of their romance in verse.

It was more usual for young men's desires to lead them to the courtesans. In the cities of the East and in Greece, these young women had been notorious for a long time: slaves, freedwomen, and a few born free, who tried to garner wealth in the company of youths of good family, merchants, and soldiers, and sometimes to occupy a place in these men's lives that their legal wives, shut up in the *gynaeceum* and excluded from normal social intercourse, could only leave empty.

It was quite natural that when Rome became essentially the capital of the Mediterranean world this same miscellaneous horde began to pour into the city, since both the local merchants and publicans drained the Eastern countries and cities of their riches In fact, the Romans did not wait until the era of the great conquests to have courtesans "of the Greek type" among them. White slavers learned the road to Rome from the days when her legions occupied Campania and the Hellenized countries of southern Italy. While Hannibal's armies had found myriad opportunities for debauchery at Capua, the reciprocal trade relations between Rome and the southern cities at the end of the third century B.C. had for a long time already familiarized the Romans with the loose morals the Greek settlers had brought with them into Italy. And the Romans must have put up even less resistance than might be expected since, as we have already stated, love was not in the least shameful in their eyes.

Plautus himself makes this clear, and Palinurus (one of the characters in the *Curculio*) frankly answers someone who was astonished to see him visit a procurer: "No one forbids us or prevents us from buying what is offered for sale to everyone who has the money to pay for it. No one is forbidden to use public thoroughfares, as long as he does not make his way through some fenced-in property. As long as one does not touch a married woman, a widow, a virgin, young persons, and free youths, everyone is entitled to make love with anyone he wants to!"

This does not mean that the calling of pimp was considered honorable. A *leno* (procurer) was deprived of his civil rights; he was "infamous." The forfeiture of his legal right was affirmed in a celebrated decision handed down by the civic Praetor Q. Metellus when the *leno* Vecillus asked the tribunal to confirm his title to assets that had been left him in due form by a citizen. Metellus had denied his request, considering that the testator had been wrong in wishing to have his fortune end up in an "impure" haven; and, on the other hand, he believed that the *leno,* having renounced living honorably, did not deserve the protection of the law.

In many comedies, too, the procurer is shown pitilessly beaten and deceived. The young people who played tricks on him well knew that if they were brought before the judge, everyone would condemn their victim. This caused pimps to be tough, wily, and merciless in their dealings; they took every possible precaution since, in the world of vice, they could not count on the good faith of their customers. Not only did persons try to seduce their "boarders" without their knowing it, not only were endless tricks devised to avoid paying them the sum agreed on, but people did not hesitate to use violence to penetrate their premises, and make off with their girls, without sparing them any kind of dirty dealings.

Let us not pity them overmuch, however: the girls they trafficked in had often been bought in the East, in countries where personal freedom was in no way protected by law; sometimes, they had been sold by parents reduced to misery, others had been kidnapped by brigands and pirates—it was as part of a criminal trade that they had sunk to the level of human merchandise. Neither was it uncommon for such traders to pick up very young children, abandoned by their parents shortly after they were born, raise them, and sell them at a large profit. Dealings of this type were not forbidden by law, but it was only natural that the men and women who engaged in them did not have a savory reputation. When a young man had really decided to take a girl away from her procurer, he did not hesitate to use any means at his command.

Young Aeschinu, in the *Adelphoe* of Terence, had just kidnapped a girl from the *leno* Sannio; the latter sued him to recover his property. But Aeschinus, unmoved by his threats, offered to buy the girl at a fair price, adding: "If you do not want to sell her, I shall go along with that; I do not want to sell her either, she is a

FREE LOVE

fine woman. I free her, on my own responsibility and afterwards, let us see which you prefer, to take the money I offer you, or take the case into court. Think it over, and let me have your answer when I come back!" At which point Sannio himself poured out a flood of recriminations:

"O great Jupiter, I am not surprised that there are people who are driven crazy by the mistreatment they have experienced! He took me from my place of residence; he beat me; he kidnapped a girl who belongs to me, and, to recompense him for all these violent deeds, he wants me to sell her to him at the price I paid for her! And he slapped me—miserable man that I am—more than five hundred times! But since after all he has made me an honest offer, so be it! It is his right, and I hope the deal goes through—on condition that he pays me. This is what I think will happen: when I say I will let her go at a given price, he will immediately find witnesses to affirm that the sale was agreed on. He will say, 'Come back tomorrow.' But as for the payments, it will be, nothing doing! 'Come back tomorrow,' he'll say. I can still stand even that, if he will only pay me sometime. It is tough, though. But I have one principle I go by: when you have undertaken the kind of trade I have, the insults of these little youths must be swallowed without complaining. . . ."

White slavers like Sannio would trade in entire lots, which they would pick up here and there according to the rise and fall in the market or to satisfy interested parties. But there were also procurers who stayed in one place, and limited themselves to maintaining a female *familia* whose services were for hire. Their young slaves had been trained to make themselves agreeable; they had been especially educated, and those who had any gift for it would recite poetry. There were schools where masters taught them music at the *leno*'s expense. Rented out by their boss for a night, they would join in banquets given by young—or not so young—persons, enlivened by their talent and their pleasant company. Later, during the drinking bouts that usually followed the repast, when wine had flowed freely, they would purvey other pleasures, unless, out of pity, they helped some young diner who had drunk too much to find the road to his home, or held him up while he spewed forth the excessive amounts of food he had eaten.

These girls who were for hire picked up their own following soon enough. They made friends, acquired habits, competed with one another, and became involved in intrigues to which they were drawn by their own coquetry.

A fragment from a comedy by Naevius called *The Young Girl of Tarentum* describes the wiles of one of these courtesans: "As a ball is tossed around a circle of players she favors each one, one after the other, with her airs and graces. She nods to one, winks at another, makes love with one while she is in the arms of another; makes good use of her hands, while rubbing her foot against someone else's; she shows her ring off to one while another's name is on her lips; she sings with this one while tracing a message with her finger for that one. . . ."

Each one of these girls had but one idea, to acquire a lover who would buy her from the *leno,* and take her to live with him, or, if he were fond enough, would be willing to liberate her. Then she would be dependent on no one, and could freely practice her trade, and—who knows?—amass a fortune! But the *leno* was rapacious; he ferreted out the plots, and when a customer had swallowed the bait, found a thousand ways of whetting his desire without satisfying it. He would banish the girl, or shut her up, pretending that she was sick or that a determined admirer had promised her a considerable sum on condition that she keep her favors for him alone. And the young man usually quite short of cash would try every means to get around his tormentor. He would send his agents out into the country to raise some ready cash no matter what the cost; he would borrow from his friends, from usurers, offering more and more without even being sure that a rival would not take the object of his desires from him.

Which is a way of saying that patrons were in great supply: they were on the lookout for the beauties who arrived in town, and did not hesitate to express their admiration loud and bold. In one

FREE LOVE

of Plautus' comedies, a city-dweller explains why he does not want to let his wife have a pretty servant girl who has been offered him:

"If a girl as pretty as that accompanied a mother, she would cause a furore when she went through the streets. She would be examined, inspected, she would be nodded at, given the eye; men would go: 'pst! pst!' at her and pinch her—and what a nuisance for us! They would come to her door and give her a 'shivaree,' there would be a regular bonfire of leaves of paper bearing verses in her honor. Not to mention that with the scandal-mongering going on today, they would not fail to accuse my wife and myself of engaging in a 'fine business!' . . ."

What a lively picture of a little southern city, where the men, apparently given over to loafing, think of nothing but possible conquests, and turn openly to leer at any passing woman. But if the woman is a matron or a girl of good family, as shown by a long dress reaching to her heels, they immediately stop staring. If it is a girl in a short dress, like that of a servant, or wrapped in the toga characteristic of professional courtesans, then they prolong their inspection, and come out with ironical comments and admiring exclamations—the whole bag of tricks of crossroad Lotharios hailing a woman of easy virtue. In the evening, when serious responsible citizens had left the Forum, the young people scattered through the streets, and, in bunches, went "to see the girls." They would pass and repass the windows of the procurer, thump a few times on the door, which was carefully kept closed. If some girl with a mind of her own took a chance and looked out the window, the crowd gathered, sang songs, and made a show of hoisting themselves up to the half-open window. Dates were made, or not, according to the credit of those who wanted them.

These melees before the doors of the lovely ladies were often described by poets in their elegies. But in real life they were sometimes dangerous, and tended to end up in the courts. A certain

Hostilius Mancinus who held the post of *aedilis curulis* once charged a courtesan named Manilia with violence. He said that he had been injured by a stone, hurled at night from the second story of the house in which the lady lived, and he showed the tribunal the wound it had caused. Manilia, on her part, appealed to the plebeian tribunes. She told how the aedile had appeared at her door one night with a band of gay followers, after a banquet, wearing a crown of flowers. She decided it was not wise to receive him, but Mancinus would not take no for an answer, and tried to force open the door. He had been repulsed with a shower of stones. The tribunes gave their decision: Mancinus had got no more than he deserved; Manilia was taking legitimate steps to protect herself. Mancinus was out of order appearing in public crowned with flowers. Accordingly the tribunes vetoed his appeal, and the legal action against Manilia was dropped.

So let us not think, when in some comedy we see a lover ordering his slaves to assault the house in which a gay lady is confined, that it is poetic license or a description of some exotic custom. The fact is that this happened often enough, but if things went wrong, the guilty party could not count on the law to defend him. If the *leno* was utterly in disfavor with the magistrates, an "independent" courtesan had a right to be protected by them, and the trade she plied did not prevent the law from shielding her if riotous "lovers" acted insultingly or used violence.

Sometimes on her threshold could be seen a "lover" who was holding a vigil. After the festive processions had stopped parading through the streets, and all was silent once more, he remained alone, waiting hope against hope for the door to open. He counted in this way on proving his love to the one who repudiated him. Did not so much patience and sacrifice deserve to be rewarded? From time to time he would sigh, he would lament, and address a moving prayer to the gods of the door and the threshold. He would hang the garlands of flowers that had encircled his brow on the doorframe—garlands that he no longer had the heart to wear. In the house, his presence had certainly been observed, the serving maids had announced to their mistress: there is a man at the door, so-and-so, he is lying on the stone threshold, poor thing! Won over by such perseverance, the lady might have pity on the supplicant—unless she had kept the door closed on him because she was already in the arms of someone else who was richer, more amusing, or more beloved.

This usage, current in Greece in Hellenic times, was brought to Rome along with other observances having to do with eroticism, to which courtesans from the East had habituated their Roman customers. In Greece it had given rise to a literary genre called the *paraklausithyron,* the "song before the closed door," and Roman poets also used it as a theme. Here once more poetic imagination was based directly on custom, and the picture it painted was on the whole an exact one.

Latin comedy, from the period preceding the Roman elegy, gives a vivid portrayal of the world of the courtesans. We see them—at least those who succeeded in escaping from the *leno,* and climbing the ladder of their profession by setting themselves up in business—putting out their snares to catch men, concocting their schemes, agreeing with one another to accept only hard cash that had been tested for weight, and above all, above everything, never to fall in love! A courtesan worthy of the name would spend many hours adorning herself. Thus, young Adelphasia on the morning of Venus' feast day (which is that of the courtesans) described to her sister, while she completed her toilet, the pains she had taken over it:

"Yes, from dawn until now, you and I have had only one task: to bathe ourselves, scrub ourselves, wipe ourselves off, put on our finery, polish ourselves, polish ourselves again, paint ourselves, bedizen ourselves—and in addition we have been given two servants who spend their whole time washing us, washing us over again, not to mention two men who wear themselves out bringing us water! Do not talk to me, I beg you, of the amount of work needed to prepare one single woman! And two of them, why, I am convinced that it would take a whole nation!"

To which the sister replied:

"I am astonished to hear you talk that way, Sister; you who are experienced and full of knowledge and wit. Although we make ourselves as pretty as possible, we are lucky if we pick up one or two miserable lovers."

Yet the sisters knew their worth. They were reluctant to go to the temple of Venus at an early hour:

"Now there will be a crowd in front of the altar. Or do you want to mingle with the girls that are waiting seated in the streets for their customers—those mistresses of mill hands, rubbish covered with bran, unfortunate creatures soaked in cheap perfume, disgusting daughters of slaves who smell of the slum and the lockup, who know nothing better than to stay on their chairs hour after hour, whom not a single freedman would want to take home with him, twopenny whores for the lowest kind of slave!"

For there was an infinite variety among courtesans. On the lowest rung of the ladder were those a *leno* had installed in a brothel. Each one was on duty in the narrow, evil-smelling street, before a cell whose doorway was covered with a curtain. Seated on a stool, she tried to arouse the customer's curiosity; half-naked, or with her body hardly veiled by a transparent tunic, she would respond to the slightest sign from the man who wanted her, and accompany him into the dark chamber, where, on a kind of concrete bench covered with coarse matting, she would give herself up for a few pennies which the madam who employed her would shortly take away. There were dozens of them in that ill-reputed street, plying their trade day and night. Their customers were slaves, poor devils buying a moment's pleasure, and in particular the feeling of not being, for once, something to be despised, the illusion of being able to receive or give a trace of tenderness.

These were the girls, deadened by sloth, incapable of hope, destined to go to pieces before their time, of whom the two pretty courtesans of the *Poenulus* were so scornful. But they themselves—with all their elegant finery, their seductive appearance—do they really delude men? Here is how a thoughtful slave describes them: "When they are in public, no one is as exquisite, as carefully groomed, as refined. When supping with a lover, they eat daintily—but to be able to see them when they are alone, at home, and observe how dirty, squalid, and miserable they are; how bad their manners are, how they devour black bread dipped in stew, how gluttonous they are—to be aware of all this, spells safety for the young."

Often these poor girls lived in their hovel with an old woman who acted partly as an adviser, partly as their protectress—called a *lena* by the poets, and who, in other days, was called the duenna or chaperone. Usually she was a former courtesan, the years having despoiled her of her charms. She tried to make a profit from the paid amours she obtained for her protégées. It was she who received the lovers, and set them right when they refused to proffer the expected gifts; she acted as go-between, carrying notes; arranged meetings, pretending to be highly respectable and full of righteous indignation which subsided when the price was met. The customers would try to rally her to their side, which could be done with a few crowns, but also sometimes by giving her spirits. For the poor old thing was always jaded; she liked wine as much as if not more than money, and after she had slaked her thirst, knew just when to doze off.

Profiting by their duenna's example, and thoroughly indoctrinated, the courtesans tried to make as much money as possible while they were still able to do it. So the comic poets had a fine time describing the myriad ways in which they extracted gifts from their admirers. No opportunity was neglected, birthdays and religious holidays multiplied. The girls' demands were insatiable: a servant here, a little slave there, jewels, fine fabrics, and new dresses. Sometimes they succeeded in having houses and estates given to them by naïve young men who soon squandered their inheritance, and had to go into exile to recoup their losses.

In Plautus' plays, courtesans are pictured as omnivorous harpies, and if young men were not morally to blame for frequenting them, nevertheless they ran a considerable risk in doing so.

And the fathers, meanwhile, often avaricious by nature or perhaps only cautious, took stringent precautions if the danger became too great. If the young man sought the company of the same courtesan too steadily, if there was a chance that he would act foolishly for her sake, he was sent off to the country. There, far from the lures of the city, he could if he wished achieve sensual satisfaction with some rustic servant girl whose company did not represent a risk—unless his body, exhausted by work in the fields, did not require any other effort to become sleepy. After all this, when he was quite cured, he would be married off, and things would resume their normal course.

That was Plautus' idea of the situation; it mirrored the conventions of his day, and one can hardly use the word "love" to describe the temporary relationships formed between young Romans and the girls who helped them get through their tender years with the least possible wear and tear.

But a half-century later, things were quite different, and it is easy to see that when Terence wrote his comedies, moral habits had changed. Just as in the works of Terence marriage had come to be based on love, so had the courtesan come to be regarded as something more than a mere means of gratifying one's pleasure, or a "gobbler of patrimonies"; now she was a companion able to inspire genuine feelings of tenderness and who was herself capable of love.

Here once again the theatre was a reflection of life. We have already related how a great many Romans, from the second century B.C. on, came to dislike marriage, and preferred less exacting partners. Terence's courtesans are very like his "concubines," freedwomen that the master kept by him from affection, once their youthful ardor had died down. The refined sentiments shown by such women as Bacchis in *Hecyra,* who overcame her jealousy and tried to conserve the marital happiness of her former lover, could also be found in real life. Thus the scandalous outbreak of the Bacchanales (which took place in 186 B.C., twenty-one years before the first performance of *Hecyra*) originated in a courtesan's denunciation: afraid that her protector's life was in danger, that he might be assassinated during the orgy following the rites of initiation, she did not hesitate to seek out the praetor, and reveal the secrets of the sect in spite of the risks she incurred.

The most human, the most modern, and the best loved of the girls who devoted their lives to pleasure, portrayed by Terence, was probably Thais, in *The Eunuch*. Her life was no different from that of a thousand others to be found all around the Mediterranean, and what, in Terence's comedy, took place in Athens certainly occurred often enough in other cities and especially in Rome. Thais was born in Rhodes, where her mother, who came from Samos, had her home. They had very little money, and one day a passing stranger seduced the young girl, who was surely still an adolescent, and took her to live with him in Athens. There the libertine, who had grown attached to her without, naturally, making her his wife, died and left her his property, which consisted of a house. Thais now had a home of her own. Young, without a protector, she could only become a recognized courtesan, but she did not hesitate to accept her lot, for which she was destined by all the circumstances of her life, and admirers visited her in a never-ending stream. Apparently her business prospered, for she maintained a household full of handmaidens and slaves, managed by an old woman holding the post of housekeeper. But one day Thais fell in love with one of her customers, who by a happy chance was also a neighbor. This young man, whose name was Phaedria, also adored Thais to distraction. Her feeling for him did not prevent her asking him for gifts, and Phaedria did not try to avoid acceding to her requests, especially as his love stimulated his generosity. But her calling distressed him: he could not abide sharing her with others. He was not rich enough, however, nor, especially, independent enough, to become her sole means of support. On her part, the young woman wished to continue in the role she had won for herself by her cleverness and persistence; she did not want to jeopardize her whole existence by refusing the gains to which her youth entitled her, in favor of a man she could never marry. But she was not wholeheartedly reconciled to fortuitous liaisons, even if they were remunerative. It distressed her to shut the door on her beloved Phaedria to receive some soldier with his money belt full of coins. So she flaunted all her wiles and became the "bad courtesan" who figures in Plautus' plays, keeping her warmth and ardor for Phaedria alone.

Thais had one aim, to become, if not a "bourgeoise," at least a "demi-bourgeoise." Since the path of matrimony was closed to her she aspired to the well-merited gratitude of some well-to-do citizen and to be taken under the protection of a great house. It happened that in Rhodes she had been brought up with a little girl whom she looked upon as a sister, who was really a citizen of Athens but who had been kidnapped by pirates. Since Thais had settled in the city, she had the adolescent girl brought to her, and conceived the idea of returning her to her family. This good deed she hoped would create a bond of gratitude for having restored the lost child, that would end by Thais' adoption once for all as the family's protégée.

After a few vicissitudes she succeeded, and at the end of the comedy she was shown as a "client" of Phaedria's father, and relieved from the necessity of following her degrading trade. Apparently there was no objection to young Phaedria's becoming her official and exclusive lover. Love triumphed, but not legitimized by marriage (which in this case was impossible) but simply the love of two persons who did not wait for a wedding in order for their personalities to be revealed to each other, since they began the relationship for the sake of the pleasure they derived from it, and did not become passionately involved until they had reached the end of the road.

FREE LOVE

Experiencing true love made the young girl marvelously compassionate. Chaerea, Phaedria's brother, seduced the young girl she had counted on returning to her family, thereby upsetting all her plans. But she kept her self-control, and pardoned the young man. He said to her: "I want you to know only this: what I did, I did not to harm you, but for love." She answered: "I know that, and that is the reason, to be sure, that I willingly pardon you. I am not so inhuman, Chaerea, nor so inexperienced not to know the power of love. . . ."

Two reasons, and only two, could thus explain someone's ignorance of the dynamism of love: inexperience (an excuse given by all legitimate wives on their wedding day) and *inhumanitas,* a lack of humane sentiments, a kind of natural brutality that makes a man incapable of feeling what other men feel—as if he was actually under a curse.

In that case love is not considered as a power to be feared, a scourge that should be kept at a distance. Love is then thought of as a god, the instinctive reaction he awakens in human hearts is divine in itself, and a person who refuses to respond to its appeal is guilty, or at least will be unhappy.

To be sure there is a great difference between such a moral attitude and that of Plautus. In actual time, the distance between them covers one or two generations. But the values on which their approach is based are as divergent as possible. Plautus, like the Romans of the early days, distrusted love. Terence accepted it as one of the most "human" sentiments that existed, one of those that expressed the profoundest human verities. To refuse to admit it, to be sly about it, to deny it, was to live "outside the truth." That was the sin committed by the graybeard in *The Man Who Was His Own Executioner*. This man, as a result of his stupid severity, exiled his son, and ended by chastising himself for his transgressions.

The new approach to love doubtless originated with the Greeks; a moral code based on nature, a new recognition of the influence of passion were part of the dogmas of several schools of philosophy. Yet it is hard to connect Terence's moral code with any specific doctrine. His work bears witness in the main to a state of mind, an assemblage of shared ideas, that one would be wrong to attribute to one philosopher alone. After all, urging young people to taste the pleasures of love does not require a mastery of dialectic. On the other hand, the strictest regulations inevitably are relaxed sooner or later, and if this process was speeded up in Rome at the beginning of the second century B.C., this can be attributed to the example of Greece and the Hellenized East, which not only offered greater temptations but revealed that life was possible without the repression of natural feelings, without submitting the relationship between men and women to the tyranny of mores whose religious and moral justification had long been forgotten and which were nothing more than a survival from a past age.

To be sure, Roman *humanitas* could not have been born if Greek thinkers had not shown the way, no more than Terence could have written his plays without Menander and the other authors of the New Comedy. But these lessons in turn, however astute, could not have been understood if the pupils had not been ready to listen to them. And no doubt in this regard the courtesans themselves played a role: to the best of the young Romans they revealed the love that is beyond mere pleasure; they helped break the old taboos, as we have tried to show, repressed the sexual urge within the family.

Cato, when he was a Censor, some twenty years before Terence began to write his comedies, had expelled a well-considered person from the senate, a certain Manilius, because he had taken the liberty of kissing his wife openly in front of his daughter. Cato felt that all acts, even the most intimate ones, should be subject to supervision: marriage, diet, gatherings and banquets, everything up to and including sexual intercourse with one's wife should—if he was to be believed—be regulated by an authority that made sure they were not performed for pleasure, and that they were in conformity with ancestral tradition and the good of the state. At

FREE LOVE

the end of the Second Punic War, Rome threatened to turn into a totalitarian state, a huge beehive, hypocritical and grim. Luckily for her, the organization Cato wanted to establish went astray while it still existed only in theory. Would it be going too far to attribute this failure at least in part to the beneficent and rebellious influence of the courtesans, to the taste for "free" love? It was a predilection deplored by the moralist, who blamed victorious Rome for it, calling it a defect and an indication of its future decadence. Yet it was to prepare human sensitivities for the discovery and conquest of new realms thanks to which the love relationship could gradually free itself from its primitive uncouthness, and develop a deep spiritual significance.

VI

LOVE AND THE POETS

THERE is a Latin poet whose name is inseparably linked with the feeling of love, and who in the course of his life paid for having acquired that reputation with exile. If Ovid had not written *Amores* and *Ars Amatoria* (*The Art of Love*) he might perhaps have continued peacefully in Rome to the end of his days, instead of becoming familiar with the hardships of the Scythian winter and the solitude of the coasts of the Black Sea, on the frontiers of the Empire. But if he had been more discreet, we should not have him to thank today for the frankest, liveliest account of Roman love during the years that marked off the Republic from the beginning of the Empire.

The Art of Love is, for all its grace, a work that bore an aura of scandal. It must not be thought that the uproar began with the Christian era. Augustus himself judged—or pretended to judge—that this little poem was not compatible with Roman dignity. Augustus, who all his life allowed himself to take any liberties he wanted and knew how to combine an appearance of the strictest virtue with the most frivolous diversions, certainly did not believe that public opinion would be completely taken in when he professed to justify the exile imposed on the poet when he was long past maturity by the immorality of his first works. Modern historians wonder about the real motive behind the sentence. They bring up obscure political or religious reasons, sometimes convincingly; none of them takes the official censure of the poet very seriously. It is nonetheless true that the Emperor thought he was right in banning these love poems from the public libraries on account of their "immorality." And Ovid himself, in the elegies he wrote in exile, voiced a repentant attitude that may have been sincere but that he felt he must proclaim, to merit being recalled. And yet—what is there in *Ars Amatoria* and the elegies of the *Amores* that cannot already be found in Terence, or, which is worse, was not in line with current practices among Roman lovers?

According to immemorial tradition, the amours of courtesans were permitted. (When Cato acquiesced in such indulgences, he doubtless did not weigh the consequences. But no matter how much authority he had over his fellow citizens, he could not expect in the eighteen months his censorship was in effect to make them over into rigid Puritans.) Ostensibly, *The Art of Love* had as its only aim to instruct persons in the practice of types of relationships that were tolerated. Ovid did not pretend to be anything more than one of those young persons whose peccadilloes were readily forgiven.

"Keep away from me," he said, "you narrow headbands, indications of decency; and you, flounce that lengthens the dress, that enwraps and conceals women's feet. What we are singing the praises of is a Venus to whom much is permitted and whose lapses are condoned, and my poem should in no way deserve any condemnation."

Horace, the official poet, had said much the same thing, and encouraged youths to sow their wild oats with girls not under the protection of the law. But Augustus could have answered in practically the same words Cato used to reprove a young rake: "I praise Horace for urging young persons to frequent the girls, but I punish Ovid for inciting them to spend their lives with them!"

Moreover, Ovid's family life was quite honorable. He loved his wife tenderly. What he tells us of his fondness for her when he was in exile, and the heartbreak they suffered when they had to separate, proves beyond any possible doubt that he was a "good husband," faithful and affectionate. But if his life was pure, his Muse was not. If Augustus in exiling the poet had been guided by moral considerations, at least to some extent, he was punishing, not a debauchee, but the chronicler of a society that the aged Emperor, whose affection for his family had been severely put to the test, seemed to have suddenly discovered indulging in perilous diversions. (Ovid's exile followed hard on the heels of the scandal of the second Julia.)

Poets before Ovid—Catullus thirty-odd years earlier, Tibullus and Propertius in the generation just prior to Ovid—had recounted their love affairs. In their verse they expressed the sentiments they strongly felt. Ovid, on the contrary, in the *Ars Amatoria* and in the *Amores,* did not seek his inspiration in his own personal experience. He could try to pretend that the heroine of *Amores,* whom he called Corinna, had been his mistress, but he had recourse to his imagination more often than to his memories; he made up most of the story, even if now and then bits of it were drawn from real life affairs. But that is just the reason why Ovid truly recorded the annals of his time. His forerunners, most of the time, set down what they themselves did. But Ovid, on the other hand, faithfully set down the idea his contemporaries had of love, their impression of its role in the lives of human beings in general, of the share that could justly be attributed to it in influencing behavior—the goal toward which it aimed.

Ovid is the last of the Latin "elegiac" poets. A type of poetry that had been created in Rome and that served specifically to sing the praises of love was reaching its end. What had started as a kind of journal of passion personally experienced every day had been transformed by him into an exposition of "universal ambition." He gathered the fruits of a development to which the sufferings of greater poets before him, and the works born of these sufferings, contributed. These writings influenced men's minds and hearts in their day, and thanks to them we are made aware of the development of an entirely new attitude toward love, which, appearing in varied forms in the works of individual writers, found its definitive shape in the poems of Ovid. Catullus, Tibullus, and

Propertius each made his contribution; without being aware of it they worked to free the new approach from the bonds that constricted it.

It fell to Ovid to assess a half century of love affairs from which a changed Rome emerged, after a moral crisis that had completely destroyed concepts seven centuries old.

On the surface, love as described by Ovid is not very different from that to be met with in Terence's plays. But the scenes that in humorous literature were laid in Greece are now transported to Rome as part of the city's daily life. Ovid's Rome is not "the Queen of cities," handing down its laws for the benefit of the human species; it is preeminently the city of love. If Ovid is to be believed, everything was an incitement to love: public esplanades, squares, and porticoes everywhere exhibited a thousand fair ladies come from every corner of the universe to captivate their captors. Young girls hardly more than children, women in the flower of youth, women who were more mature (their group was the largest) passed and repassed ceaselessly before men's eyes, waiting to be loved. No place was exempt, not even the ancient Forum—transformed into a place of assignation, and spreading its tentacles to catch austere men of the law. Ovid's Rome, then, was quite like the "little city" pictured by Plautus where every man, on the alert, spent his time ogling the foreign women. Now, however, their salutations in dubious taste were no longer addressed to a handful of servant girls but to members of an immense throng, always changing, ever renewed, that seemed to have come to Rome only to exacerbate the yearnings of the male.

Love, for Ovid—and no doubt for most of his contemporaries— meant above all, desire. And in Latin, moreover, *amare,* to love, meant at first to be someone's lover or mistress, and *The Art of Love* was a compilation in which could be found the best advice on how to win a woman's favors. Now, as we said, Ovid did not allow himself to think of any woman in this connection who did not make a living from love, and whose only *raison d'être* was just that: to acquire and hold lovers.

Married life is not mentioned, primarily in order to respect the proprieties, but also because marriage was obviously not considered the setting for "love." Even if Ovid loved his wife, this was his attitude toward legitimate alliances, the regular bonds sanctioned by custom. At one point in his book, he insists on the need for lovers to be good-natured with each other: "Let the legal wife and the husband quarrel with each other," he says, "let them feel as if they were forever suing each other. But as for the mistress, let her turn a deaf ear to the words she doesn't want to hear. It was not the law that ordered you to go to bed with that woman among all others, it is love that plays the role of the law where you are concerned."

Without the constraints provided by the law, true love became what it had been at the beginning. It could not thrive on deceit, unless one was very rich, and could by means of gifts keep the person one wanted in perpetual bondage. Whatever our moral code may lead us to think of such complete freedom of indulgence, it is nonetheless true that it set the stage for an experience of love "in its pure state." A threat to the social structure, even to the future of Rome, in the long run bringing about the destruction of the family and even the persons involved, it nevertheless allowed the feeling of love to experience its own fulfillment, and opened the door to new refinements of taste.

Ovid's endeavors led him to adhere to some universal notions—because of his efforts to be objective and impersonal—in particular, current Roman prejudices regarding feminine psychology. How could he have introduced subtle modifications of his own since he was not really speaking from personal experience, and the women he conjured up were not real persons but all abstractions to some degree? There is "the blonde," there is "the brunette," the big one, the small one, the cultivated woman and the ignorant one, the mistress and the servant. In trying to give advice that will be helpful to everyone, the poet tends to forget that love between two human beings in each instance has its own particular character, that if passion is the most banal experience in the world, it is nevertheless the most personal.

In Ovid's eyes, every woman was a passionate being and consequently a willing victim, ready to welcome her seducer. He is not thinking only of courtesans, whose calling it is to captivate, but like all Romans who, as we have said, took extraordinary precautions to protect their companions from concupiscence, he was convinced that this failing was an essential trait of the female character. "Their desire is stronger than ours," he wrote, "and is characterized by more violence and aberration." This is just about the same attitude as that of the philosophers who tried to justify the laws authorizing girls to marry at twelve "because of their desire for sex." It is one of creation's laws, and Ovid did not hesitate to cite examples of that voluptuous frenzy commonly attributed to women. He was content, at the end of his poem, to mention discreetly such women as experienced no pleasure because Nature did not make them sensual; as well-trained courtesans, their job was to simulate the most lively reactions.

Avid for love, and obviously thinking of nothing else, women indulged in every form of coquetry. Whoever wanted to captivate them had only to sing their praises. Any kind of compliment would do, whether it applied to their physical charms, their dresses, their finery, or their wit. There was nothing that could not serve as the subject of a eulogy no doubt partly sincere. It was up to the lover to realize just how far he could go without overdoing it, and letting the flattery become too obvious. The older the woman, the less sure she was of her power to attract men, the easier the task became. We have now reached the time when a woman, even a courtesan, even one freed the day before, was, for her lover, the *domina,* the "dame," who dominated him. *Domina* is the word used by slaves to designate their mistress. The Greek language has an equivalent: κυρία. Roman lovers used the term to give the one they loved the dignity of a "dame," and to describe their complete submission to her. For others, she was only a *puella,* a "girl"; but for the lover, she was the "mistress," and in fact he performed all the ministrations usually required of slaves. In hot weather, walking together, he would hold her parasol; if she fixed her hair, he held the mirror before her, which was usually the task of the *ornatrix*. And Ovid did not scruple to conjure up the myth of Hercules becoming the servant of Omphale.

Love was a powerful god, capable of altering a person's true nature, and forcing him to go against his own tendencies. Women were delighted with the power the god accorded them, and were willing to risk defeat to make it felt.

Such dependence, such devotion, which were supposed to be rewarded by attaining satisfaction, were, in a rather curious way, compared by Ovid to those of the soldier. That "love is a kind of military service" is a thesis he propounds with some assurance, and which, besides, he did not invent. Tibullus had already said the same thing, but Ovid repeats it with conviction, and draws far-reaching conclusions from it. In Rome, soldiers were bound to their leaders by an oath of fealty. They no longer belonged to themselves, and did not become free men again until after their tour of duty was over.

Similarly, in love, one has to give up one's freedom, tramp the roads at night in all weather, and never think of oneself, but brave all dangers to find one's mistress! Doubtless such complete submission is an instinctive force, many examples of which can be found in the animal world. But the remarkable thing here is that this natural impulse had been justified and regulated. A total abnegation of the male will is predicated—and this attitude is completely different from what we encountered in ancient Roman society.

In olden times the woman was respected because she was a wife. She was honored, but great care was taken to restrict her field of action to the interior of the household. When important matters were involved, no Roman worthy of the name would be guided by his wife's fancy. But in the social system that Ovid describes—and which was that of "respectable persons" in Augustan times—the free man became a slave, the lover became the votary of an idol whose slightest gesture could plunge him into despair or fill his cup of happiness to the brim. Until then the wife was "mother" and "mistress"—"mother" in her husband's eyes, "mistress" for the servants and other members of the household. But now the companion (and not only the paramour for a night or a season) had complete power. Her dominion was exercised first and foremost over the one to whom in earlier days (in conformity with old-style marriage customs) she owed respect and obedience. By a strange reversal, man became a slave because he was in love, because the law did not protect him; if he wanted to seek a liaison that made him happy, he had to realize that his felicity did not depend on himself but on one of those creatures said to be fickle, a prey to passion, deceitful, and unfaithful. And, to influence this capricious goddess in his favor, his devotion must be complete.

In *The Art of Love* Ovid even goes so far as to advise the lover to connive at his mistress' infidelity. At the same time he also can allow himself some passing gratifications: "Do not," he writes, "let my disapproval condemn you to sticking to one girl . . . which is about all a legally married woman can hope to expect. Keep your indiscretions hidden and don't overdo it." So far, nothing very surprising. But what are we to think of this advice: "If you have a rival, be patient. You will win out in the end. The best thing is to ignore the whole matter; let her keep her infidelities a secret, so that she may not have to lose face by admitting them."

From this point of view, to deprive a mistress of the right to pick and choose was to act like a boor. So the Romans, who were more jealous than anybody, learned to show forbearance when they were in love.

Cato had already acted with self-restraint regarding Claudia's first infidelities. Sharing the loved one, which was inevitable in the case of a courtesan, should have seemed unbearable if she was a person whose way of life classed her among the "matrons"—and yet it was not so. Jealousy, apparently, was allowed only in marriage. The jealousy felt when one loved someone who was free had to be concealed if one were not to be thought coarse and disagreeable. It is rather strange that in those days the selfsame man who would have wreaked exemplary vengeance on a rival surprised making love to his own legal wife, could not even show his displeasure if he was deceived by his mistress! In that social system where freedom was precarious, it was feared that feelings should not be circumscribed if they were of the type that did not come under the law.

This shows, in a society where freedom was at a premium, to what extent emotional responses thought to be natural and spontaneous were really dictated by custom and morals! Perhaps the ancient Romans thought less of putting their wives under restraint than of accustoming them to discipline, and using reason in regulating their mutual relations.

In Ovid's day, there is no getting around it, this attempt had completely failed. Love, the most unreasonable of human passions, had taken its revenge. The proud descendants of Romulus had to go down on their knees to women whom they could not make their legal wives, whom they could never force to share their lives, but who, on the contrary, would have the right at any time to abandon them and bestow their love on another.

But Ovid indicates that there is another aspect, in compensation, to the generally rather pessimistic picture he paints: and that is that women are no less desirous than men of hanging on to their "victims." After repeating complacently that women are wily and deceitful; that it does not trouble them at all to commit perjury, Ovid admits that they are more faithful than men. An unexpected compliment, addressed to professional "beauties." "Virtue is a feeling," he points out. "Both her name and her dress show it, and it is not surprising that she appeals to her own sex." And even the women who did not acknowledge that it was their duty to be virtuous—those to whom *The Art of Love* was addressed—

nevertheless, despite themselves, were not beyond showing the fidelity that goes with their true nature.

So *The Art of Love* seems at first glance to be nothing more than a manual for the "compleat" seducer, and to have no other aim than to provide weapons for the pleasure-hunter. But gradually it evolves and covers more ground as the sentiments it describes become deeper. Beyond coquetry and the wiles of courtship, love is born. Pleasure is no longer sought for its own sake but in order to be shared.

"I hate an embrace that does not leave both bodies quivering with passion," he writes, adding, "and that is the reason I am less drawn to love with a young boy. I hate the woman who yields to it only because she has to, who stays as stiff as a piece of wood, and is thinking all the while of her spinning. Pleasure rendered out of politeness is disagreeable to me; I do not want my mistress to be polite with me. What I like is to hear the words that reveal her ecstasy, to have her ask me to slow down, and have her hold me back. Ah! let me but see my mistress's fluttering eyelids as she lies there only half-conscious. May she feel helpless, yet forbid me for a long time to touch her!"

Having reached the point of shared fulfillment, love blossoms out into tenderness, and unites the two lovers in a mutual self-forgetfulness, more effectively than the law ever could.

All these revelations of the poet are quite indelicate to be sure, but they have the advantage of going to the heart of the real problem without reservations. Gradually Ovid discovers—and discloses to his readers—that love, if it combines tenderness and gratitude in just proportion, is enough to fill one's life and create a durable bond between two human beings. Let us suppose—Ovid is suggesting this without coming right out and saying it—that a married couple have attained this understanding: a mutual comprehension allied with continual attention to each other's desires, which would be based less on the law's restraints than on courtesy and amiability to guarantee the stability of their marriage—would not this couple be happy? Content, since, first of all, they would be lovers. This, which seems to be a verity derived from his own experience, he was prevented from asserting by Roman moral conventions, but it is the lesson that can be drawn from all his works. He described the ideal relation between lovers, human love carried to its completion, in a thousand forms in the *Metamorphoses* and the *Heroides*. Is it not Ovid who bequeathed us the most touching of all myths, Philemon and Baucis, whose love has become famous—the peasant couple who spent their whole lives together because they loved each other, and who begged the gods not to separate them even in death? Similarly, the *Heroides,* which are imaginary letters attributed to legendary heroines, imputed to the lovers of the early days the feelings analyzed in the *Amores* and the *Ars Amatoria:* Penelope, Ariadne, and Laodamia think and feel like courtesans—but because the love of courtesans is the best equipped to allow for the genuine fulfillment of passion.

Ovid's "immorality" lay in this, and not in the vividness or indecency of the incidents he painted. He revealed to his times what the era already dimly perceived: that there is not one kind of love "permitted" and other kinds "tolerated," but, as Virgil wrote after Lucretius, love is "the same for all that lives," the passion has its roots in the human creature, and is neither an illness nor a shameful aberration.

In a society where unrestricted love affairs were becoming more and more important and where the courtesan was asserting her dominion, "respectable" women could hardly fail to seek their revenge. Many, without a doubt, continued to honor the virtues of their ancestors in practice, and, if they had recourse to secret liaisons, in order to hang on to their husbands all the better, that is something we know nothing about. But some of them, too, were determined to win their freedom and, since courtesans were more loved, to act as they did. And of course many of them went to extremes.

This tendency was already marked in Cicero's time, during the last years of the Republic. Quite a few examples are commonly given of women who belonged by birth to the aristocracy, but whose conduct suggested that they were better suited to a lower rank. They were as determined "to live their life" as their mothers had been to exercise their authority in the home, and some did not hesitate to commit crimes in order to satisfy their passions. Cicero's letters are full of descriptions of debauched and violent women, and tend to give an impression of a society in which the ancient moral values were scorned more and more. These "matrons" sang, danced, played the lyre like courtesans, wore flimsy fabrics that revealed more than they hid, changed husbands many times in the course of their lives, gave little thought to having children and still less to their upbringing, since, as Ovid recalled later, having many children hurts good looks. These same women, we are told, were not content with one husband at a time, but carried on many intrigues simultaneously that catered to their sensuality or their desire for variety, or served their interests. We shall also see that they took part in politics, wove spells (there were several women of this type among Catalina's accomplices), plotted to maneuver men into power, held salons, and expended their efforts and gave of themselves without stint, contributing in large part to the creation of that atmosphere of intrigue and effervescent agitation in which the regime collapsed.

This is a standard portrayal, based on authentic accounts. But let us not forget that in the eyes of Roman historians any woman who did not confine herself to her traditional role, who did not spend most of her life in her home directing the servants, not to mention spinning wool, was for that reason alone considered to be acting shockingly. So we, on our part, hesitate to admit that most of the ladies of those days were already insatiable Messalinas.

While modern historians condemn the society of those days, they lack flexibility when they are not Pharisaic. Here, for example, is how Drumann judged it: "There were few women in the public eye at that time who did not provoke scandals or who were not unfaithful to their husbands. Their misconduct had more influence on young people and on their own children than on the men, although the men, too, were to blame for neglecting their wives and having culpable relations with other women. But the state in those days had no foundation of religion, and private life, similarly, was not on a solid basis since it too must be imbued with religious faith to become strong and prosperous."

Which amounts to saying that the essential immorality (or what passes for it) of certain women at that time justified and prepared an expected religious renaissance. *Felix culpa!* . . . O happy fault! But Drumann, who was writing long before the modern studies concerned with Roman religious history, could not know that the society of those days, far from being atheistic, was pervaded by religion, that the minds of men had never before been so preoccupied with trying to solve the mysteries of the deity. Some turned to philosophy, which spoke to them of god in almost Christian terms; others practiced oriental cults. Isis had no more fervent and meticulous devotees than "loose women." And can one be sure that if in the old days matrons behaved better, the reason was that they believed devoutly in Jupiter Capitolinus and in the efficacy of ritual? No, the problem is not as simple as one could wish!

What seems sure is that there was a certain uneasiness, that traditional morals remained attached to some values that were no longer valid and refused to approve others that were replacing them, as Ovid has pointed out. If in theory all family life was based on woman's self-denial, in actual fact, woman's role and her place in a profoundly changed society—and what men, tired of washed-out or dismal companions expected of them—showed this theory of self-denial to be an illusion. It was the turbulent and sometimes anarchic revenge wreaked by nature and reality.

This dramatic development has been portrayed by the poet Catullus. The woman he cherished typifies a whole generation of loving partners caught between two worlds. He called her Lesbia.

Her name was Clodia and she belonged to a branch of the ancient family of the Clodii, a great house permeated with aristocratic prejudice, and celebrated for the pride and violent character of its men and women.

He himself was from the provinces, a young bourgeois from Cisalpine Gaul, born in Verona. He belonged to Rome's allies, and at the time he was born, none of his compatriots had the same rights as Roman citizens. As for her, she was descended from the conquerors; when she came to Cisalpine Gaul for the first time it was with her husband, Caecilius Metellus Celer, who was its governor. At least, one can assume that their first meeting took place at this time, in 62 B.C., when Catullus was twenty-one and Clodia probably twenty. Truth to tell, although it is sure that Metellus governed Gaul in that year, there is no certain proof that Clodia accompanied him to the Province. However, it is quite likely that Catullus' father, who was an important personage in the Colony of Verona, was the Governor's host on this occasion, and that the bond of hospitality linked the young man with the Roman magistrate. Perhaps Catullus knew Clodia only in Rome when he came there the following year to pursue his studies, and paid a courtesy call on the former Governor.

Clodia's marriage was not a happy one. That same year Cicero says that she "was at war with her husband." The difference between them originated in a political incident. Clodia had a brother, Publius Clodius, who was very boisterous, and she felt a strong affection for him—more than was due a brother, said Cicero, who in all probability knew nothing about it. But Clodius was very elegant and very charming, and Clodia was, we are told, the most perfect, seductive beauty of her day. And this was enough to have a lawyer, who was also Clodius' political adversary, give himself authority to spread the vilest calumnies. Now Clodius had decided to become the leader of the Popular party, and in order to do so he had to be made the plebeian Tribune, which was impossible since he belonged to a patrician family. There was only one conceivable solution: that a law be passed authorizing him to relinquish his patrician status, and move into the ranks of the plebeians. It was to get this law voted that Clodius mobilized all his friends and all those of his sister. But not long after that, Metellus, under pressure from his allies in the Conservative party, campaigned against Clodius. Hence the conflict in Clodius' home on the Palatine Hill.

At this point Catullus appeared on the scene. He has described the impression Clodia made on him when he saw her for the first time in a famous poem:

"Yes, I think he is the equal of the gods, or, if that is possible, superior to the gods, who is privileged to sit before you and look at you, and listen to you at leisure.

"When you laugh softly—alas, unfortunate that I am, I can no longer express what I feel, for when I see you, Lesbia, not a word can I speak.

"My tongue is heavy, a delicate flame pours through my veins, a muffled buzzing vibrates in my ears, and a dual veil spreads the night over my eyes."

Three stanzas of the poem (there are four in all) are essentially a repetition of one of Sappho's odes. In choosing it for a model, Catullus expresses the subtle nuances of his passion: brutal, overpowering desire that is also hopeless. Early critics considered that these verses of the poetess contained "a mixture of every kind of passion." Sappho had written them, we are told, for one of her "girls," who left her to get married. They evoke at one and the same time the (probable) feelings of the fiancé, but in particular Sappho's own emotion. It is significant that Catullus turned to such a violent poem in which love is felt to be an illness, a fever that grips the body and destroys the will. It should not be thought that this was just a device on the part of an adept, or the fancy of a poet going back to archaic times. Catullus really held to this brutal concept of love: otherwise would he have named the one he cherished Lesbia—that is, from Lesbos? It was Sappho's patronage he wanted from the first; the rapport between his poem and hers was a proof that he shared the intensity of her emotions.

But he was not proud of it, as is shown by his conclusion after three stanzas with this passionate outburst: "It is leisure, Catullus, that negates you; it is leisure that sweeps you off your feet and drives you to excesses. Leisure in the old days led kings and prosperous cities to their doom!"

Ensnared by his love of Clodia, Catullus suffered pangs of conscience. He could not resist, but saw the depth of the chaos into which he was about to fall. A young provincial, having only lately left a city where the traditional moral code was very much in force, Catullus, who willingly passed along the scandalous gossip of the little city of Verona, found himself in love with Clodia, one of Rome's first ladies and wife of Metellus, who yesterday governed Cisalpine Gaul and tomorrow would be Consul! He blamed himself in the tone of a scolding uncle or father: "You're lazy, Catullus, and that leads you into wrongdoing. . . ."

Too impulsive, and prone to think of the material risks such an affair might entail, his only scruples were moral ones. This was the last balk, caused by his provincial training; after that he would abandon himself to the torrent that swept him along.

Soon the unexpected happened. Clodia was not indifferent to him. She accepted his naïve, burning love, and easily overcame his scruples, provoking this outcry:

"Let us live, my Lesbia, let us live and love, and let us not pay a shred of attention to the muttered criticism of stubborn old men. Suns may set and be born again; as for us, when our brief day has drawn to a close, we must sleep through an endless night. Give me a thousand kisses, and another hundred, and a thousand more, and still another hundred and then still another thousand, and a hundred again. And then, when we are running into the thousands, let us mix up the reckoning, so as not to be aware of the score, and so that no envious person can wish us harm, if he comes to know the total of all those kisses!"

While Clodia was thus receiving Catullus' homage, Metellus was conscientiously, if not brilliantly, carrying out the duties of Consul. Between her lover's visits, Clodia mitigated her impatience by playing with her favorite sparrow. She would hold her finger out to him; he would peck it greedily; she would clutch him to her breast as if this living presence could somehow be an answer to the desire that stirred her.

It was seldom possible for the lovers to be together, which is not surprising when one thinks of the myriad duties incumbent on a Consul's wife, of the interminable comings and goings in the home on the Palatine Hill. Once, nevertheless, Clodia was able to give a whole night to her lover, having "escaped from the arms of her husband."

Most of the time they met in the house of a common friend, Manlius Torquatus, who was also a poet. For some reason of which we are ignorant, Clodia could go to his house without causing a scandal. But to go openly to Catullus' home would have been to admit the liaison. All these precautions indicate that the mores of society in those days were not as dissolute as people like to think. An effort was made, at least, to keep up appearances. Clodia might be frivolous, imprudent, and sometimes guilty; still she did not want to be pointed out as an adulteress.

At this time several incidents interrupted the course of the poet's affair. One was a bereavement: the death of his brother, who had been near Troy, in Asia, caused him deep sorrow. Since he could not bear to stay in Rome any longer, he went back to Verona to conceal his grief. Maybe the sudden death of Metellus during the first months of 59 B.C., when Caesar was Consul, had something to do with this decision. The circumstances surrounding the nature of Metellus' disease, which occurred after a brief illness, struck some persons as mysterious. It was whispered in Rome (at least among the political enemies of Clodius and his sister) that Metellus might have been poisoned. Cicero, a few years later, echoed these rumors when, to defend young Caelius, he made the gravest possible charges against Clodia, Caelius' accuser. It would be a mistake to put too much credence in what could hardly be more than a gratuitous calumny. Whatever may have been the reason—

perhaps the cruel death of Metellus—Clodia's mood changed, and she decided not to see Catullus again, at least for a while. But the mourning of Clodia, whose married life with Metellus had not been harmonious in any case, did not last long. The year was hardly over when she had another affair. This one was with Caelius, who was also a neighbor on the Palatine Hill, and whose political career promised to be better than the poet's. And he was older. In short, he had no difficulty in winning her over—even if once again we refuse to believe Cicero, who this time asserts that Clodia was the temptress and Caelius the innocent victim. A kind friend, it appears, took it upon himself to apprise Catullus, who answered in indulgent vein: "Even if she is not content with Catullus alone, I shall tolerate the few infidelities my lady, usually so reserved, has indulged in. I don't want to be like all the fools who act insupportably. . . ."

But soon Catullus had to bow before the facts. His relationship to Clodia had been only a passing fancy for her. She had seemed to love him to distraction. In a moment of abandon she had gone so far as to promise to marry him: "The woman who belongs to me assures me she wants to marry me; that she would prefer me to anyone, even if Jupiter himself should ask for her hand. This is what she asserts, but what a woman declares to a man who is overcome with desire for her should be written on the wind and on the driving rain."

"I want to become your wife. I want you to be my husband." That is what Clodia said. Apparently she was ready to enter into the one paramount relationship of her life, and Catullus had been naïve enough to believe her. In his opinion their desire sufficed to create a permanent bond that would have sanctified their union. In another poem can be found these significant words: "I loved you, not the way anyone dotes on his mistress, but the way a father cherishes his children and his sons-in-law."

But this was exactly what Clodia did not want: a burdensome affection that put her back into the usual fetters of family life, making her feel like a prisoner. It was certainly true that, legally as well as morally, a husband and a father were considered the same. But what a strange idea, for a lover of Clodia, to want to restore the ancient custom of the *manus*—even in his thoughts, even in his dreams! During her raptures, Clodia might seem to want her lover to become a husband; did this mean anything more than the quite natural desire to have the moment they belonged to each other last forever? When "real" life took over again, the truth looked quite different. Meanwhile Catullus dallied, while Clodia was already far away.

From then on the misunderstanding between them was exacerbated. Catullus' passion, as exclusive as ever, prevented him from finding a mistress elsewhere who might satisfy him. But the other half of his love, that protective tenderness seeking instinctively to hem in the woman he loved with the imperious respect bestowed on wives—this, the best part of his feeling, was dying.

"Now I know you, and that is why if the fire consuming me is more ardent, you are nevertheless much less precious to me and much less worthy of respect. How is that possible? you will ask. Because such a betrayal makes a love more burning but less tender."

Amare, bene velle: sexual desire, affection. Catullus' whole conflict and that of his generation is contained in the opposition between the two. The men of the early days started with affection, with benevolent goodwill, and were not permitted to reach complete sexual fulfillment with their wives.

With a courtesan, one started with carnal satisfaction without being sure that one wanted to go as far as to experience tender feelings. Who would bring the two elements into harmony? For a while, Clodia, because she was a "lady," and because their affair had started with mutual satisfaction, had seemed able to gratify Catullus' desires fully. But Clodia stopped halfway. What maddened her lover was not so much, at first, that she was unfaithful, as the impression that he had been duped.

"I hate her and I want her. How can I do that, you may ask. I do not know, but I feel that it is so, and I am a martyr."

Catullus felt that he had acted in accordance with divine law, that he had practiced *pietas*. It was Clodia who was guilty of perjury. He himself was pure; he had never taken an oath that he had not intended to keep. Might the gods, as a reward, give him peace!

But peace was a long time in coming. He could not forget Clodia, compromised in a resounding scandal with Caelius in 56 B.C. But Catullus revenged himself on her with bitter epigrams. Once, perhaps in the following year, she tried to patch things up. And Catullus answered her in insulting terms:

"May she live happily with her lovers; may she kiss three hundred of them at the same time without really loving a single one, but ceaselessly wearing them out on every side. Let her never think of my love as she used to do; it perished through her own fault like a flower at the edge of a field that the passing plow has crushed with its iron share."

Was Clodia the depraved, insatiable woman described by Catullus? We may allow ourselves to remain skeptical. Caelius himself, after their reverberating rupture, asserted that "She said yes in the dining room, but no when she got to the bedroom." The independence of a woman who refused to relinquish her liberty even in love aroused a lot of resentment in her lovers; it is by no means sure that all the wrong was on her side. Certainly she was a violent woman, as relentless in her hatred as her brother Clodius. And there is no doubt either that she had a taste for sensual pleasures. Cicero brings up the gatherings of young people with whom she liked to surround herself, in her gardens on the edge of the Tiber. But his comment, that she went there to watch youths swimming in the river and admire handsome male bodies seems typical of small-town gossip, and proves only that the public Cicero addressed still affected a narrow Puritanism. This makes us suspicious of the righteous indignation of the lawyer and even of the insults heaped by Catullus on the woman he had loved so much.

As for her, her only fault, no doubt, was to refuse to throw in her lot permanently with a poet younger than she, without a fortune, and fiercely determined to love the way people used to in Rome and as they still did in Verona.

It was doubtless not by chance that among Catullus' most successful poems are two epithalamiums, but he did not write them in his own honor.

Between the love affairs of Catullus and those of Tibullus, more than thirty years elapsed. The first took place when Caesar was Consul, the second during the wars between Antony and Octavian that irrevocably ended all hope for a return of the Republic. During these years Rome was thrown into confusion by perpetual disorders. The old aristocracy lost an incredible number of its members; it became necessary to create senators by the dozen to fill the gaps in the curia. Unbelievable eddies and backwashes lifted people to high place who had been born in a state of servitude. But it must not be thought that the primordial moral concepts were undermined. The men first summoned by Caesar and then by the triumvirs to sit in the senate were men from the provinces where morals had remained as strict as in the old days. It would even appear that the decline of certain great families helped to slow down the slackening process manifested at the end of the Republic. It was true that there were no more censors but masters who, if they did not always give a good example, were determined in spite of all to prevent the spread of lawlessness. Disorder was soon to become a characteristic of Court circles.

It has often been repeated that Augustus' legal code of morals was imposed because of the need to check the horrifying and speedy deterioration of mores. In reality, it seems likely that the Emperor, in promulgating his law "on marriage between castes," wanted above all to restore observances that had fallen into disuse, and stamp out an incontestable tendency for marriage to grow more democratic and for married couples to have fewer children. We have already said that "old-style" marriage was more and more neglected, and was being replaced by unions less encumbered with responsibilities. But this brought in its train the progressive extinction of the great families, since legally these extramarital unions were the equivalent of celibacy. If it was desirable to preserve the traditional framework of the Roman City-State, which was aristocratic in type and was founded on the stability and continuity of the clans, steps should be taken—but in the domain of law rather than morals.

The Emperor, after thinking, in 27 B.C., of making marriage obligatory, and then giving up the idea of imposing such a coercive measure, which ran counter to all Roman legal traditions, thought of a way of encouraging legal marriage by according certain privileges to men who agreed to found a home, and, what is more, to those who produced more than three children "in a legitimate marriage." It was not a question of increasing the birthrate, as is done in some modern states, for the citizens covered by this legislation were in a minority. Augustus wanted to maintain certain social classes, the governing classes, who, in his eyes, constituted the framework of the Empire. To this end the Emperor created a "privileged status for the parents of three children" (*jus trium liberorum*), which gave them a special position before the law. Later, the Emperor extended these privileges to certain persons he wished to reward, even if they did not fulfill the specific conditions he had fixed. This status conferred reductions in taxes and charges, an acceleration of the climb up the political ladder, and special honors, and exempted women from the necessity of having a legal guardian.

Another law, regarding adultery, may strike us as narrower and more Puritan. In reality the events that led Augustus to promulgate it were rather complicated. According to Republican tradition, the repression of adultery was the concern of the Council of Fathers. But this archaic institution no longer existed except in a few particularly conservative families.

Augustus wanted to change the crime of adultery into a public offense. Under the Republic, the state certainly had a right to look into the private lives of citizens, but it exercised it through the censors, whose intervention was not controlled by generalized legal provisions. Now the office of censor had in fact been legally abolished by Caesar since the beginning of the Civil Wars. Augustus assumed some of Caesar's functions; others were turned over to the regular tribunals. And that is, we believe, what lay behind the law concerning adultery. It was a part of a reorganization of the judicial system. Instead of being a reactionary measure made necessary by the state of public morals, it was a step forward in a development begun long before, which gave the magistrates more and more jurisdiction over domains that had formerly been considered strictly private.

When Tibullus met the woman he called Delia (that is to say, from Delos)—and this was also the epithet applied to the goddess Artemis—Octavian had not yet consolidated his hold on the Roman Empire, and the question of introducing laws regulating morals did not arise. But hints from Tibullus' romance help us better to understand the precise nature of the dangers Augustus was trying to circumvent a few years later. It was the story, to begin with, of a banal affair. A young man belonging to an aristocratic family, but half ruined by the depredations during the outbreaks preceding the Civil Wars, met a young courtesan in Rome, and fell in love with her. He was not quite twenty. It was necessary for him to recoup his fortune, and all he had to do to accomplish this was start on the career that opened up before him. A great personage, Valerius Messala Corvinus, after following Antony's party, came back from the East, his patience exhausted by his chief's extravagances, to put himself at the disposition of Octavian. Messala agreed to become Tibullus' patron, which meant for the latter, first, inclusion in Messala's cohorts, where he would be trained to fight, then, at the right time, admission to different magistratures that little by little would make him into a respected—and rich—senator.

But, on the threshold of his twenty years, none of these possibilities looked very attractive to Tibullus. He had always lived in the country, with his mother and sister, on the slopes of Frascati amid the vineyards and forests, among the villagers. He had no desire to leave his familiar surroundings and engage in warlike adventures in the Orient, even if they should turn out to be profitable. This state of mind found expression in a poem—the first that has been preserved. He had not yet met Delia but he already spoke of his horror of war, his fondness for the country, the abounding harvest and the fruits of peace. He looked forward to romance; he liked gratification of the senses, and the only banner he wanted to serve under was the banner of love.

Nevertheless Tibullus was reasonable, and he went along with those who were seeking his advantage. Messala was already preparing to rejoin the army being assembled, with Octavian at its head, for the inevitable clash between the two halves of the known world. Tibullus was resigned to going with him. But as he was finishing the preparations—this was probably during the winter of 32–31 B.C.—something fateful occurred: he met Delia. Suddenly the vague aspirations that had been troubling him, and in particular his need for love, found a goal. He rebelled. Let someone else go and win success on the battlefield. As for him, he wanted to stay in Rome.

"It's up to you, Messala, to make war on land and sea, so that one day your house will be bedecked with enemy trophies. I—am a prisoner, shackled by a woman's beauty, and I remain seated, like a sentinel, before a door that remains pitilessly closed."

For Delia's love, he gave up not only wealth, but glory—which is more serious for a young Roman.

"If only I can be with you, I ask to be called lazy and cowardly; if only I can see you, when the supreme, ultimate moment comes, and clasp you in my failing arms, as I die."

Tibullus was acting out in real life a situation made familiar by Terence. A young man, overwhelmed by his passion for a courtesan, renounced everything but his love. But what was only play-acting on the stage now became a tragic reality. It was no longer a question of having his fun before settling down, it was a question of the delights of love consuming his whole existence. Or rather, this pleasure was only a prelude to tenderness. Delia was surrounded as in a procession by visions dear to the poet's youth.

"I am willing to pass my whole life in poverty, if only, every day, the fire can glow on my hearth, if only I can graft my tender vines myself, at the right season, like a peasant, and my fruit trees, with a skilled hand—and that my hopes be not deceived, but bring me always a heaping harvest and the thick must of grapes filling the vats."

Around the experience, trite enough, that began like so many others on the doorstep of a girl of easy virtue, there is an aura that can be traditionally described as "Virgilian" (except that Virgil's works were only half written at the time), and which is in line with the dreams familiar to the Romans, those peasants exiled to the city.

Trying to trace the beginnings of this type of poetry, one can be sure that it is Greek in origin. It is not hard to find, in these rustic outpourings, an echo of *Works and Days,* written by Hesiod six centuries before. But this still leaves unanswered the question of why Tibullus chose it for a model. Just as Catullus had chosen as his patron the poetess of Lesbos because, as we said, Sappho's writings were in tune with his feverish passion, so Tibullus, a villager of Latium, found in Hesiod's epic an echo of the feelings that country life awoke in him. But it is remarkable that he brought love into Hesiod's world. Of all the poets Hesiod was the greatest woman-hater. Woman was to him (as the ancient Romans said of the courtesan) only a "disaster for the crops." He could not find words strong enough to condemn the loose women of the city "with their dressed-up rumps, whose only talent is to bewilder the peasant and drain off the funds he has so laboriously acquired."

Well, Tibullus specifically associates the tenderest and also the most dangerous of feelings, love for a woman, with Hesiod's universe. He transforms what was no more than peasant caution on the part of the old poet into a broader and more subtle congruity. If the Roman of the early days enjoyed evoking the image of the "mother" in the heart of the rustic household, that mother was the legitimate wife, the *domina*. But he, Tibullus, conferred dignity on a girl he could not marry, and required his love, which convention called ephemeral, to carry the burden of all the elements involved in a legal marriage. And here is where we discover the true "scandal," the real significance of the decadence that the legislation of Augustus was soon to try to counteract. Love no longer took social classes into account when a young man destined for the senate wanted to take a courtesan as his legitimate spouse! What would happen to the Empire if young aristocrats were allowed without further ado to marry according to the dictates of their hearts?

In Tibullus' love for Delia there was no disturbing element, nothing that went beyond a happy sensuality well on the safe side of Catullus' flaming strophes, or, later, the lessons disseminated by Ovid. Curiously enough—and this gives his poems a strangely modern tone—the presence of the beloved is associated with the myriad expressions, the thousands of messages that Nature transmits to the soul. "How I love to listen to the unchained winds as I lie in bed, clasping my mistress tenderly, or when the tempestuous West Wind spreads an icy downfall, to go tranquilly to sleep, warmed by the fire on the hearth!"

Love takes its place in the aggregate of created things, among the loveliest and best that this world offers. All the other values of our society are worthless beside it. It represents the supreme good in this world and the next. The poet's willingness to follow the commandments of the God of Love will, he tells us, guarantee him eternal happiness in the Kingdom of Shades.

"Because I have always submitted to the tender dictates of love, Venus herself will lead me to the Elysian Fields, where there is always dancing and singing, where, flitting about, birds make sweet music with their soft voices. There uncultivated ground produces cinnamon, and the abundant earth bears sweet-smelling roses. Troupes of young men among whom are gentle young girls disport themselves, and Love presides forever over their games.

Here are to be found those whom death has taken while they were in love; myrtle crowns adorn their hair."

One should not make the mistake of thinking that this was purely poetic license. Venus and Amor were truly believed to be gods who could save people and guarantee them immortality. Here Tibullus echoes the beliefs, probably Syrian in origin, that had found their way into Rome many years before, brought, we suspect, by courtesans from Syria, where the goddess the Romans called Venus and they called Astarte or Ishtar was worshipped with unusual fervor.

Despite his reluctance to abandon Delia and in leaving her to break with a love into which he had put so much of himself, Tibullus could not avoid following Messala. They left for the East in the spring of the year 31 B.C. But fortunately (no doubt) for Tibullus, he went no farther than the port of Corcyra, where they made a stop. Illness forced him to let his companions go on without him. It was a malady serious enough for him to fear for his life. Willingly enough, as a matter of fact, this young man of twenty looked forward to breathing his last. We have already seen him, at the beginning of the affair, derive satisfaction from thinking of his last moments, happy if he could clasp the object of his love in his arms. Such an evocation could hardly be considered morbid. Never, perhaps, were death and love more naturally connected in the mind of a suitor, considering that love as experienced by Tibullus was the primordial act of life, a willing compliance with the world's supreme law.

During the moments that he thought were his last, he conjured up his memories of passion. The sad weeks before he left had been compensated for by Delia's love; she was heartbroken over his departure, consulted fortune-tellers, and tried in every way to put off the moment when they must separate.

All these recollections were sweet in the shadow of death. And since at bottom he was convinced he would survive, he began to think what it would be like to return. He pictured Delia, sitting by the hearth, near the old housekeeper who shared her existence.

Together they passed many a vigil; the old woman told stories, while Delia spun wool. One could imagine an evening in Lucretia's home. And Tibullus saw himself arriving suddenly, without warning, as if Heaven had sent him: "Then, Delia, you run to meet me just as you are, your long hair hanging loose, your feet bare. I shall ask the gods to bid Aurora bring you to me in the luminous dawn with its rose-colored horses."

Convalescent, Tibullus returned to Rome and Delia. But the reality turned out to be very different from the dream. The happy moments he had spent with her were not to be repeated. It was not a "chaste Lucretia" that he saw in Rome, but the courtesan that his mistress had never ceased to be. During his absence she had taken a new protector, as was only natural, and her door was bolted against him. All-powerful Venus no longer favored her fervent devotee. And the poet's rustic dreams were pitilessly shattered. Never again would Delia come to count the sheaves on the threshing floor or supervise the harvest. She spent her time lying beside a rich man; a courtesan would never change her ways, she would never be willing to be the companion of just one man!

So that is the story of this unfortunate affair: a shattered dream, because Delia was herself, because Tibullus, in spite of the strength of his passion, could not change the whole pattern of society. It was a society where, with the best will in the world, a young man of senatorial rank could not be allowed to marry a courtesan, and the courtesans were not naïve enough to believe it possible.

Tibullus' escapade had a very moral ending. When Messala returned from the East, where he had carried out several missions for Octavian, the latter gave him a new command, this time to put down a revolt of the Gauls in Aquitania. Tibullus, who had completely recovered from his illness, and, apparently, was cured of his love, left with Messala, and conducted himself brilliantly during the campaign. But since the poet, even when covered with glory, could not fail to be in love, he sang the praises of another kind of passion: the one he felt for a boy, young Marathus, who was a professional in these particular pleasures. And also of another woman, like Delia a courtesan, whom he referred to as Nemesis. What led him to choose the name? Did Nemesis, who made him suffer, represent retribution? Was she sent by the gods to punish Tibullus for being unfaithful to Delia? A romantic but unlikely supposition, since it was not Tibullus who had betrayed his mistress, but the latter who had spurned him for a wealthier protector. One could get closer to the truth by recalling that the name Nemesis appears in the *Theogony*, where Hesiod tells us that the goddess was the "sister of tenderness and deceit." Would not Nemesis then stand for the daemon of the contradictions that the gods like to put in the way of human desires? If someone hopes for happiness, and flatters himself that he is achieving it, Nemesis steps in and inflicts some suffering on him.

Tibullus, disillusioned, transformed into a misogynist as the result of his disillusions, believed that his new "victim" was in fact the instrument the gods were using to drive him still further from his dream. Perhaps they wanted to punish him for thinking a new Golden Age was possible, that would not only be an era of abundance but of happiness in love. Nemesis was the sister of Tenderness and simultaneously of Deceit. In giving this name to his second mistress, was not Tibullus making a confession whose meaning is cruelly manifest? When he was in love with Delia, he thought that Hesiod, the woman-hater, was wrong. Now he perceived that it was he himself who had been a prey to illusion: "This, the 'Age of Iron,' sings the praises not of Venus, but of gain. . . . Alas! Alas! I see that women are drawn only to riches!"

And totally defeated, all passion spent, he was willing to give up everything he once thought could not be separated from love: "Adieu to the harvests, if only pretty girls will keep from going to the country. Let us feed on acorns, and let water be our drink, as it was in the old days. . . ."

Tibullus died very young, in the year 19 B.C., and Ovid reports that Delia and Nemesis were present at the funeral beside his mother and sister, and quarreled about which of them he had loved the better! It seems, unless to be sure Ovid made the scene up to suit his fancy, that Nemesis was present at Tibullus' bedside as he lay dying, and Delia implied that Nemesis' unfaithfulness and her severity had shortened the life of the man they had both loved. In any case it is sure that the poet's love for Nemesis darkened his last days, even if he was not continuously and entirely unhappy. To keep that love as it was, he had been obliged to sacrifice himself and everything that life held dear—a heavy penalty to pay for the occasional complaisance of a courtesan.

When Propertius knew Cynthia, he too was only about twenty years old. He belonged to the aristocracy; his family's fortunes had suffered in the Civil Wars. But in matters of the heart, he was not as raw as Tibullus, since before tying up with Cynthia, he had already had an affair with Lycinna, a courtesan, no doubt, who had initiated him into the arts of Venus. But with Cynthia he discovered love.

Cynthia was not the young woman's real name. She was almost certainly named Hostia, and she may possibly have belonged to a respectable family, if the report is true that one of her ancestors was a poet who, a century earlier, had won some renown writing epics. But she had chosen what seemed to be an "easy" life, and earned her living by selling her favors.

Nevertheless, there was nothing vulgar about her. Quite elegant, she was cultivated as well, and lacked nothing—neither "the gifts of Venus nor of Minerva," for Apollo had given her a talent for writing poetry, and the Muse Calliope the capacity to sing her verses accompanying herself on the lyre. Her lyric poems and the songs she composed appear to have been influenced by the poetess Corinna. This was a proof of Cynthia's good taste, almost of erudition, since she had gone back five centuries to choose her model, who was esteemed by sages, and had acquired renewed popularity in circles as refined as those of Maecenas. But Cynthia, in spite of her learning, knew how to keep her conversation witty rather than ponderous. And she danced admirably. All these talents, especially the last (for dancing, in those days, included the art of mimicry), would have made an old-time Roman uncomfortable. Outside of courtesans, only a few very emancipated women of the highest aristocracy possessed them.

Propertius, who had no desire to describe his mistress' charms, tells us only that she was tall and blonde, with black eyes. He was intrigued by her beauty, and mentions her perfect figure, which a "veil from Cos" rendered voluptuously discernible. But he wished she did not take such an interest in finery. He wanted her to be satisfied with her natural perfection, without the seductive ornaments and artifices of which he disapproved.

He objected to them first of all because they indicated a disturbing coquettishness. But also for a more subtle reason: all those dresses, all that makeup, jewelry, and ointments, hid the real Cynthia from him, the one who should be his alone. Whereas, instead of acceding to his desires, she wasted a lot of time rearranging a hairdo that was already perfect, putting on makeup, and choosing one by one the precious stones that would decorate her bosom. Where was the real Cynthia? Would he find her behind that panoply?

Catullus and Tibullus were looking for a love within themselves. It was their own feeling they tried to express, and find mirrored in the eyes of their mistresses. Propertius was less preoccupied with himself than he was with Cynthia. It was Cynthia he was seeking. This is to some extent the main theme of the *Elegies*. Cynthia represented a world for him that he was never tired of exploring. Every pose, every gesture, held him spellbound. In a word, in a look, in the language revealed in the eyes ready for sleep, a whole universe was offered to him and refused at the same time. It seemed to him that all this might sometime be caught and held in verse, but in the long run would never yield its secret. Before Cynthia, it was as if he were standing before a statue, a mysterious *objet d'art* offered to his gaze, whose beauty itself was an enigma. The sculptor might know the secret of his statue. But Cynthia's secret?

Coming back to her late one night, he found her asleep. He had drunk a bit, which only served to kindle his ardor. She was lying in a state of abandon on her bed, but instead of harkening to the promptings of love and liquor, Propertius became intrigued with the way she was sleeping. He replaced her tresses, which had come unloosed, back around her brow, curled a stray lock of hair around his finger, but what he wanted above all was to recapture her dream, to interpret every sigh, every movement she made as she slept—until a ray of moonlight, filtering in through a chink in the shutter, roused her from slumber.

Inevitably, and rapidly, his curiosity turned into jealousy. Propertius knew perfectly well that Cynthia had not been a model of faithfulness in the past. But there had been a moment, because she accorded him her favors without asking for payment, when he believed that this would be his only love. And it is probable that she was faithful to him for a while. At the end of a year, perhaps after only a few months, he could not blind himself to the facts: she had gone back to her old way of life. He wanted to give her up, because the adoration he felt for her alone prevented him from being as tolerant as Catullus or Ovid, or as Tibullus was toward Nemesis. And at this point he discovered he could not break the chain that bound him. Defeated and humbled, he not only went as far as to surrender his pride but his manly dignity.

The first book in the volume, entitled *"Cynthia Monobiblos"* (*Cynthia, a Unique Book*) and highly indicative of his total immolation on the altar of his beloved, was a mixture of joy and misery. Without some happy moments, or the expectation of some, a love cannot survive. But, when all was said and done, even at the beginning suffering prevailed over happiness. Even when it was Cynthia's prayers that held him back and prevented him from following his friend Tullus to the East, as he should have done to be worthy of his race, the last verse of the elegy describing the episode is full of resentment. "If you remember me," he said, "you can be sure that I live under a star that has no mercy."

This does not mean, as some commentators rather superficially assert, that Propertius' passion was not returned—the whole poem implies just the opposite since it is Cynthia who proclaims her love, and implores her admirer to remain at her side. But in the midst of the joy of shared gratification, the poet realizes that his very happiness is a curse that weighs on him, paralyzes him, and deprives him of liberty, just as a star controls the actions of a person who is under its influence.

Propertius once told his mistress that he wanted to be her brother and her son. Julien Benda, in a famous essay, insisted on interpreting this wish as a somewhat perverse taste for humiliating situations. Benda assumes that Cynthia has the right to complain of this state of affairs, and that she would have preferred a more virile lover.

Of course we do not know how Cynthia really felt. No doubt her feelings were less complicated than those of Propertius. It is even possible that she might sometimes have leaned toward an admirer more like what was then the Roman masculine ideal. There was certainly an indication of such a preference in her hot-blooded indiscretion with a Praetor who had been holding the post of Governor of Illyria. Here was a man who had not turned his back on his political responsibilities, and who was satisfied to indulge in what was called "a soldier's relaxation with Cynthia." But whatever our assumptions, right or wrong, regarding Cynthia's likes and dislikes, they should not prevent our understanding what Propertius really meant by the words "son" and "brother." We would be wrong in suspecting the slightest perverse inclination or semiconscious taste for incest. For a Roman woman, as we have said before, the man of her family, whether he was either her brother or her son, was still her master. In some cases the son could become his mother's guardian. But the tutelage of a brother or a son is naturally less onerous and more tender—with a nuance of deference otherwise lacking—than the authority of a husband or father. It shows a greater respect for the woman's freedom, and tries to exercise less domination over her feelings.

Now Cynthia, like Clodia before her, wanted to be a free woman. And Propertius, because of his sensitivity and the very nature of his feeling for her, did not consider that he had the right to exercise the rather tyrannical ascendancy of a husband where she was concerned—the husband he was not and never would be. In this, perhaps, he was mistaken and revealed himself to be a poor strategist. Cynthia wanted to be free too, but the only way she could manifest her independence was by having many lovers. During the moments she devoted to each of her patrons, she acted the part of a dutiful mistress. Propertius once alluded to this dependence, in connection with another man, which suggests that she was married. But there are too many indications to the contrary: legally she was free, although in the course of her various affairs she wanted to be the *de facto* wife of the man she accepted as her master, even if only temporarily.

Now that was exactly what Propertius did not want. He refused to owe his happiness to the authority attributed by custom to the *vir*, the man. He could love only a woman who did not feel bound and who could love him freely in return. And therein lay the whole cause of the tragedy. You cannot run counter to the habits and instincts of a race without the cruel risk of breaking your heart. Propertius knew that his overweening passion was insane and was drawing him to his doom, but it was the only way he could love.

Even before it had become a reality, Propertius felt that love was a curse. Not because of his love for Cynthia (she was only the instrument of Destiny), but because he loved differently from other men, who find it easy to be satisfied with the enjoyment afforded by a familiar—and complaisant—presence.

The poem that served as a preface to the first book struck this note. It pictured Propertius as a humble slave. Prostrate, his face in the dirt, he felt the foot of the God of Love resting heavily on his neck. Far from experiencing some secret pleasure, as Julien Benda suggests, he was fully cognizant of his aberration, while recognizing that there was no way to restore his reason. So he addressed a pathetic appeal to his friends, begging them to take him away by force—elsewhere, anywhere, as long as it is far from Cynthia, or any woman who might play the same role. He should certainly have been annoyed with Cynthia, and he should have been brave enough to vent his spleen, but he could not do it: the presence of the loved one, even her image in his mind, prevented his complaining. What doctor could cure him, what doctor could, even at the cost of burning his flesh, of opening his heart, give him back his lost willpower?

In the same way, a century earlier, Catullus had both adored and hated Clodia. When he wrote the first elegy in the *Book of Cynthia,* Propertius obviously had his predecessor in mind, but it was so that he could make the difference between them clear right from the start. Catullus had had the courage to write the most outrageously cruel verses about Clodia because she had deceived him. In his eyes she had committed adultery. As for Propertius, he was sadly incapable of such courage. In Cynthia's hands he became inert, a passive, helpless victim. But the realization tortured him and brought him even more suffering than his mistress' infidelities. If he should cease to be in her good graces, he would become as nothing.

Perhaps there were other remedies. He had the right, according to custom, to seek sensual gratification with other, less cruel women. It was true enough that Cynthia was unfaithful, but Propertius now let himself seek the solace of other loving arms. He even managed to fall in love with several women at once; he would not have boasted of these easy conquests if he had not thought, with Horace, that these chance affairs were a tribute to his sagacity and powers of discernment. That worldly wisdom, futile as it was, he tried vainly to make use of when Cynthia was away from Rome, in her villa at Tibur, or in Campania, or, again, while she was taking a trip with some admirer. But he soon became afraid that he would find a new Cynthia somewhere else. No longer was he fighting against the disdain of a faithless mistress, but against the madness within himself that lured him on.

"You ask me, Demophon, why it is so easy for me to give way to the vice of woman-chasing? But love, it does not know this question, this 'why.' Why do men scarify their arms with sacred knives, and mutilate themselves to the demented sound of Phrygian flutes? Nature gave each of us one fault at birth; Fate condemned me never to stop loving."

Propertius vainly tried to go back to what he called "normal" amours, those that do not deprive the lover of his self-esteem. But when this instant of complete satisfaction was over, his humiliation returned, increased by the ill repute he acquired for indulging in so many fleeting escapades.

For in his poems, after all, he had professed to love Cynthia, and to compare her to a real wife. And now he was publicly compromising himself with others! In the eyes of the public, if he was already ashamed of binding himself so solemnly to a courtesan and swearing to be faithful to her—was it not still more disgraceful to be untrue to that vow? Propertius was defeated on all sides. It was as if he were caught in a net that was drawn tighter each day. His passion had stripped him bare of the approval of his fellowmen, of Cynthia's affection, and also of his own self-respect. It is not surprising that in such a shipwreck he should often think of letting himself slip into the abyss of self-destruction. And yet, faced with annihilation, bereft of all hope, he was now to find the road to salvation.

The idea of death is always present in Propertius' poetry. It is often said that for this frustrated voluptuary, death was one more voluptuous experience, adding a touch of charm to his rather self-pitying melancholy. On the other hand, he is accused of trading—rather dishonestly—on the pity of his mistress. Was he an over-refined Epicurean? A spoiled child? Or a rabid romantic?

An Epicurean taste for death was not uncommon in that century. We see Antony, at Cleopatra's side, make a death pact with her; his own life, in her arms, was hardly more than a voluptuous death-agony. Tibullus too, in his thoughts, died next to his Delia. But what savor would there be for Propertius in the extinction toward which his passion drew him?

Death was not the last limit of sensual delight for the poet, and the thought of death was not allied to fulfillment in love, as it was with Tibullus. None of his poems brings us to the edge of consciousness and annihilation as some of Lucretius' poems do, for instance. The images Propertius conjured up in connection with death are gentle and have at the same time a less obvious significance. The death he evokes is not so much that of the lover, completely fulfilled or destroyed, as that of the Roman he could become again through the ransom of his soul.

Love was not one of the sentiments in which, usually, the Romans took pride. According to ancestral tradition it was a natural weakness, whose effect on one's existence should be only temporary. Even women, if they had loved, were careful not to admit it; their epitaphs, rarely containing more than a few lines, told how they had spun wool, brought up their children, and dying, were consoled by the affection of those near and dear to them. All else was veiled in shadows. But now, at this point in the century, the elegiac poets brought the hitherto dark areas into the full light of day, and Propertius dared to hope that what would be remembered of his existence could be epitomized in these lines: "He who lies here, in the form of forbidding dust—an odious heap of dirt—was once the slavish victim of a single love."

He would have none of pompous inscriptions listing his offices and victories. His only glory was his unique infatuation. And, he tells us, his tomb, sanctified by love, would be as well known to fame as the bloody pyre that honored the heroes of Phthia. If Propertius, fettered by his devotion to Cynthia, had to turn his back on the political and military fame that were the dream of every true Roman, he continued to hope that death would confer on him a glory that was equally enviable.

It would not, it is true, be that of the conqueror or the invincible fighting man, as symbolized by the name of Achilles, Prince of Phthia, but the everlasting fame of an exceptional devotion that could inspire many thousands of lovers as the valor of Achilles had inspired thousands upon thousands of warriors.

Reading Propertius, one is inclined to forget that he was a Roman, and that among men of his race the idea of death was all-pervasive.

Human destiny is not fulfilled and does not reach its full significance until death. What Solon said to Croesus, in the home of Herodotus, was to be repeated by Seneca, and was deeply felt by all Romans in the past. Through death, life becomes perfect. A dead man, simply because he lived his life, because he can no longer be affected by Destiny, because he belongs irrevocably to the past, is an inspiration, an example to the living. The Romans did not believe in personal immortality, or if they did, it was in a rather confused way. But they held to one kind, that guaranteed their immortality in the minds of the living—a son's pious recollection of them, the admiration of a passerby who deciphers a glorious epitaph beside the road. Otherwise what would be the significance of so many tombs in serried rank along the highways?

The warrior wanted to die in battle so that his name would not be forgotten. Propertius, because he identified himself wholly with his passion, wanted his immortal being perpetuated by his monument with its inscription to be nothing but—love. Death at one and the same time frees a man from his weaknesses and his uncertainty, and purges his soul of everything imperfect, from treachery, from negation. It sums up and characterizes. It was natural that Propertius, in order to be so "defined," should foresee his death and want a name and an image that would symbolize love.

When a passion was over, no matter how much it dominated one's personal life, it could only be considered fortuitous. It did not become an ideal, like the "virtue" of a Scaevola or a Horatius Cocles, unless it was put on a pedestal for everyone to admire and in which, if one dared, one could recognize something of himself.

"O lucky Achilles," sighed Alexander, "to have found a poet such as Homer." But Propertius would be both hero and poet of a new Iliad, an epic of love. The force of his poetry would melt the episodes of his personal life like wax, and though he could not avoid his body turning to ashes, his passion would change into bronze, and survive the onslaughts of time.

As the years passed, and the intervals when the two lovers were apart became longer as a result of Cynthia's infidelities, Propertius' poems grew more intense, but also less taken up with specific incidents. His poetry seemed to be gradually rising to a higher plane than the reality in which it had originated. At the same time his love transcended temporal considerations. Loving as he did no longer humiliated Propertius; he was no longer tortured by his quarrels with Cynthia, or, at least, he realized that his suffering itself contributed to his fame and were a part, as we would put it, of the message of his poetry.

Modern commentators do not try to conceal their astonishment over what they call Propertius' "mythological lack of restraint." They say they would prefer not to have passionate outcries interrupted by long, learned digressions. Blaming the Alexandrine poets for what they consider lapses from good taste, they are inclined to think that Propertius used ancient myths to enrich and lengthen his poems.

No doubt legendary accounts in Roman elegies are indeed a holdover from the past. But if Propertius so often has recourse to myths, it is because they help him explain his most intimate thoughts. The ones he draws on rarely fail to reveal, when analyzed, a profound rapport with the subject of the poem in which they are used. These legends are not stories gratuitously introduced for the reader's delectation, but "genuine myths," that is to say recognizable symbols of a secret truth, a hidden verity that his experience of love enabled him to perceive intuitively.

When Propertius watched Cynthia when she was asleep, he was already haunted by a vision: his mistress' slumber reminded him irresistibly of the legendary Ariadne asleep on the shore of Naxos, a heroine whose supernatural trance prepared her to receive a divine revelation.

The mystic revery that protected Ariadne from the embraces of Theseus and promised her those of Dionysus delighted and disturbed the poet simultaneously. When Cynthia woke up, would she still belong to him? Similarly he never tired of studying the myths left over from the past: the myth of Ulysses, that of Dirce, all those that portray heroes or heroines overcoming the sorrows of love. A Christian poet cannot prevent his passion from becoming purified and transcendental, to lose itself finally in divine love. Propertius followed much the same road.

In the end, he too discovered the divine, ontological significance of love. And in this his experience was analogous to that of Tibullus, for whom Venus and the God of Love are redeeming divinities. The Roman elegiac poets, prepared by their Greek models to experience divine manifestation, to whom a tremor running through their consciousness implied the presence of a god, discovered a force in amorous passion that ancestral custom denied or tried to deny. Love became what it was for Plato, an intermediary between what is accidental and ephemeral and what is eternal, beyond the lapses and inconstancy of the heart's desire.

When Propertius wrote the last poems of Book III, his relations with Cynthia had become still more intermittent. He even went so far as to extol his liberation from the bondage of earlier days: "Now my ships, crowned with wreaths, have reached port; they have crossed the Syrtes; they are at anchor. Today at last, worn out by the ocean's surge, I am back where it is calm, and now my wounds are closed and healed. . . ."

Even though he said he was healed—and he was, since his suffering was alleviated—he did not owe his newfound poise to being able to forget Cynthia, but to a new conquest with a different value. Forgetfulness is but a kind of defacement. Propertius' love for Cynthia continued even if it no longer made him suffer. It was no longer a form of servitude, it was not even sensual desire anymore. It was an eternal reality, κτῆμα εἰς ἀεί. And this had been revealed to Propertius by the time he had composed the elegies that make up Book IV, the last of his works.

Cynthia, whom one might have thought out of the picture from then on, after the farewells, heavy with resentment, with which Book III ends, reappears most unexpectedly as the subject of two more poems. One takes us back to the time when the young woman, intoxicated with freedom, gave herself with no attempt at concealment to a chance admirer, and betrayed Propertius. The latter, as he often did, sought consolation with two girls of easy virtue, and the three of them began to drink and carouse on the Esquiline. But the orgy brought the poet no joy. The flame of the lamp, instead of rising straight as it should, fluttered and gave out a feeble light. The dice thrown on the table came up in unlucky combinations. Although the girls were pretty, the poet remained unmoved. And suddenly, right in the middle of the banquet, the door opened and Cynthia burst into the room. She had not been able to stand the idea of her absent admirer paying attention to other women. In a frenzy she attacked the two unfortunate creatures, scratched their cheeks, pummeled them, drove them out, and then, supreme on the field of battle, turned on Propertius and battered him mercilessly until he surrendered ignominiously—before she capitulated in turn.

The other poem, stranger still, is the story of a dream. It takes place after Cynthia's death, the poet having survived her. It seemed to him, that night, that the young woman drew near his bed. And the ghost began to speak. It recalled the happy days of their early love, when they exchanged vows. Then it reproached the poet bitterly; why did he not keep her memory green? Why was the place beside him not empty, as it should have been if he had remained faithful? As for her, she swore she had never been untrue!

A strange poem at the end of a love affair. It is based on a macabre evocation: the dead woman who waits, watching for her former lover, sure that she will feel his beloved ashes mingle with her own one day. And this ghost, despite all proofs to the contrary, dares to proclaim herself faithful!

But where death is involved, fidelity has a different sense. When the soul is freed from the flesh, there can be no more jealous anxiety. There is certainty at last in the eternal. Returning in his dream, Cynthia proves her faithfulness, because she turns to him when all else has been annihilated. Reduced to its essential purity, love is simply *fides,* loyalty, with each person completely revealed to the other. In the sleep of death when no awakening can be expected, there are no secrets, no room for doubt. Now at the end of that long and dolorous climb toward the eternal, love finds again one of the essential elements of the Roman mentality, that *fides* in whose honor temples are built and on which is founded the entire life of a city.

Thus, even in the most liberated love, free of all constraint, the poets tried to safeguard the essential covenant that united the couple.

Catullus, Tibullus, Propertius—all three followed the same road. But Propertius is the one who went furthest, so far, in fact, that he went beyond the limits of his own amorous venture. Significantly, this same Book IV of the *Elegies* contains two other poems devoted to glorifying "legitimate" love. One purports to be a letter written by a young Roman woman to her husband whose military service keeps him far away. The other, which has been called "the queen of elegies," purports to be a long apologia, a regular funeral oration, that Cornelia, Augustus' daughter-in-law, composed in her own honor. Cornelia was virtuous, worthy of the most austere matrons of olden times. But instead of stopping with a eulogy, as custom required, the poet penetrated the intimate secrets of his heroine. He put tender words into her mouth; the secret of a Roman conjugal love relationship was publicly disclosed for the first time. Propertius would never have thought of that, nor dared to do it, if he had not learned through pain the power and dignity of love. By suffering and persistent struggle he gained the strength to break the spell that for a long time hid—in the depths of the Roman heart—the nobility of a sentiment no one would have to blush for after him.

From then on the way was open for Ovid—to gather, in *Amores* and *Ars Amatoria,* the fruits of a long experience which he would make readily accessible to his readers. After the Augustinian poet, morals evolved. The two aspects of Roman love would from that time on tend to resemble each other, and tend soon to be mingled. There would be legal marriages that were love marriages, and there would be liaisons in which the partners remained faithful to each other.

The moral revolution we have been able to witness, thanks to the poets, and to which they contributed, consisted in bringing love, passion, and desire and its fulfillment into relationships that develop moral ties, duties, and rights between two human beings. To the Romans goes the credit of having discovered that there is an ethic of sentiment. Ancestral tradition certainly accorded high honors to filial affection, respect for the wife, and the duties of fatherhood and motherhood, but feigned to ignore the lusts of the flesh, which are nevertheless the nexus of that whole constellation. One was expected to be a good husband, and one could over and above that love one's wife, but the latter concept was neither essential nor exactly admissible. After Terence, the poets of the Augustan epoch helped in large measure to put love back where it belonged, and at the same time free woman from the prison in which she was held by custom and a purely *pro forma* respect, in order to return to her the right to love, to choose, and remain faithful by choice.

But this upheaval, with its incalculable consequences, appeared to be a triumph of depravity. When new moral values take over, their positive side is less in evidence than the negative, and so it turned out for those that upset ideas accepted for so many centuries. Ovid paid with exile for his imprudence and for his ability to sing so effectively the praises of the most seductive and lighthearted aspects of a way of life politicians thought detrimental to the state. But even before Ovid's exile, there was a poem, which expressed a reaction whose Puritanism was so strict as to be inhuman, against the new privileges accorded to love. That may be why Dido's romance, to which Virgil devoted a whole canto of the Aeneid, so often proved shocking to modern commentators.

Aeneas, in letting Dido love him, did not conduct himself differently from "young people" in the Roman tradition. As we see it, he thereby gave pledges to Queen Dido that he should have held sacred. But there could be no question of a "legitimate marriage" between him and this foreign woman, and in such circumstances individual promises lost all their validity. What would be immoral, precisely, would be to persevere in an affair that would end by causing the shipwreck of all Rome's hopes. Virgil was closer to old Cato than the poets who were his contemporaries and his friends. That was because he had chosen myths for his epic that could justify the essential values of the City-State. Love as such, with whatever personal and antisocial elements it might contain, was to be condemned, even if that meant opening the door to cruel frustrations.

Yet Virgil was not callous where tender feelings were concerned. Sometimes he is even considered the poet of sensibility par excellence. But the latter must not be in conflict with essential duties. He would depict it in the games of the *Bucolics* and in the Aeneid, but only marginally as compared with primordial motives. When Aeneas went to Pallantium to seek allies, his own army remained in the camp, which was besieged by enemy troops. It was indispensable to send a message to the chief, at which point two young men volunteered for this dangerous mission, Nisus and Euryalus.

Nisus was an experienced soldier, and Euryalus was his companion: "The handsomest of all Aeneas' companions, of all those who had ever borne Trojan arms. He was hardly more than a child, and on his cheeks the first growth of beard which had never been cut, showed that he was an adolescent. They loved each other equally, and hurled themselves into the thick of the fighting with the same ardor."

Nisus wanted to go alone to join Aeneas but Euryalus insisted on going with him. So the two filtered through the enemy lines at night. At first they were successful, butchering sleeping soldiers, but Euryalus, easygoing as the young tend to be, lingered to strip the victims of their arms. Soon they fell upon a cavalry patrol. Euryalus, whose presence was revealed by the clatter of a helmet he had just laid hands on, was surrounded and attacked. Nisus, more cautious and cleverer at concealing himself, was not discovered. He could have escaped and accomplished his mission, but he preferred to stick by his friend. Euryalus was transfixed by an enemy sword. He fell "like a purple flower, struck down by the plow, or like a poppy, bowing its head beneath the weight of the falling rain." Then Nisus threw himself into the fray, and overcome in turn by sheer numbers, fell across the body of his friend, where he found repose at last.

What a strange love story Virgil sketched in a corner of his immense fresco, and how un-Roman! Did he simply want to extol the heroism of the warrior? Why, then, make the two heroes lovers? We are told that he himself was susceptible to the beauty of young boys, and if Roman moral conventions prevented his portraying a love affair with a woman for a heroine, he was not able in spite of all to keep silent about the strength of love shared between men. In this he echoed one of the themes dearest to the heart of the Hellenistic poets, and he wanted—with the love of two youths thinly veiled beneath an appearance of fraternal feeling—to show that an affection of this kind gave birth to a heroic ardor in the souls of those affected by it, an innocence in self-denial that sufficed to justify it.

LOVE AND THE POETS

Virgil stood at the border between two worlds—the past, which refused to consider love justified, and the present, which tended to make it one of the essential elements of moral life. By his own hesitation, he symbolized the malaise from which Rome suffered and the complexity of a universe seeking its path.

VII

LOVE AND POLITICS

UNDER the Republic, it was the men who held the center of the stage; it was they who to all intents and purposes held the life of the City-State in their grasp. Political alliances in the senate and in the assemblies, the selection of magistrates, the conduct of wars, the administration of provinces, the great trials, all were negotiated in the meeting place or *curia;* in any case, outside the home. And the old Romans would have thought it disgraceful to be accused in all seriousness of taking their wives' advice on the conduct of their affairs.

Sometimes, it is true, an orator allowed himself to assert, as a kind of joke: "All men everywhere command women. As for us, we command men, and, in turn, obey women." But that was only a misogynous witticism on the part of a man of letters, who paraphrased a sally attributed to Themistocles. Cato himself, for he is credited with the jest, liked to relate that only three times in his life did he regret an act he had committed: once when he had taken a trip by sea he could have made by land; another time when he had neglected for a whole day to draw up his will; and the third time, finally, when he had one day trusted his wife with a secret.

Nevertheless he was the best of husbands and fathers: he stopped whatever he was doing to supervise his son's being bathed and put in swaddling clothes, the son his wife nursed and brought up herself. He thought that a husband who beat his wife or a father who struck his son was committing a veritable sacrilege. This did not prevent his keeping his public life entirely separate from his private life: the Roman "ideal," which Cato wished to incarnate, should show two faces, like the god Janus. One was turned to the outside—this was the visage of the "public man"; the other, which was entirely different, was known only to his intimates. This dual existence was a duty that it would have been "immoral" not to observe.

But Cato himself—and his ironic quip proves it—indicated that in practice his contemporaries were far from conforming to this principle. And, assuredly, it was inconceivable that family life, the affection of individuals for each other, not to mention affairs carried on outside marriage (and we have already said that these were not absolutely condemned) should play no role whatever, should have absolutely no influence on the personality, the moral choices, and the daily conduct of citizens. The imperious "matrons" we have come to know were not easily reconciled to ignorance of their husbands' whole public lives, and one anecdote gives us to understand that their curiosity was sometimes punished. It is nonetheless true that custom, to the extent that it admitted political influence on the part of women, contradicted an idea that had often been proclaimed.

It is hard, after so many centuries, to know how much of a role tender affection, not to say love, played in public life. Too many elements are lacking to enable us to arrive at a sound conclusion. The examples we can cite were exceptional—and that is why they seemed worth recalling and why they were handed down to us. Nothing prevents us from trying to analyze them, and the legend of Coriolanus, for example, can help us understand the ambiguous attitude of the Romans in this respect.

The story is told that a long time ago, not long before the Republic was established, when Rome was at war with the Volsci, a certain Gnaeus Marcius had won a striking victory over the enemy; he had, in particular, taken the Volscian capital of Corioli by assault, which had won him the triumphal surname of Coriolanus. Whatever his merits were, Coriolanus was a diehard conservative, which caused the people to become irritated with him, and finally got him exiled. Coriolanus took refuge with the Volsci, and offered to join forces with them against his own country. Soon, at the head of an army, he camped before Rome, and all the people trembled. The senate sent a mission to him asking for peace. Coriolanus refused. A second mission was no more successful; then priests were sent, wearing their sacerdotal garments, but they were also repulsed. Finally, the wife and the mother of Coriolanus were given the task of begging the conqueror for peace. This time his anger was appeased: "The embraces of his wife and children, the cries of despair arising from the procession of women, their lamentations over him and the nation finally brought him, this man with the heart of a savage, to see the light. He kissed his family and told them to go back, then raised the siege and left the vicinity of Rome."

Such is, in the half-legendary history of the Republic, the first instance when the affection of a husband and father clashed with the determination of a leader. Livy, in his account of the dramatic confrontation between Coriolanus and those near and dear to him, told what his old mother said, the brave, imperious Veturia. But it was the embraces of Volumnia, the wife from whom he was separated by exile, that broke his furious determination. And Livy adds naïvely: "The men of Rome were not jealous of the women for what they had accomplished—since life in those days was free of malevolent envy with regard to the glory of others."

Livy had a vague feeling that the measures the women took, and, even more, their success, were "improper," contrary to the pattern of public morals, and almost "abominable" in character. They resembled the reproaches before that time made by the too-famous Horatia, who reproached her brother Horatius, when he brought back the bloody remains of the three Curiatii to Rome. It is not surprising that Coriolanus' adventure, and his weakness when faced with "his women," was in a way expiated by the erection of a temple dedicated to "Women's Good Fortune" (*Fortuna Muliebris*) on the exact site where the interview had taken place. Such a lapse from social and moral convention could be explained and rendered legitimate only by an intervention of the gods.

Old-time custom, which decreed that marriages should serve the formation or consolidation of political alliances, also tended to belie in practice the principle according to which women were excluded from public life. A young fiancée, brought into the gens as the guarantee of an alliance; the children she bore her husband, in whose veins the bloodstreams of the two families were united, were reminders for the husband, willy-nilly, of his responsibilities as a citizen, senator, and magistrate. As long as no tenderness and love existed, or were not supposed to prevail between husband and wife, the principle of two separate lives for each man was safe. But that necessitated certain qualities: strength, or, if one prefers, a mental and emotional toughness that was hard to maintain. Let us recall how Plautus' Amphitryon, a true Roman *Imperator,* furtively slipped into Alkmene's house—to the utter delight of the audience who considered such an action a weakness unworthy of a magistrate, and were amused to see one of the city's great men lay bare emotions that a simple burgher would not dare to show.

We are aware that natural feelings, held for long in check, finally took their revenge as the Roman soul became more human. This transformation, as we said, manifested itself at the beginning of the second century B.C., and was nearly completed by Terence's time. That is why Cato, who observed it in his ripe old age, is a privileged witness.

His scoldings, and the accounts of the scandals in which he intervened, constitute highly valuable documentation of this development. When his contemporaries were too complaisant toward their wives, Cato could only nag. He acted with greater severity when the guilty party abused the power conferred on him by the Roman people to court a favorite, or worse still, an attractive youth. A few years before he became Censor, there was an example of this: L. Quinctius Flaminius, the brother of the very men who "gave the Greeks their liberty," when he was Proconsul had had a man, condemned to death, executed before the eyes of a youth Flaminius loved. The young man had spent a day with Flaminius, and had revealed to him that he had thereby missed a combat of gladiators. "Still," he added, "I wanted to go very much, because I have never yet happened to see a man die." "Nothing to it," answered the Proconsul. And he gave orders that a deserter awaiting execution be brought before them, and had him decapitated on the spot. The deed became notorious; once before, when his brother was Censor, Flaminius had escaped disgrace. Cato did not want him to go unpunished: his passionate action put him to shame both as a man and as a Magistrate, and cast a slur on the majesty of the *imperium*. Once Cato became Censor, he hastened to banish the guilty man from the senate.

The influence of women on political life in the days of the Scipios and the Gracchi has often been studied. It is one significant aspect of woman's emancipation to which we have already called attention; it was to become accentuated up to and during the Empire, and ended by giving Roman society a deplorable reputation that is familiar to all.

But the first woman—as far as we know—who played an important role in the history of her times, was anything but a profligate. She was even considered one of the most virtuous of Roman women and her name—linked with that of her son—has remained famous.

"Cornelia, daughter of the African, mother of the Gracchi"—this was the inscription engraved on the pedestal of the statue in the portico of Metellus, dedicated to her after her death. The story of her life has an aura of legend, and her image, despite the calumny heaped upon her, was one of the most noble and humane in the history of Rome.

Cornelia was the second daughter of Scipio, victor at Zama. We do not know just when she was born. Cicero tells us that while still young (*adulescens*), she lost her husband, Tiberius Sempronius Gracchus—the date is sometimes given as 154 (in which case her last son, Gaius Gracchus, would have been born after his father's death), and sometimes as 148 or 147. In any case, Cornelia was much younger than her husband. One cannot take exception in general to Cicero's dates, even if they are not very precise. Sempronius was extremely fond of her, and, so the legend runs, he chose death to save her life. It happened that one day Sempronius saw two serpents that had slithered into the house. Upset by this marvel, he consulted the soothsayers, who declared that their presence was indeed an omen. If Sempronius killed the female one, his wife would die. If he slaughtered the male, he himself would perish. Sempronius thought things over, reflected that he was old while his wife was young, and slew the serpent whose life was symbolically united to his own. A few days later he died. This is the story as Cicero recounts it, and its authenticity is guaranteed by its source, since Gaius Gracchus himself, the youngest of Cornelia's sons, had related the happening. The reasons that led Sempronius to give up his life are worthy of a Roman: first of all his age, which made his death part of the natural order of things, and his respect for the memory of the great African. But there was certainly another, which his Roman reserve prevented his mentioning, but which was conclusive: he loved Cornelia.

Widowed, Cornelia wished to devote herself to the education of her children, and a group of noteworthy parents soon gathered around her. She had borne twelve children, but most had died at a tender age; at this time only two sons were left: Tiberius (who was no doubt the older since he had his father's name) and the younger, Gaius, as well as a girl, Sempronia. The latter, perhaps around 152, married her first cousin by adoption, Publius Cornelius Scipio Aemilianus, "the second African," and a first cousin of Cornelia. The latter thus became illustrious not only through her father's memory, which continued to dominate Roman political thinking, and whose spiritual legacy was to remain an effective influence beyond the century in which he lived, but by the fact that her son-in-law's destruction of Carthage a few years later was to make him as famous as Hannibal. Through her, moreover, the gens of the Sempronii, one of the most representative plebes, survived and stayed vigorous. The Sempronii and the Cornelii had not always been political allies in the past, but the personal influence Cornelia could bring to bear on her son-in-law and her sons, who had become the nominal leaders of the two houses, appeared to be enough to guarantee a fruitful collaboration for a long time to come. It is not surprising under such circumstances that not long after she became a widow (after 154 or only later, in 143—we do not know for sure) she received an offer of marriage from the King of Egypt, Ptolemy Euergetes. Ptolemy, who was at war with his own brother, hoped, thanks to Cornelia and the family alliances resulting from the marriage, to obtain the active goodwill of the men on whom Rome's attitude depended. The King had failed to take into account the instinctive reaction of a Roman lady, to whom even the word "royalty" was odious. It should be added that such a union, with a plain "King" would have seemed discreditable to any patrician lady, even if her father had not been "the African." Finally, Ptolemy was not attractive; his nickname of Physcon, "fat paunch," given him by the Egyptians, suggests why. Cornelia did not accept his offer, and remained among her own people.

A very cultivated woman, she listened to the discussions that went on around her, in which her sons, her son-in-law, and their friends took part—all those who formed what is called today the "Scipio group." It included some of the greatest names in literature, philosophy, and politics. Cornelia knew how to bring her sons into contact with the most brilliant men, men whose daring ideas would finally lead them in directions that were contrary to the interests of their own class.

And Tiberius, like Gaius, was deeply fond of her as long as she lived, even though, we suspect, she did not always approve of their projects.

Nevertheless during Cornelia's last years suspicion was rife: cer-

LOVE AND POLITICS

tain of the old-time authors accused her of having had her son-in-law Scipio Aemilianus poisoned, with the collusion of her daughter Sempronia. Scipio died a violent death in 129, just when everyone expected him to use his immense authority to set at naught the agrarian legislation of Tiberius Gracchus. He had spoken in the course of the day before the people and the senate; in the evening he returned home followed by a crowd of admirers, and withdrew to his room to prepare a speech he planned to deliver the following day. In the morning he was found dead in bed. His demise seemed so opportune for the Popular party, who were behind Gaius Gracchus, that the rumor immediately spread that he had been assassinated, although no one at first dared to say who was guilty. But little by little names began to be heard. People remembered that Scipio had openly taken the part of Tiberius' murderers, and that when he had learned of Tiberius' death he had quoted a line of the Odyssey: "Let anyone who wants to do what he did die as he did!"

Family ties meant less to him under the circumstances than political convictions. It was not forgotten either on the Capitoline Hill that Tiberius had received the *coup de grâce* from his first cousin Scipio Nasica, son of the other Cornelia, the oldest daughter of "the African." By now enough hatred had piled up in that family to make anything—the most desperate measures—seem possible. People became convinced that Sempronia, the daughter of the man who gave his own life to save his wife, would have had the frightful courage to poison her own husband. She would have done so, it was said, not only to appease Cornelia's anger and her own, and at the same time (she might have thought) to make Gaius' political position secure, but also for more intimate reasons: to forestall an inevitable divorce, since her husband hated her for being sterile.

It is almost certain that these terrible accusations, which do not appear to have been made by her contemporaries, loomed up only during the following generation. This was the period when the memory of the Gracchi was the target of venomous attacks by the aristocrats. They wanted to sully forever the honor—and even the names—of their mother and sister, the two women who had watched them grow up and who had loved them. But all these calumnies, of which Cornelia was doubtless ignorant, did not prevent her from enjoying an honorable old age. After the death of Gaius, she returned to her villa at Misenum. Even the sight of Rome, whose soil had sopped up the blood of her children, was hateful to her.

She was not left alone in her retirement. The leading intellectuals of Rome, and the Greek philosophers who were then beginning to come to Italy in considerable numbers, were happy to visit her, and she received them courteously. She was faithful to the memory of her sons and also her husband who loved her to the point of preferring death to a life she could not share.

Involved in all the streams of thought that stirred her times, responsible in part for the feelings and the ideals that inspired Tiberius and Gaius and, in that very way, for the violent crisis that marked the decline of the old aristocratic Republic, Cornelia contributed, as a woman respectful to her duties as a Roman mother, proud, intelligent, and tender, to making the City-State more humane. It is highly significant that her statue, erected in the old portico of her contemporary, Metellus Macedonicus, was preserved by Octavius in the one which was built in 33 B.C. to honor Octavia, and which surrounded a temple to Juno, guardian of matrons. Meaningful, too, was her association with Octavia, who brought great influence to bear on the political life of her day, and who also tried, and failed, to reconcile two men—by the strength of her affection and dignified restraint—whose ambition brought them into merciless conflict with each other, one of them her brother and the other her husband. Thus Cornelia was, at the beginning of the Empire, considered an example and a model. The statue conserved by Octavius is tantamount to official recognition of the role that from then on women were expected to play in the struggles of the City-State, and that they already performed in fact, but with less restraint than the mother of the Gracchi.

Roman matrons, greedy for authority, proud of their birth, used every possible means to influence their husbands. To that end they often had recourse to religion: they had had a dream, or had observed some omen; or a god had spoken to them. If the husband seemed too preoccupied to listen, they hurried off to a fortune-teller, and once home again, took the liberty of giving advice, their hand strengthened by the predictions they had been told.

A word here, an observation there, let fall at the right moment—or just having a conjecture turn out right by pure luck—gave them the victory.

During the first days of December, 63 B.C., Terentia, the wife of Cicero, presided as the Consul's wife over the ceremonies held in her own house in honor of "the Good Goddess." This was at the time when the Consul and the whole senate, which had just received eagerly-awaited proofs that the plotters associated with Catiline were guilty of high treason, were deliberating the fate of the men they had arrested. Should they be executed, or, as Caesar proposed, be dispersed in the outlying cities under heavy guard while awaiting decisions to be made when feelings were not running so high and when the tribunal was less agitated? At this point Terentia hurried to her husband. The gods had spoken, she told him. During the rites in honor of the goddess, the sacred flame had risen high on the sacrificial altar, as if it wanted to devour everything within reach. The vestal virgins had interpreted the omen. It was necessary to act vigorously; the conspirators should be put to death without mercy.

It is possible that in proffering this advice Terentia acted in pious good faith. It is, however, also conceivable that, in agreement with the vestal virgins, she wanted to avenge herself on Catiline, who had before that compromised Fabia, herself a vestal virgin and Terentia's own sister.

This hypothesis is all the more likely in that Terentia, as Cicero has told us, was more inclined to give her attention to public affairs than to what went on in her own house, and that in the past she had employed a similar stratagem. That was when Cicero became a candidate for Consul. Apparently he hesitated to run, since the risks seemed great. But Terentia stiffened his vacillating will by telling him that a miraculous flame had leaped up from the altar before which she was performing the sacrificial rites. Far from being ashamed of the episode, Cicero told all about it in the poem he wrote giving an account of his consulship.

Caesar was less easily persuaded. On the morning of the Ides of March, refusing to heed the warnings of his wife, who had had baleful dreams the night before, he was fatally stabbed by conspirators.

But Terentia's inspirations were not always happy ones. If she was really responsible for the severity with which her husband treated the conspirators, by so doing she aroused opposition toward him for what was called his "cruelty" and which finally, six years later, resulted in his being exiled.

This is simply another instance, no less important in its effect on her husband's career, in which Terentia appears to have played a decisive part, with most unfortunate consequences for Rome itself.

During the Catiline affair, Cicero had nothing but praise for the attitude of young Publius Clodius Pulcher, the brother of Clodia, whose love affair with the poet Catullus we have already related. As it turned out, two years later Clodius became enamoured of Pompeia, Caesar's wife, who returned his love. The night during which the rites in honor of "the Good Goddess" were being celebrated in Caesar's own house, Clodius had the idea of mingling with the women, disguised as a lyre player. Beardless, he was still young enough to pass for a girl. The servant who received him left him in an antechamber for a moment, and, telling him she would soon be back, asked him to wait. But as she was slow

LOVE AND POLITICS

to return, Clodius decided to go to look for Pompeia himself. The house was a large one, and it was not long before he became lost. As he was wandering in the corridors, another servant came across him, and asked him what he wanted. She took him for one of the women taking part in the ceremonies, but when Clodius answered her, his voice betrayed him. The servant gave the alarm, all exits were closed, the house was searched, and Clodius was found in a servant's room.

According to another version, he was able to escape through a window, but was recognized. The next day the scandal broke, spread with relish by Aurelia, Caesar's mother. A man had taken part in the ritual observance; this was a sacrilege, and everyone knew why he had come into Caesar's house at night. As for Caesar, he pretended to know nothing of the escapade; he was satisfied to get a divorce without giving any reasons. As clumsy bunglers continued to question him, he replied that "Caesar's wife should be above suspicion." By his discretion he won Clodius' affection for all time. Cicero, on the other hand, was to lose it irrevocably.

As a result of the scandal, Clodius was called before the tribunal on the charge of having committed a sacrilege.

In his defense, Clodius denied everything. He declared that he was away from Rome the night of the crime, and produced witnesses. Among them was Cicero. But instead of confirming the alibi, Cicero swore that on that night the accused had indeed been in Rome, since he had visited Cicero to discuss some business. This was true. But it was equally certain that Cicero could have refrained from testifying. If he testified, it was to please Terentia. The latter was very jealous of Clodia, whom she accused of wanting to steal her husband. Clodia, as we have said, was young, pretty, and gay. She was also imprudent, seeing a great deal of a certain Tullus, who was a friend of Cicero, and who was suspected by Terentia of acting as a go-between. So, it is said, Terentia forced her husband to make sure that Clodius was found guilty, by his testimony. She hoped in this way to make Cicero hated by the young woman, who loved her brother tenderly (too tenderly, if he himself can be taken at his word).

Terentia's ruse did not have quite the result she had counted on. It is true that Clodia now hated Cicero, and so did Clodius. But the latter was not found guilty. Under popular pressure, and thanks to generosity shown at the right times and in the proper places by Clodius' friends, and, as malicious gossips would have it, thanks to the complaisance shown by Clodia to certain of the judges, the tribunal did not take Cicero's testimony into account. Clodius was acquitted. From then on, Cicero could count on the opposition of a redoubtable enemy whose hatred had been aroused against him by Terentia's jealousy. Later, when Clodius had succeeded in having Cicero exiled, with the help of Caesar's troops waiting massed on the Plain of Mars for the edict to be passed, Clodia indulged her resentment of Terentia and mistreated her cruelly.

The last days of the Republic, when women were almost fully emancipated, were those in which passionate affairs, intrigues that were often culpable—not just conjugal tenderness—began to play an important role in political life. The era was over when widowed matrons (and the big age difference between husbands and wives, when they married for the first time, resulted in a multiplicity of widows) refused to marry again, like Cornelia and other great ladies of the past. Married during adolescence or when they had hardly outgrown infancy, to bring about some political alignment their fathers judged useful, they revenged themselves afterward by selecting their new husbands themselves, to fit in with their schemes or further their ambitions, or, more often perhaps, because they loved them. These great ladies were usually very competent in business. Once no longer married, they were completely free to manage their fortune as they saw fit, even when they had not exercised this privilege from the beginning of their married lives. Men sought them in preference to young girls, because they were richer and also because they had usually made a place for themselves in the social structure, and were in positions to further their new husbands' political careers. Perhaps they were desired because their personalities had blossomed out, and men enjoyed companions who were their equals.

Generally speaking, money matters took on a particular importance in conjugal relations at that time. The combination of love, money, and ambition, three driving forces whose effects complicate the rapport between men and women to a striking extent, explains the fragility of the marriage tie in those days and the ease with which it was broken, not to mention the complexity of intrigues that became inextricably tangled.

The story of the marriage between Cicero and Terentia, which is one of those we have the least trouble in piecing together thanks to the *Correspondence* (or at least what has come down to us from it) is an example of those dramas in which the deepest feelings and the most sordid self-interest confront each other.

Terentia, in spite of her obvious faults, her fits of temperament, her desire to dominate, and her independent bearing, seems to have been devotedly loved by her husband for a long time. His more sensitive nature and his self-doubt (surely the basis of his disturbing vanity, which often led him to proclaim his own merit, more from uncertainty than arrogance) were reassured by his spouse's personality. In a letter written in exile, we take note of this apostrophe: "Now you are unhappy and persecuted—you, Terentia, whose help was sought by everyone!"

And that was no vain assertion. Everyone who hoped for help from Cicero knew well that there was no better and no more powerful intermediary than Terentia. When catastrophe struck them both, she did not indulge in recriminations. "It is all the fault of Destiny," she said, when her husband was blaming himself and regretting that he had not been more careful. It seemed as if misfortune had spurred her on to even greater efforts. She pursued Cicero's interests more vigorously, which did not save her from a few clashes with her brother-in-law.

She had no intention of seeking financial help from Cicero's friends; she sold an apartment building to cope with the money problems created by the confiscation of the exiled man's property. In a word, she was very active and helpful, while Cicero addressed her from afar as "Thou, Terentia, the most devoted and the best of women." They were apparently in complete harmony. Yet Cicero let fall a shred of evidence to the contrary in a letter addressed to Atticus, his most secret confidant. At the beginning of October, 57, he wrote him: "My other worries are more confidential . . . I have my brother's and daughter's affection." And Terentia's? Did he no longer have her affection? Once the crisis was over, did these two beings who clearly moved on different planes, and who at bottom were as different as possible, no longer take pleasure in each other's company?

During the years following Cicero's recall, we have little information on their feelings for each other. They were still apparently a happy couple, but all in all we may assume that Terentia's dominating attitude, and the advice, perhaps, that she tried as usual to give the Consul, whose popularity was on the wane and who was faced with a thousand political problems, was no longer as tolerantly accepted. But we do not find any precise indications until the year 50, when Cicero was Governor of Cilicia; from then on we perceive that the situation had changed.

First, there was the marriage of Tullia, Cicero's well-beloved daughter. She had lost her first husband, and her second marriage (with Furius Crassipes) had just ended in divorce. Her father wanted to find her a third husband, but "a good catch" was needed and the time was not opportune. Cicero was far from Rome. All that would be hard to handle by mail. But the Proconsul in his province received a visit from a man who might be able to settle the whole matter. Tiberius Claudius Nero, a young aristocrat (the very one who a little later was to become Livia's first husband), came to see him, and the two envisaged the possibility of an alliance. Cicero immediately wrote to his family, who had stayed in Rome, about it. But when the letter arrived, Terentia had already decided that Tullia was to marry Dolabella,

LOVE AND POLITICS

whose charming manners had won over the future mother-in-law as well as the prospective bride. It was not to be a marriage of convenience or common sense, as in the old days, but a new-style marriage, and to bring it about the prospective groom must court his sweetheart, must act tenderly toward her, and show himself to be both tractable and attentive. As for Cicero, it seemed to him that the road to marriage was strewn in this case with more thorns than roses. The project put a thousand difficulties in his path, and jeopardized the political alliances he had thought he could rely on. He did not complain. He even wrote to Appius Claudius, who might have proved a stumbling block to the marriage: "It was all arranged without me, but, since I had to be so far away, I wrote to my family not to consult me. . . . And if I had been there? Well, I would have approved." He would certainly have given his consent; he would have yielded to Terentia's importunities in behalf of Tullia.

Faced with Appius Claudius, Cicero did not hesitate to accept a responsibility that confirmed his standing as head of the family. But his real feelings were quite different. When he wrote freely to Atticus, one could guess from his reticence that he did not approve of the steps his wife had taken. He had doubts, from that time on, about Dolabella's character—and Dolabella was to prove the most despicable of husbands. From the vantage point of his distant province, Cicero could judge Terentia's actions more objectively than ever, and he was beginning to lose every shred of confidence in her judgment. What was only a slight wound when he returned from exile, grew worse from day to day, perhaps without his knowing it.

And Tullia's marriage, which struck him as absurd, and which was eventually to result in the young woman's death, was not the only event to disturb him.

Terentia had a steward whom she held in high esteem, a freedman named Philotimus. The latter had managed the family's affairs. After Milo had been sentenced to exile for having Clodius assassinated, Cicero tried secretly to buy back the property of the condemned man in order to save as much of his friend's fortune as he could. To this end he organized a stock company, in which of course the freedman acted as an intermediary for his master, who could not appear in it openly. But when Philotimus came to Laodicea to give an account of his activities to Cicero, his explanations were so involved and confused that Cicero realized beyond any doubt that he had been cheated. What was worse, he got the impression, rightly or wrongly, that Terentia was mixed up in the affair. He suggested this possibility in a letter to Atticus, and asked him to clear things up. Three years later, on August 6, 47, Cicero could make his accusation specific: Terentia was supposed to have sent him a bill of exchange from Atticus for 12,000 sesterces, but she had sent only 10,000!

"If she was not above making such a trifling profit where such a small sum was involved," he wrote, "think what she would have gained if the amount had been larger." The difference, paltry in itself, would not really have had any importance if it had not been the culminating episode in a prolonged crisis—Cicero did not separate from Terentia because she had defrauded him of 2,000 sesterces (an amount in the neighborhood of four hundred dollars) but because this act followed many other annoyances. Terentia realized that her husband would never become the state's leading citizen. So she renounced her propensity for political intrigue, and gave herself up entirely to her passion for money. It is easy to guess that she made an independent life for herself, and devoted all her efforts to managing her affairs. Cicero would certainly not have thought of criticizing her for that any more than he would have done earlier, if it had not been an indication of the distance she maintained between them, of that *de facto* divorce that preceded their legal separation by several years.

It is not up to us to judge the rights and wrongs of this drama. There is no doubt that Cicero was always inclined to spend unreasonable amounts of money. And it may have been quite legitimate for Terentia to have felt she should keep her own financial interests more and more separate from those of the family as a whole, even if she did so with an offensive ineptitude that transgressed the limits of honesty.

One might assume that the proud and noble Terentia did not approve the old Consul's reluctance to join Pompey and the "legitimate" senate, nor the care he took not to offend Caesar, as if he were making things ready for an eventual pardon. Why should Terentia, who was directly involved in the revolution taking place before her eyes, have been more indulgent and more understanding than so many modern historians who criticize Cicero for the same shortcomings?

The supposition is true, no doubt. Politics and self-interest collaborated to destroy the union, which, after lasting more than thirty years, came to an end under the most painful circumstances. When Cicero returned, after defeating the followers of Pompey, did he go back to Terentia? She offered to join him at Brindisi, but he dissuaded her. What would such a voyage accomplish? Why begin a return from exile with its joys and hopes followed by such bitter tomorrows? Why reopen the old wounds? But, as is often the case with weak persons, Cicero did not give the real reasons.

"I cannot imagine what you can do for me," he wrote to Terentia. "There can be no question of your starting on a trip under these circumstances. The road is long and unsafe and I don't see what would be gained if you came."

He had already made his decision: he refused to go back to a life together that was devoid of tenderness, that consisted of nothing more than mutual distrust and deception. But he was worried about the consequences a legal separation might entail for his children. He wrote to Atticus, his usual mediator, recommending that he get Terentia to make out a will in favor of Tullia. "Circumstances make it desirable," he said, "that she take care to do what is necessary for those to whom she owes so much."

It was in this atmosphere (during the month of August) that the incident of the bill of exchange occurred, which Cicero took as proof that his wife had wronged him by misappropriating funds due him. Evidently this was not the deciding motive for a divorce that had been inevitable for a long time. Here is what Cicero says in his last letter to his wife, in October:

"I think we will arrive at the estate in Tusculum the seventh or the eighth. Have everything made ready. There may be a lot of us, and we may stay a long time—at least, so it seems to me. If there is no basin in the bathroom, have one put there; and let everything be made ready for people to live and take care of themselves. Good-bye."

Thus, punctuated by a letter that seems more like one addressed to a negligent steward than a wife, ended the marital life of Cicero and Terentia.

Everyone knows that Cicero remarried immediately, and that on her part, Terentia married Sallust, a follower of Caesar and the orator's sworn enemy. Terentia's apparent belief that Caesar was wrong could not have been very firm; perhaps it had been asserted simply as a reaction to Cicero's ambiguous attitude—since it did not interfere with the marriage. It is true that Sallust, on whom Caesar had heaped riches, was one of the wealthiest men of his day, that he could afford luxuries of which Cicero could only dream, and owned a villa in Rome itself surrounded by magnificent gardens. With such a husband, Terentia no longer had to fear that she would be pressed for money.

Cicero had the weakness, at sixty, to take a very young girl as his second wife. She was his ward, and he looked after her property. The marriage took place during the last months of 46 or the beginning of 45. It did not last. The question of a divorce arose in July, 45, and was discussed from then on. Cicero's contemporaries wondered what reason, what motives, had led him to act so strangely. Some saw a flare-up of senile love, others (including Tiro, his secretary and intimate friend) declared that Cicero had found the means to dodge having to render accounts and pay debts in his capacity of guardian.

It is not easy to find out the truth today. We know only that after his divorce Cicero thought of remarrying and that he hesitated between several candidates but that Publilia did not figure among them. The idea of marrying her was an afterthought. Should it be assumed that the young girl herself suggested it to him, and that he accepted because, after all was said and done, it seemed to solve the problem of whether to give back an inheritance of which he was only the trustee? One can also adduce the testimony of Plutarch, who asserted that Terentia, in a scurrilous attack on Cicero, claimed he had married Publilia because his desire was stimulated by her youthfulness. Tiro, on the other hand, with the opposite intention, and obviously in order to defend the orator, brought up the question of financial interest. How far people were then from passing judgment, morally, on the basis of proofs that we assume as self-evident today!

Obviously Tiro thought it less shameful to marry a girl for her money than for her youthful freshness. And, for a Roman of that day, Tiro was right.

When all the evidence was in, it would appear that Cicero's standing was not diminished by the episode. And with good reason, since he did not hesitate to break off the unequal marriage, thereby renouncing the financial benefits he was alleged to have reckoned on. The reason for the rupture was undoubtedly Publilia's attitude: she was not able to conceal her joy at the death of her stepdaughter. Cicero, overcome by grief at the loss of Tullia, no doubt the only human being to whom he had shown real tenderness, could not abide the young woman's presence, and soon he divorced her.

It is possible that the settlement of an advantageous legacy which Cicero came into at that time provided him with sufficient means to live alone. But if he did manage to free himself, does not this mean that the marriage weighed heavily on him, that Terentia had slandered him, and that he was not in love with Publilia? And by the same token, since he could have kept everything— both his new wife's dowry and the inheritance—that he was not a man who put money above everything else, but tried to reconcile his amorous desires and his need for the means of subsistence?

His heart belonged entirely to Tullia. Let us pay no attention to the calumniators—motivated by hatred for the old statesman—who dared from the earliest times to insinuate that their relations were culpable. Let us be satisfied to recall that he loved her enough to make Publilia jealous. Would this have been so if she had not on her part felt one of those passionate attachments for him which are impervious to a difference in age, a love like that which a few years earlier had bound Julia, Caesar's daughter, to Pompey until she died? It is more likely that Cicero let Publilia do what she wanted with him: he was so accustomed to giving in to Terentia! He may have felt that his ward's youthfulness would make her less dominating and give him greater freedom. (In this he was quite wrong.) The union could not meet the test of reality. A psychologist might suggest that there was an attempt to substitute Publilia for Tullia, his ward taking the place of his daughter as his closest companion—until the day when the loss of Tullia brought the conflict out into the open and made even the sight of Publilia intolerable, since now he could only hate her for the same reasons that had made him love her before. We suspect that in this drama, money and ambition counted for very little—except perhaps in Publilia's case; her motives were certainly complicated—no matter what Tiro said when trying to defend his master's memory in accord with the attitude of his time. The whole business took place on a higher plane than that of pettiness: it reveals a Cicero who was no longer just an "author" or a "Consul," but a man, and this removes all temptation we might have to condemn his conduct in any way.

Dramas motivated by love—or money—were by no means unusual. This was true not only in Rome, where the social standing of the chief actors gave them more importance than those who lived elsewhere, because of the consequences for the whole civilized world, but also in little provincial Italian cities where feelings ran just as high and intrigues were just as Machiavellian as in earlier days.

One of Cicero's speeches for the defense has preserved for us the circumstances of a trial that was, in 66 B.C., a *cause célèbre*. The hero was a Roman knight, Aulus Cluentius Habitus, an upper bourgeois inhabitant of the little city of Larinum, on the Adriatic side of the Apennines at about the same latitude as Rome; it is called "Larino" today. The story is a highly complicated one involving a great many persons and just about all the outstanding families of Larinum, who, like the great Roman *gentes*, did not hesitate to form alliances among themselves without fearing the consequences of inbreeding.

Cluentius was on trial, charged with assassinating a certain Oppianicus six years earlier. The latter was then in exile, having himself been condemned for an attempted murder. His accuser in that trial—which had been a public scandal in its day because the decision was handed down by an obviously corrupt tribunal—was none other than this selfsame Cluentius. So, in 66—before our eyes, thanks to Cicero's defense—the last act was played out of a series of vendettas which were all the blacker because of the close family ties between Cluentius and Oppianicus.

A woman, of course, was the focal point of this drama: a great lady of Larinum named Sassia. Married in her tender years to Cluentius' father, she had borne him two children, Cicero's client and a girl named Cluentia, probably somewhat younger. Cluentius' father died in 88, when his son was fifteen years old. Not long after that, young Cluentia married a cousin, Aulus Aurius Melinus, also from an excellent family. Two years later Melinus got rid of his wife. For some time he had been the lover of his mother-in-law, who, according to Cicero, had done her best to win his affections. He was, we are told, a weak young man, incapable of resisting the wiles of an experienced and shameless woman. To make a long story short, once he was free, and despite the scandal his action provoked, Melinus married Sassia.

The marriage did not last long. Because Melinus, having become involved in a complicated matter regarding an inheritance, trying to protect the property of a cousin of his who had been done away with by an unscrupulous relative, was assassinated in his turn. And the guilty party was none other than Oppianicus himself!

To perpetrate these two crimes and then escape the retribution that public opinion in Larinum was calling for, Oppianicus took advantage of the outbreaks that were keeping Italy in a ferment. This was during the Social War, the revolt of the Apennine mountaineers. Oppianicus joined Sulla, who was in charge of repressing the insurrection, and returned to Larinum a conqueror. At which point he played the same role in the little city as the dictator did in Rome. He outlawed his enemies, and had them executed—specifically, those who condemned his assassinations. This gave him control of the political activity of the city. He became wealthy by pocketing the property of those he had executed. Then, as a means of further increasing his fortune and becoming the head of one of the most important houses of the city, he conceived the idea of marrying Sassia, his victim's widow. Sassia herself was not shocked by the idea of such a union, anymore than she was by this candidate stained with the blood of the person she had loved. Nevertheless she did raise one objection. Oppianicus had three sons by three former marriages. This, she averred, was the only obstacle in the way. Two of these children, still extremely young, died most opportunely, one after the other. Cicero had no hesitation in asserting that they were murdered by their father, and it may be true. If Oppianicus let the third child live, this was doubtless because the infant was related to Aurius Melinus through its mother, and because as a consequence it would be possible to take into his own hands the fortunes of the different houses. Besides, there was no guarantee that Sassia's union with Oppianicus would prove to be fertile; prudence required that someone be left to carry on the line.

LOVE AND POLITICS

Cicero alludes to the other murders: all the parents and allies of Oppianicus, the issue of the numerous marriages concluded between the different families, perished in their turn. Oppianicus did not even hesitate to thwart the desires of one of his relatives who was pregnant, after the death of her husband, and in return for the gift of a large sum of money, persuaded her to get rid of the child, whose existence as an heir might have proved highly inconvenient, even before it was born. After which he married her, and they had a son. All this happened, naturally, before his marriage to Sassia, which was his last, and the high point of his criminal career.

Finally Oppianicus tried to murder Cluentius as well, Cicero's client and Sassia's last surviving child, and as a consequence heir to a large part of the family fortune. Cluentius had not made a will. Oppianicus knew it. In case of accident Sassia would legally inherit his fortune.

But this time Oppianicus failed, and Cluentius had him brought to trial. He was found guilty, and from then on lived in exile. And it was there, according to the charge, that Cluentius tracked him down and ultimately poisoned him. It was against this accusation that Cicero defended him. And who was the guiding spirit behind the charge? Who moved heaven and earth to have Cluentius adjudged guilty? His own mother, Sassia.

To accomplish this end, she bought witnesses, tortured slaves, came in person to Rome, and had recourse to magic and the black arts, so that, according to Cicero, her hatred for her son, at least, might be satisfied. It was no longer cupidity that pervaded her soul, nor her craving for dominance, but the spirit of revenge. Cicero was moved to ask whether she deserved to be called a mother.

Cluentius may not have been innocent of the crime he was accused of having committed. His lawyers admitted later that throughout the trial he had "thrown powder in the judges' eyes." But the facts he relates, the ambience of violence, avidity, lust, and ambition, in which after long years of dissimulation the scores were paid off in the most horrible ways—this is certainly all too true.

If Oppianicus had been the only person guilty of these machinations, the curse would have died with him. But in Sassia he found a worthy companion. Past crimes do not cause remorse, they pave the way for future violence.

One would like to think that these lurid items, which, thanks to Cicero's talent, grew into a classic drama in the schools of rhetoric from antiquity onward, were simply the aberrations of a few human monsters. But is it not possible that such a "pathological" phenomenon was at bottom the morbid exaggeration of a more or less normal state of things? Even if the structure of that introverted society, hermetically sealed within each city, did not itself foster the growth of such tragedies, wealth and family alliances, with the expectation of inheritances they brought in their train, played a considerable role. The temptation to discount the maturing of these "promissory notes" could become irresistible. And it may be added that the women, once freed from the restraints that had hemmed them in from childhood onward, would suddenly be likely to give free rein to their immoderate cravings, and put no obstacle in the way of their full satisfaction. *Impotentia muliebris*—women's inability to control themselves—the expression is often found in the works of authors, and it is not just a preconceived idea that they appropriated.

Reading Greek novels of the second and third centuries A.D., and the stories included by Apuleius in his *Metamorphoses,* gives a remarkably clear picture of the bloody intrigues that often tore families apart and frequently originated in a feminine caprice.

One can easily recall, for example, that in Catiline's career there was an episode similar to the story of the marriage between Oppianicus and Sassia. After a tumultuous adolescence followed by a marriage that resulted in the birth of a boy, Catiline fell in love with a young woman named Aurelia Orestilla. And this woman, a member of the highest aristocracy, of whom Sallust said that except for her beauty, no honest man could find anything to praise, insisted on the extermination of the son-in-law, whose presence was embarrassing. And Sallust adds that it was in a house where room had been made by the murder of a son, that an essentially criminal marriage had been celebrated.

Such deeds of extreme violence were fortunately rare. If tradition is to be believed, Catiline suffered remorse for this crime until his dying day, and this is the explanation sometimes given of the unstable fit of madness that led him to plot a conspiracy doomed to failure from the moment it was conceived.

There were women's faces, at least a few, that could be distinguished in the miasma of torment surrounding Catiline. Among them can be made out that of a certain Sempronia, a descendant perhaps of the Sempronia who was the spouse of Scipio Aemilianus. Sallust painted her portrait in lively colors.

"By her birth and beauty, and because of her husband and children, this woman could only congratulate herself on her good fortune. Well educated in the Greek and Roman languages and letters, she played the cithara and danced, more skillfully than is becoming in an honest woman, not to mention many other talents that are employed in the art of seduction. Nothing found less favor in her eyes than honor and modesty; it would have been hard to say which she valued less, her fortune or her reputation. Burning with sensual desire, it was more common for her to make advances to men than to receive theirs. She had broken her word many times in the past, had solemnly refused to recognize her obligations, and had steeped her hands in the blood of murdered men. Adversity and dissipation had hastened her downfall. Yet she did not lack finesse; she knew how to turn a verse, make a joke, and vary her way of speaking, at times modest, at others, tender or provocative. In a word, her refinement was only equaled by her charm."

Not satisfied with playing the part of Egeria to the conspirators, Sempronia was active in helping the cause, lending her house, for instance, for the interviews Catiline's leading representatives gave the ambassadors of the Allobroges. Apparently widowed or divorced at the time, Sempronia took advantage of the absence of her son Decimus Junius Brutus, who would one day be found among Caesar's assassins, to facilitate these meetings, since he would certainly have opposed such doings.

In spite of all her defects, Sempronia was loyal, at least, to her fellow conspirators. The same cannot be said for another of their "friends," a certain Fulvia. She too belonged to the highest aristocracy, but lived in fact like a courtesan, since she was kept by an admirer named Curius, who had been banned from the senate by the censors on account of the many scandals in which he had been involved. Their affair had already lasted a long time when the conspiracy was organized. But Fulvia was getting tired of it, specifically since Curius had very little money, and his presents were getting sparser all the time. And since she denied him her favors, he began one day to promise her everything under the sun, while threatening to stab her if she would not resume their relationship—on credit.

This sudden change aroused the lady's curiosity, and she had no difficulty in persuading her lover to confess his secret and reveal the nature of his hopes. Catiline was about to take the reins of power into his hands, and when he was head of the state, he would certainly know how to reward his friends! Astounded, Fulvia was not able to keep what she had just learned to herself for long. She began to let drop mysterious hints, proclaiming to anyone who cared to listen that a grave threat to the security of Rome was being prepared. But she did not name any names.

This occurred during the consular elections, and Sallust avers that these rumors helped Cicero get elected. The latter, as soon as he took up the responsibilities of his office, made it his first duty to sound out Fulvia, who was always short of money, and bribed her into becoming his informer. She immediately read Curius a lecture, and, once again, he did not hesitate to betray his accomplices. Day by day, through Fulvia's efforts, Cicero learned of the deliberations of Catiline's friends, their plans and their hopes. Everyone was astonished to discover how well informed he was. Curius and Fulvia should nevertheless be given credit for one thing: they were loyal to the man who was paying them: as soon as they learned that some of the conspirators planned to assassinate him on the very next day, they took the initiative and alerted him. In the middle of the night Fulvia ran to Cicero and warned him to be on his guard. In the morning, when the two men charged with the mission came to his door as if they wished to greet him, they were refused admittance.

Not all the stories of love affairs in which politics mingled with passion were as sordid. During those troubled times there were women who, gaining the ascendancy over the men they loved, did not take advantage of it for deplorable and criminal ends, just as there were others who were beyond any doubt drawn into committing atrocious acts but whose conduct was not lacking in dignity.

The former were probably the more numerous: persons who simply had a taste for intrigue, and who liked to think that they could manage affairs of state from their boudoirs. But more often, dupes of their own vanity, they were manipulated by men who made use of them to advance their careers. One of these, for example, was Praecia; Plutarch has described her. When her beauty was at its height, she had, by bestowing her favors judiciously, collected a whole court of influential friends.

Unscrupulous enough so far as her conduct was concerned, but intelligent and clever, she had the reputation of being a dependable friend. When she had decided to further the career of a man she was attracted to, she succeeded. Soon she numbered among her lovers Cornelius Cegethus, then at the height of his power. From that moment on, said Plutarch—drawing a long bow—"the whole city was in her hands. For nothing was done in the City-State without the approval of Cegethus, and Cegethus did nothing without Praecia's advice."

Lucullus, who ardently desired a high command in the East,

where Mithridates had embarked on a war against Rome, decided to court Praecia. He plied her with presents, and showered her with attentions and compliments. And Cegethus, who had until then been inimical to Lucullus—a man who was far from being considered unattractive—changed his attitude completely. Thanks to him, the obstacles in Lucullus' path were removed, and he was put in charge of the war.

One can assume that Praecia was not the only example, and that many women who wanted to convince themselves of the influence their attraction gave them over men maneuvered in the same way in the circles of the great. But historians have not recorded their successes and failures. It is usually some accident, some isolated account, that reveals the counterplay of those incidents behind great historical events. Cicero gave them the agreeable name of "nocturnal intercessions."

Of course the victorious Clodia, whose unhappy amours with the great Catullus have already been related, did not hesitate to use her undeniable powers of seduction in the service of the political causes she championed. Even when she was married to Metellus, she made every effort to further the interests of her brother, Publius Clodius. And once she was free, it would seem likely that she continued to help him all she could.

But it is hard to figure out today exactly what part she played in the complicated intrigues characteristic of those times. Nevertheless we can guess that her difficult dealings with Marcus Caelius Rufus (after her affair with Catullus was over), who was perhaps her lover, and in any case her fervent admirer, were not caused merely by a lovers' quarrel. It is clear, in spite of Cicero's oratorical cunning when he defended Caelius against the accusers Clodia had pitted against him, that the truth was both more complex and more somber.

After breaking with Caelius, Clodia had him charged with trying to poison her, which was apparently false. But she also accused him, with more plausibility, of having taken part in a conspiracy in which she herself was involved. In 58 the Egyptians had again revolted against their King, Ptolemy Auletes, who without further ado had taken refuge in Rome. Here, with Pompey's support, he tried to win over the senate by distributing largesse and—especially—promises, with a view to the day when he should be restored to the throne. His daughter Berenice, who had been made Queen in his place by the Egyptians, wanted a hearing, and sent a delegation that landed at Pozzuoli. There the plenipotentiaries were harassed by a band of young persons that included Caelius himself. Not long after that, Dion, the head of the delegation, who was the guest of Lucceius, a friend of Pompey's, in Rome, died of poisoning.

At Caelius' trial, his accusers declared that he was the murderer, and—an extremely dangerous disclosure for Clodia—that he had borrowed money from her to hatch the plot. As a matter of fact, they added that Caelius had not revealed his real intentions to his friend, but in view of the closeness of their intimacy at that time, it is hardly likely that she did not know about it. This played into Cicero's hands.

One gets the impression that if Caelius played a leading part with funds furnished by Clodia, he was simply his mistress' tool.

And behind Clodia was Clodius, who took advantage of his sister's dominion over this scatterbrained young man to lure him into a Machiavellian conspiracy.

Ostensibly, to be sure, Ptolemy Auletes was the protégé of Pompey, who counted on being commissioned by the senate to put the King back on his throne. This would have been highly profitable to Pompey. But Clodius would have none of it. Just when Pompey seemed about to gain his ends, Clodius raised obstacles of a religious nature that prevented the senate from reaching a decision.

But Clodius did not want Berenice's plenipotentiaries to have an opportunity to tell the senate how things were really going in Egypt, since he had others in mind for the role Pompey wanted to play. In all this Clodius was really serving the interests of Caesar. And in the end it was Caesar who reaped the benefits of the illegal expedition organized—later by Gabinius, Proconsul of Syria, that brought Egypt completely under Rome's sway. Such were the strangely tortuous ways of politics in the last days of the Republic.

After the death of Clodius, assassinated on the Appian Way by the followers of Milo, Clodia disappeared from the political scene, either because the loss of her beloved brother had drained all her vitality or because she did not long survive him. Forever dishonored by the insults heaped on her by Cicero in the *Pro Caelio* and the curses proffered by Catullus, Clodia was typical of the corrupt Roman woman, unworthy of her great ancestors. No accusation made against her, however horrible, was thought incredible by historians. But she really owes this reputation more to the hatred of two of the most brilliant writers of her day than to her "vices" or to some special perversion. Compared to Fulvia, who was her sister-in-law for awhile, she seems, if not "an angel of sweetness and purity," at least a woman whose greatest sin was to have been a coquette, to have forfeited the affections of a poet, and, because of her devotion to her brother, to have become involved in shady intrigues in which, ultimately, her honor was compromised.

Fulvia, on the other hand, who did not surround herself with poets, took an active part in tragedies that were far more sanguinary, and that imperiled the existence of Rome itself. This Fulvia—we must be careful not to confuse her with the other, whose activities during the conspiracy against Catiline we have already related—did not have the good (or bad) luck to belong to the upper aristocracy. She came from the little town of Tusculum; her father was a certain Fulvius Bambalio, called "the Stutterer," because of an impediment in his speech. According to Cicero, he was a contemptible, stupid man.

Through her mother, Fulvia was the granddaughter of a very strange character named Sempronius Tuditanus, who died insane after doing a number of odd things, among them scattering money among the crowd from the tops of the Rostra. Perhaps it was from this ancestor that Fulvia inherited a taint revealed not only in the disharmony of her countenance but in outbursts of cruelty and violence.

Clodia was pretty and gracious. But the portraits of Fulvia that have come down to us show a pointed profile, thin lips, eyes sunk deep in their sockets, and a long, bony neck. A historian—who, it must be said, was antagonistic to her—declared that "there was nothing feminine about her but her body." Her first husband was Clodius, who took her everywhere with him, and was always willing to be guided by her advice even when she counseled violence. This did not prevent Fulvia from having a weakness even at that time for Mark Antony, who was assiduous in his visits to the Tribune's home. When Clodius died, she gave way to outbreaks of despair. Perhaps they were sincere, but the effect was to increase the people's anger and indignation against the murderers. And the riots that followed augmented the political confusion, helping to prepare the crisis that culminated in the collapse of the regime.

A few months later Fulvia married young Scribonius Curio. Why did she choose him? Without a doubt Curio was one of the most brilliant men of the new generation. He had the esteem and the support of Cicero. It was obvious that he was very ambitious. But was not Fulvia's choice determined by other more personal and more secret reasons? Cicero informs us (and since it was a public scandal, there is no reason to be skeptical) that when they were very young, Antony and Curio had loved each other with a passion that was sordid and romantic at the same time, and that they had given free rein to their juvenile ardor. Curio's father, who could not abide this degrading situation, stepped in and separated the two boys.

Young Curio, "burning with love, declared that he could not endure Antony's absence, and that he would go into exile." His confidant, who has given an account of the episode, was none other than Cicero himself. And Cicero also told how Antony, despite the precautions taken by the father, used to enter the house by way of the roof to rejoin his love!

When this affair was over, Antony again became intimate with Clodius, whom he helped in his career, and it is at this time that he probably had his first relations with Fulvia. Then, since he was wretchedly poor, he left for the East to seek his fortune, joining Gabinius, who was about to leave to put Ptolemy Auletes back on the throne at Alexandria. Once this had been accomplished, he went to Gaul where he had been summoned by Caesar. He was doubtless away from Rome when Fulvia married Curio. After being the mistress of one of the two lovers, she became the wife of the other one.

Until then Curio had been hostile to Caesar. It may well be that he showed it too violently, which suggests that he might have been playing the role of *agent provocateur,* while he really sympathized with the man whose enemy he pretended to be. In any case, not long after his marriage to Fulvia, he dropped the mask, and turned up as a Tribune in Caesar's service. If he really had not rallied to Caesar's cause until then, it may have been Fulvia who influenced his decision.

But the union between Curio and Fulvia was not to last long. The Civil War soon broke out; Curio, to whom Caesar gave the mission of organizing and leading an expeditionary force in Africa, was killed in combat during the month of July, 49.

Having lost two husbands by violent death, Fulvia married Antony. And it was at that point that her "political career" really began.

Antony had already been married twice. His first wife was a certain Fadia, the daughter of a freedman. Next he married his cousin, the daughter of Antonius Hybrida (an associate of Cicero's during the 63 consulship), but repudiated her on the pretext that she had deceived him with Dolabella, Cicero's third son-in-law. In view of Dolabella's reputation as a wild profligate and a chaser par excellence, the accusation was probably true. Cicero makes a

LOVE AND POLITICS

show of believing that Antony got a divorce so as to marry Fulvia. If that is true, it is hard to explain why he led the life of a rake at the same time, parading the actress Cytheris everywhere, and a host of shady characters, including Sergius, the mime, who had a great hold on Antony. But quite possibly it was Fulvia who loved Antony, and that the marriage was based at least in part on love. It seems likely too that Caesar, tired of the way his lieutenant was carrying on (he had made him "Master of the Cavalry," which ranked him as second highest personage in the state), had brought his influence to bear, in the hope that the marriage would calm Antony down. No matter how little the latter was able to curb his instincts and his taste for debauchery, it is certain that he was quite fond of Fulvia and was even, at times, really in love with her.

This lies back of a curious anecdote that Cicero tells in the Second Philippic. Antony had left for Spain to join Caesar during the Munda campaign. But he did not finish the trip. He suddenly came home, without having gone beyond Narbonne. As to how he entered Rome—here is the incident as Cicero describes it:

"Arriving at the Red Rocks on the via Flaminia, about twelve kilometers north of Rome, he hid in a low-class dive and, keeping out of sight, did not stop eating until evening. Then, going to Rome in a fast carriage, he arrived at his house, keeping his face hidden. 'Who are you?' asked the porter. 'A messenger from Mark Antony.' He was taken to the person he had come to see—his wife Fulvia—and he handed her a letter. She wept as she read it, since it was quite tender in tone: the gist of it was that Antony would no longer have anything to do with the actress (Cytheris); that he no longer paid her any attention, so that he could give all his affection to his wife. As she cried still harder, the sensitive Antony could no longer control himself. He uncovered his head and embraced his wife."

This scene, obviously authentic, since it is described in almost the same terms in Plutarch's *Life of Antony,* shows that Fulvia was unusually sentimental. Plutarch said that she was not one to spin wool or keep house, that she would consider it beneath her dignity to marry an ordinary individual, but wanted to rule over a man in a position of power, to exercise her dominion over a leader. So there she was, weeping for joy, because of the very intensity of her feelings, because her husband, disregarding his official responsibilities, had come back to her to tell her that he loved her! Is not this a striking proof that the union of these two human creatures was more than an understanding between two schemers who wanted to turn their influence to account?

For a while, at least, Antony and Fulvia led an existence that did not belie the impression afforded by the romantic episode described by Cicero and Plutarch. After Caesar's death, in the course of the year in which so many dramatic events took place, and while Antony worked to save the political heritage of the fallen dictator, Fulvia was by his side. Perhaps she was responsible for several happy ideas that helped him reach the goal he had set for himself. It is noteworthy that when he became a *triumvir* he showed his gratitude by awarding Fulvia a distinction that had never been accorded a Roman woman until then: as was done in the case of queens in the East, he had coins struck bearing her effigy.

Cicero wrote a malicious account of Fulvia's political activities in 44 and 43. He said that in Antony's house she carried on a shameful traffic: "A woman who was luckier when she was working for herself than for her husband, she put up provinces and kingdoms for auction. . . ."

But these are the utterances of a partisan and a polemicist. No attention need be paid them except for the implication that Fulvia, like so many other matrons of her time and of previous epochs, had the right to put in a word when affairs of state were being deliberated, and her husband paid attention to her advice. And she was brave: she did not hesitate to accompany him to Brundisium in October, 44, when he was given the mission of reorganizing the legions repatriated from Macedonia. It was Antony's job then to check military uprisings, and she was present at the

LOVE AND POLITICS

execution of a number of deserters. According to Cicero, she was even splashed with their blood, but this touch conjured up by an orator need not be taken literally.

When Antony "decimated" the rebellious troops, he was only conforming to custom, and applying the harsh rules of discipline. But Fulvia? We are not aware what her deepest feelings were. We know only that she did not hold back while her husband was fulfilling his duties as a leader. Which is true: that there was no room in her heart for pity, or that she thought it unworthy to show any?

The same question came up a little later in a somewhat similar situation. To prepare for the war against the murderers of Caesar, the triumvirs Antony, Lepidus, and Octavian had decided that the richest women in Rome—they drew up a list of 1,400 names—were to furnish an estimate of their wealth to be the basis of a special tax. The ladies, who had not protested when their husbands and their sons were proscribed (a measure that carried the death penalty), raised a huge outcry when their worldly wealth was threatened. Forming a procession, they sought out the women who had the most influence with the triumvirs. Octavia, sister of Octavian, and Julia, mother of Antony, received them cordially. But Fulvia closed the door on them, which made her very unpopular. She was accused of harshness and pride. But perhaps she simply shared the viewpoint of her husband, who found the selfishness of the Roman ladies, more attached to their worldly goods than to the men of their families, unbearable!

But if we are inclined to judge Fulvia and her behavior during those troublous times too leniently, one incident should be recalled, which Appian too records, and which seems prophetic of the charges Tacitus later brought against the Empresses. The Senator Caesetius Rufus owned a handsome house next to Fulvia's. She wanted to buy it, but the senator refused. At the time of the proscriptions, Rufus lost his nerve and offered it to her as a gift. She preferred to have him proscribed by Antony. When the bloody head of Rufus was brought to Antony, he said that it was no business of his, and sent the executioner on to Fulvia, who had the sinister trophy stuck on the house that had caused all the trouble, instead of having it nailed to one of the Rostra as custom demanded. A true Roman woman, Fulvia liked the taste of revenge above all, even though her greed could have been satisfied at less cost than the life of the senator.

Violent and passionate, Fulvia certainly used Antony and the love he bore her to satisfy her rancor. The story goes that when Cicero's head was exposed on one of the Rostra, she pierced his tongue with a needle. Some historians do not mention this episode, which is not incredible in the dramatic atmosphere of the proscriptions. The gesture reveals the old malevolence of the woman who had been Clodius' wife, and whom Cicero had deeply insulted in the *Philippics*.

Plutarch has told of the atrocious vengeance wreaked by Pomponia, wife of Quintus Cicero, on a freedman named Philologus, who had played the orator false. Handed over by Antony himself to Pomponia (whose husband and whose son had been killed in the course of these very proscriptions), Philologus was first tortured in a thousand ways, then forced to cut off pieces of his flesh that he was obliged to cook and then eat. Such were the women called "adorable Furies" during the cruel times of the Civil Wars!

After the Battle of Philippi that clinched the victory of the triumvirs over Caesar's assassins, the victors divided up the civilized world among themselves. Antony was given the mission of pacifying the East, which he desired, and went off alone, leaving Fulvia in Italy. Octavian, who had the task of restoring order in Italy, was faced with highly complex problems. Certainly Fulvia had already guessed that the young man who owed so much to Antony, and above all the victory at Philippi, would take advantage of the situation to establish his personal dominion at the expense of his comrade. She decided to make every effort to prevent this, and found an ally in her brother-in-law, Lucius Antonius. Together they organized the opposition that the application of measures giving lands to veterans had aroused. This resulted in what was practically a war, ending in the siege and capture of Perugia.

Was it only her wish to guide the affairs of state as she pleased that led Fulvia to provoke such a conflict? Did she believe herself to be Antony's agent? Classic historians adduce other and much more feminine motives. They remind us that as early as 41, Antony had met Cleopatra in the East, and Fulvia had conceived the notion of setting Italy afire and drenching the country in a bloodbath to force her husband to return and demand an accounting from Octavian.

Perhaps, as Appian alleges, the idea was suggested to her by Manius, one of Antony's freedmen, who acted as bailiff. However this may be, once the plan was conceived, Fulvia did not hesitate. Prepared to take the consequences, she defied Octavian's troops, and, after the defeat, fled with her children to Athens, where Antony came to find her. Fulvia had attained her object, as she thought. But Antony's attitude was not what she expected. The difficulties she had created between him and Octavian ran counter to the schemes of the man who felt obligated to continue Caesar's policies in the East. They harshly interrupted his dreams of power, in which another woman, Queen Cleopatra, played the leading part, and in which Fulvia had no place.

Instead of enjoying the happy reunion she had hoped for, Fulvia found herself facing a man who had grown distant and hostile. Antony reproached her for starting a cabal whose consequences she had not foreseen, and left her brusquely to try to redress what he called her blunders.

This was more than such a woman, deeply wounded in both her pride and her love, could stand. She fell ill, and in her despair did not have the strength to throw off her malady. She was ill when Antony left Athens without coming to see her. A little later she died at Sicyonia, while Antony, at Brundisium, was having a reconciliation with Octavian. It is said that the news of her death greatly facilitated their rapprochement, and both men were only too glad to make her responsible for what they called a "misunderstanding." Their peace pact was sealed by a marriage between Antony and Octavia, his comrade's sister.

Thus died—and was forgotten before her corpse had hardly grown cold—a woman who had raised armies during the Perusian War, lived in the camps, and assumed all the functions of an *imperator*. But her indomitable energy could not withstand the collapse of her love, or, perhaps, the defeat that would have been the ineluctable consequence of her failure.

Fulvia's career is not the only example, in that epoch, of the enormous effect some marriages had on political events, even when the partners did not go to such lengths to establish their influence. In the life of Pompey, who was one of the principal actors in the drama that marked the downfall of the Republic, the women he married one after another played an increasingly influential role, and one of them just missed sparing the world the tragedy of the Civil War.

The image of Pompey provided by his busts, which show him aged and bloated, do not correspond at all to the description given by his biographers. In his youth Pompey was strikingly handsome in a way that had something noble and royal about it. The curl of his hair and the curve of his cheeks irresistibly reminded one of the portraits of Alexander. This gained him the favor of the multitude and the affection of womenfolk. When still very young he aroused a flaming passion in the breast of the courtesan Flora. Later she enjoyed recalling that he never quitted her without leaving the marks of his teeth on her body. Nevertheless Pompey had not hesitated to turn her over to one of his friends, Geminius, who had fallen in love with her. He had released her "in spite of himself and in spite of her." On his side, in the role of friend; on her side, in the part of a courtesan who must do as she was told. But she suffered so much, on losing him, that she remained ill for a long time.

Another beauty of Pompey's day, the wife of his friend Demetrius, did not receive such courteous treatment at his hands. Apparently he did not trust himself where the seductive power of women was concerned, so, mindful of his reputation, made an effort to curb his feelings and desires.

It was not long before the powerful personages of the day wanted to make sure of him as an ally, and one of them, Antistius, who presided over the tribunal before which young Pompey was then appearing (the victim of a vengeance attempt directed against his father Strabo), did not even wait until the trial was over to promise him his daughter's hand. When the dictator Sulla, after his victory, also wanted to organize a party of supporters, he took special notice of Pompey, who had rendered him considerable service during the Civil War by raising an army on his own initiative. With the help of his wife Metella he got Pompey, partly by persuasion and partly by force, to repudiate Antistia and marry Aemilia, Metella's daughter by a previous marriage. This was a shocking union, for Aemilia was already married and expecting a baby. But Pompey was unable to resist and married the young woman, who, as it turned out, died in childbirth.

We do not know when Pompey married for the third time, nor under what circumstances. His new wife's name was Mucia, and he may have wanted to strengthen his ties through her with the Metellus clan, to which she belonged. We only know that he was genuinely fond of her.

When he was put in command of the Roman forces in the war against the pirates, he exclaimed—not without a nuance of hypocrisy, for it was a post he had ardently desired: "Ah! Always working! How I would prefer to be someone quite obscure, if I am never to stop fighting and never cast off this odious role, without being able to live quietly in the country with my wife."

As for Mucia, she was not able to wait for him. She deceived him while he was away, perhaps with Caesar, perhaps with others. As long as he was in the East, Pompey refused to listen to the reports brought him, but when he was back in Italy, and no longer distracted from his own concerns by those of the Republic, he learned of the exact state of affairs, and announced that he was getting a divorce without even agreeing to see her again. Mucia's misconduct was apparently so flagrant that everyone approved his decision.

Pompey, then, was free. The major problem before him, now that he was back from the East, was to stabilize his political situation. His victories had aroused animosity in several quarters, and the senate was jealous of his popularity. Cato's hostility, in particular, was so outspoken that it attracted attention. Pompey figured that if he could win over Cato his position would be stronger in the senate. Cato had two nieces; Pompey asked for the hand of one in marriage and that of the other for his son. A strange scheme, which ill concealed the self-interest that prompted it. But were not such alliances entered into every day in this milieu?

Cato's wife and his half-sister Servilia advised him to accept; they were delighted at the prospect of including Pompey, who was already called *Magnus,* "the Great,"—among their allies. Despite the authority—like that of a mother—that Servilia exercised over him, Cato refused. He did not wish to jeopardize his political independence by aligning himself with a man whose ambition he discerned, whose methods he disapproved of, and who, he believed, was a danger to the Republican regime. But Pompey did not wait long before making another match, also motivated by political ambition, but which was to grow into a marriage of love.

Since Cato had rejected Pompey, the latter, seeking allies, agreed to conclude a secret pact with two other ambitious leaders, Caesar and Crassus. This was the first triumvirate. The political covenant was sealed by a marriage between Pompey and Julia, Caesar's daughter. Born around 83, Julia was the child of Caesar's first marriage, with Cornelia, the daughter of Anna. Her father had affianced her to a certain Servilius Caepio. The latter was no doubt really M. Junius Brutus, son of Servilia, Cato's half-sister, and, as will become apparent, one of Caesar's closest friends. It

LOVE AND POLITICS

would seem that the same idea had occurred to him as to Pompey, and he was trying to ally himself with the powerful clan of which Cato was the most eminent—unless his own relationship to Servilia suggested the plan to him.

But when the triumvirate was formed, he was in fact compelled to turn the pyramid of alliances he had so carefully built up on its head. And the following year, 59, since Julia's engagement to Junius Brutus had been abruptly broken off, Pompey married her.

She was hardly more than twenty-two or twenty-three at the time. Pompey was nearly fifty, and he quickly fell in love with his young bride. Plutarch tells how he began to neglect political life more and more, seldom going to the Forum, and leaving Clodius, the demagogue, every opportunity to pursue his mad schemes. As for Pompey, he spent all his time with Julia in their gardens in the Plain of Mars, and in the villas he owned in other parts of Italy, so that the wish he had expressed when he was married to Mucia came true, but this time with a companion who was worthy of him. For—and this never ceased to astonish Plutarch—Julia loved Pompey as deeply as he cherished her, and if he never left her side, it may have been less in order not to be deprived of her presence than that she should not be deprived of his. This was an attitude better suited to an "irresponsible" poet like Catullus than to a man whose political responsibilities were onerous. And Clodius never lost a chance to mock him for it in public. But the people could not help feeling a warm admiration for this love affair, which became proverbial. The rumor spread, generating surprise and not a little amazement, that Pompey was faithful to his wife, that he was having no liaisons on the side, but belonged entirely to her.

Yet this happiness was not to last. In 55 an incident occurred that was to have serious consequences. During a clash on the Plain of Mars, several rioters were killed so near Pompey that his toga was splashed with blood. He immediately ordered one of his servants to take the soiled garment back to the house and bring another. The manservant, still badly shaken, appeared at Pompey's home bearing the bloody toga, and as luck would have it, Julia saw him bring it.

The blood on the toga, which she recognized immediately, and the remarks the servant uttered in a broken voice, made her think Pompey was seriously wounded, perhaps dead. She fainted. Julia was pregnant; the violent emotion she had experienced brought on an abortion. A few months later she became pregnant again and was able to give birth to a little girl, but she herself did not survive.

The whole Roman people was profoundly affected by her death. And, since Pompey planned to have the funeral rites observed on their estate at Alba, the crowd took possession of the body and installed it in a sepulcher in the Plain of Mars. Was this to honor Pompey or Caesar? Had the sad fate of this young woman fired the imagination of the people? Because through the strength of her love alone she had been able to maintain harmonious relations between two men whose disunity might have brought on a catastrophe? Julia was to become the everlasting symbol, in the writings of historians and poets, of the power of love: "If destiny had let you live longer in the light of day," wrote Lucan, "you alone might have restrained the hitherto unfettered madness of a father here; a husband there; you might have torn their weapons from them and joined their hands together, just as the Sabine women, acting as mediators, joined those of fathers and sons-in-law. . . ."

The following year Pompey remarried. In a solemn ceremony he was wedded to Cornelia, the daughter of Metellus Scipio, who belonged to the highest nobility. But what was more important in Pompey's eyes, young Cornelia had been the wife—in her first marriage—of Crassus the Younger, who had just died in Syria after taking part in the expedition that had cost the life of his father, Crassus the Triumvir. This marriage, Pompey figured, would gain for young Crassus' successor the backing that the latter had lined up from a number of senators.

LOVE AND POLITICS

This was the time when Pompey, courted by the nobles, who had come to fear Caesar more and more, began to loosen the ties that bound him to his old friend. The old statesman's marriage with Cornelia defined his new political position with considerable exactitude. But there were other possible matches, just as advantageous, and we can assume that he chose Cornelia among many because of her charm and her feminine qualities. This was the opinion of Plutarch, who declares: "The young woman had many characteristics that made her worth loving, in addition to her youth. She was well versed in literature, the art of playing the lyre, and in geometry; and she had been taught to benefit by listening to the utterances of the philosophers. Moreover, her nature lacked the unpleasant tendency to indiscretion that such capacities usually bring out in young women."

Finally, Cornelia, like Julia, was so young that Pompey's adversaries observed that the match would have been more suitable for his son, and public opinion criticized him for giving his new love the careful attention he should have dedicated to the problems of government.

Pompey took advantage of the marriage to back up his policies. He used his father-in-law Scipio, whom he made his associate during the last months of his "unique" consulate, as his mouthpiece during the sessions of the senate that preceded the Civil War and made it inevitable. But this by no means signifies that he did not love Cornelia and was not loved in return. Yet it does not appear that he was able to live again with her the days of enchantment he had known with Julia. Perhaps because such great happiness comes only once in a lifetime. In any case, historical events crowded in on them at precipitous speed. Two years after they were married the Civil War broke out and they had to leave for the East, hard pressed by Caesar's armies.

While Pompey was leading the fray on the slopes of Illyria, in the neighborhood of Dyrrachium, Cornelia had taken refuge at Mytilene, where, alternating between hope and fear, she anxiously waited for news of her husband. One day a messenger appeared and informed her of the defeat at Pharsalus. On board the ship that had brought the messenger was Pompey. Cornelia ran to the port and threw herself into her husband's arms. The first thing she said, according to Plutarch, was to take the blame for the catastrophe in which Pompey's armies went down into defeat. Suddenly remembering that she had previously been the wife of young Crassus, she felt that she must be under a curse: each man whose mate she had been had met with disaster!

Pompey comforted her as best he could and tried to buoy her up with hopes he himself no longer shared. The senators' fleet was intact, he pointed out, and it was still possible to go back to war. But at the same time, in a talk with a philosopher, he admitted that he could hope for nothing more from Divine Providence.

And it was Cornelia who indirectly caused the final debacle. Pompey's first idea had been to seek refuge with the King of the Parthians. Caesar would certainly not have pursued Pompey into Parthia, at least not for the moment. But on thinking it over, he decided that he could not make an appearance in that oriental court with a great Roman lady whose honor would not permit her to accept the humiliations and even perhaps opprobrious attentions to which she might be exposed. So he decided to return to Egypt—where the assassins awaited him.

With his trail as a politician staked out by successive marriages, Pompey's career was greatly influenced by women. But traditionally even the greatest detractors of the leader defeated at Pharsalus never accused him of immoral conduct.

The same cannot be said for his adversary. Caesar's own soldiers used an insulting nickname for him in their songs celebrating his victory.

"Citizens!" they sang. "Look out for your wives: we are bringing back the rake, the plucked rooster!"

In his biography of Caesar, Suetonius has compiled a list of the dictator's love affairs. Most of his "victims" were from the upper crust: Postumia, wife of Servius Sulpicius, probably Sulpicius

Rufus, who was Consul in 51. Then Lollia, the wife of Aulus Gabinus, Consul in 58, who was first a follower of Pompey, then sentenced to exile, then reinstated by Caesar, and given a command in his army during the Civil War. The third name Suetonius cites is that of Tertulla, wife of Crassus the Triumvir; next comes Mucia, Pompey's second wife. It would thus seem that the political alliance represented by the triumvirate had a clandestine parallel in relationships of a more congenial nature, from which Caesar, to tell the truth, was the only one to benefit. However, it should not be forgotten that the liaison with Mucia, which took place during Pompey's absence, resulted in the lady being divorced—repudiated by her husband a few months before the triumvirate ended. Over this affair, Pompey suffered bitterly. Mucia had given him three sons; it made him very unhappy to separate from her. And it was his habit in those days to curse Caesar, whom he called "Aegisthus." But this did not prevent his marrying Julia a few months later. The recital of these complicated intrigues makes it easier to understand what ambivalent feelings such men aroused in each other. Ambition forced them into these alliances, while for that very reason they were obliged to conceal their antipathy, not to say hatred, for each other, and forget their old wounds.

According to Suetonius, the Roman mistress Caesar loved the most was Servilia, mother of M. Junius Brutus and Cato's half-sister. The happiest period in their relationship was in 63, when Cicero was Consul. They were about the same age. (Caesar was going on thirty-eight. We do not know exactly when Servilia was born but she was probably a close contemporary of her lover.) They were passionately fond of each other, so much so that they found the moments when they were separated interminable. An anecdote told by Plutarch provides an intriguing, if scandalous, reminiscence of the relationship.

It was in the month of December, 63, during one of the senate sessions deliberating how to treat the conspirators who had been Catiline's accomplices. Caesar happened to be sitting next to Cato;

their opinions on the matter were quite different. Cato wanted the guilty parties to be executed. Caesar was for having them spared, which provided grounds for suspecting that he had been somehow involved in the conspiracy.

At one moment, right in the middle of the session, a note was brought to Caesar from outside the senate. He began to read it forthwith. Cato jumped from his seat and cried out that Caesar's conduct was intolerable, that he was receiving messages from enemies of the state, and was betraying the cause of law and order. And since the senators were beginning to take sides in the quarrel, Caesar calmly handed the note to Cato and told him to read it. No sooner had Cato glanced at it than he recognized the handwriting of Servilia, his own sister, and the contents, couched in the most passionate possible language, left no doubt as to the nature of the relationship between her and Caesar.

"Here, you oaf, take it!" growled Cato, throwing the note in Caesar's face. And the session was resumed.

Thus we see Caesar, his cup of love filled to the brim, receiving billets-doux from a mistress in the middle of senate deliberations—which he did not hesitate to let his half-brother read, the greatest prude of his day. Such airy persiflage was typical of a great noble unhindered by bourgeois scruples.

Three years later the liaison between Caesar and Servilia was still going strong. During his consulship, in 59, he gave her a pearl worth six million sesterces. And in addition, according to Pharsalus he let her make a profit on property confiscated from those who had been defeated. Probably by then their youthful ardor had given way to a calmer friendship.

But slander, echoed by Cicero, would have it that the youngest daughter of Servilia, named Tertia, took her mother's place with Caesar, abetted by her mother. The fact that Junia Tertia was the wife of Cassius, one of the leaders in the Ides of March conspiracy, is worthy of remark. But it is by no means sure that Caesar and Tertia had an affair, so it is idle to think of adducing it as one of Cassius' motives.

The declaration, repeated by some historians, that Junius Brutus was the child of Caesar and Servilia is probably also calumny. Other reasons can certainly be given for the affection Caesar undoubtedly bore him. Partly, no doubt, it was the bond between Caesar and Servilia, but there were also political reasons. It seems that the young man had early attracted Caesar's attention; he was one of the most brilliant of the younger generation of his day. A family feud had brought him into conflict with Pompey, since the latter had in 77 had his father, M. Junius Brutus senior, Servilia's first husband, brutally assassinated. It could mean a great deal to Caesar to get Brutus as an ally, and that is why Caesar conceived the idea of a marriage between Julia and Brutus. It also explains why, even when Julia was married to Pompey, he continued to protect the young man, even though he was involved in an attempt to assassinate Pompey. Later, again, Brutus, who rebelled in no uncertain terms against Caesar's offer of friendship, allied himself with the dictator's enemies. This he achieved by first marrying Claudia, then his cousin Porcia, the widow of Bibulus, Caesar's implacable rival and his associate during the consulship of 59. And at Pharsalus he fought in the ranks of the followers of Pompey. Before the battle Caesar was careful to urge his officers to spare the young man. When Caesar emerged the victor, he heaped offices and honors on Brutus, because it was highly necessary for the dictator to gain the loyalty of the best elements of the aristocracy and the regime. To have Brutus in his camp was to exorcise the memory of Cato, who turned out to be even more of a menace dead than he had been alive with his meanness, his narrow-mindedness, and his insupportable pride. Caesar had planned to promote Brutus and Cassius to the consulship together for the year 41. Thus the son and son-in-law of Servilia would attain to the magistrature at the same time, which would make them members of the *consulares,* the personages who had the highest authority in the state, and who in a crisis would make the necessary decisions.

When he was preparing for the future, Caesar called to mind the men who usually grumbled against him, but whom he did not despair of transforming, come what may, into supporters of the new regime—thanks to Servilia, an ally of whom he felt sure. Everyone knows how his hopes fell through. Brutus and Cassius carried out the counterplot of the Ides of March. It is easy to understand why Caesar, that day, ceased to struggle against the assassins when he recognized Brutus among them. "You too, Brutus, my son." This is not an admission of illegitimate paternity—which is contradicted by the facts—but that of a spiritual fatherhood desired and dreamed of, the symbol of the great reconciliation between Caesar and the senate on which the future of Rome was to be based. The machinations of a few unimportant adversaries could only be fortuitous. But the presence of Brutus among the conspirators signified the complete failure of the political program of a lifetime.

So the relationship between Caesar and Servilia appears highly complicated. It would be futile to argue that they were exempt from the lusts of the flesh, but it would be equally vain to maintain that politics did not play a major role. The example of Cornelia, mother of the Gracchi, and the matrons whose power within the City-State was gauged as much by their personal influence as by the alliances they had their sons and daughters contract, came to life again in Servilia. It was with her as a focal point that, after the death of the dictator, the tyrannicides held a singular council of war at Antium that also included Cicero, Brutus, Cassius, and a few others. At Antony's instigation the senate had chosen Brutus and Cassius to carry out a mission in the East that would keep them out of political activities for a while. Should they accept? Servilia made a strenuous effort to obtain a revocation from the leading jurists of the senate. Apparently she had not lost all her influence there with the death of her former lover. And her attitude toward Cicero, whom she cut short in the middle of a speech, showed that she was faithful to the traditions of the aristocrats to whom he was never anything but a parvenu.

During those days of anguish, until the Battle of Philippi, Servilia was the devoted helper of the Republicans, but she was also able to keep the goodwill of Caesar's followers. Perhaps her political activities at this period disclosed the depths of her nature: devoted to her gens, a born schemer, she had staked her charms and her friendship without always being able to tell each time whether she was guided by her heart or her reason. What can appear to us in the perspective of history as a conflict of ideas, or classes, or temperaments, must have been to her no more than a skein of intrigues that she happily tried—by every means available to a woman—to unravel on the one hand, or tangle up on the other. She had every right to think that she could remain loyal to an old love without, for that, staying faithful to a cause. Did Caesar, on his part, do anything else when he utilized that same liaison to pry Brutus and Cassius loose from their political principles?

Always methodical, Suetonius devoted an entire chapter to the "exotic mistresses." It is true that the chapter contains but two names, Eunoe, wife of King Bogud of Mauretania, and Cleopatra.

We know nothing about the love affair between Caesar and the Mauretanian Queen.

As for his amours with Cleopatra, it is highly probable that historians gave free rein to their imagination, and made a romance out of what was a passing liaison.

Cleopatra, the second daughter of King Ptolemy Auletes—who, we have seen, was Crassus' protégé—was born in 69, and found herself from her early years drawn into the incredible machinations in which the Egyptians were usually involved. When her father died she was named Queen, sharing the throne with her brother and husband, Ptolemy XIV, in accordance with the royal laws of Egypt. Then, in the conflict between Caesar and the Roman senate, brought about by Pompey, she unhesitatingly took the latter's part. She helped him in some ways, and may have had an affair with one of his sons, Gnaeus, who had headed a mission to Alexandria. But she soon embarked on a struggle against her brother, and had to flee the capital. She was away when Caesar arrived, on October second, 48 (August nineteenth of the Julian calendar). Caesar offered to act as arbiter. He wanted to restore peace in the kingdom, and to that end summoned the young Queen. It was now up to her to find a way to obey his orders.

It was necessary to cut through the curtain of troops led by the regents acting in Ptolemy's name. Cleopatra took a boat to the lighthouse commanding the entrance to the port. Of course it was guarded. She bribed the guards, and managed to disembark near the palace. But how could she get to Caesar, inside the palace where everyone knew her and where any servant might be hostile? So Cleopatra resorted to a stratagem. She ordered her companion, the only one with her, a Sicilian named Apollodorus, to envelop her in a blanket, which he was to sling over his shoulder, and have himself taken to Caesar. It is said, adds Plutarch, who tells the story, that it was this ruse that won over the Roman. And apparently, in the tête-à-tête that followed, she conducted herself with consummate coquetry. Historians have been a little hasty in deducing that Caesar lost his head, fell madly in love, and that he was nothing but the young Queen's slave from then on.

It does not matter much whether Cleopatra was as beautiful as legend would have it. Perhaps her most authentic portraits did not do her justice. The powers of an enchantress do not always depend on the regularity of her features. In any case, Caesar did not abstain from having an affair with her. But far from forgetting the interests of Rome during his amorous transports, he seems to have taken full advantage of his easy conquest to tighten Rome's grip on Egypt. It was a kingdom that could not easily be subjugated, as was well known, and that no one would dream of annexing. So Cleopatra was really a tool in Caesar's hands. He used her to get rid of Ptolemy XIV, and immediately gave her another brother in marriage, whose youth made him less redoubtable. He ruled under the name of Ptolemy XV. In this way Caesar hoped to dismember the party dedicated to national independence that supported Ptolemy XIV. Having done this, reassured, he went for a cruise with Cleopatra in the royal galley, going up the

LOVE AND POLITICS

Nile as far as the first falls. During these early days of enchantment, in this exotic country, Caesar may have had dreams of becoming a royal sovereign. But the idea of being King of Egypt did not detain him for long; the time was past when he could dally with the temptation of being "first" anywhere but in Rome. Moreover, at the beginning of the summer of 47, he left Egypt to pacify Asia. Only a simple trace remained of Caesar's visit to Alexandria: a garrison of three legions, which effectively turned the kingdom of the Egyptians into a Roman protectorate.

About eighteen months later, Caesar summoned Cleopatra to Rome. It must not be thought that he wanted to have her near him for romantic reasons: she had hardly reached Rome when he left for Spain. And when he returned, he lingered in his own villas instead of living as near to her as possible. In Rome, Cleopatra was more like a prize hostage than the chief's favorite—he had other concerns. And the first of these was his own dignity: he did not wish to alienate public opinion, which he tried to win over by every possible means. Roman diplomatic custom favored keeping allied rulers away from their countries for a while so that they might provide an example, in Rome, of the subjection in which they were held.

During Cleopatra's months in Rome, Caesar brought Egypt completely under control. He added a fourth legion to the garrison in Alexandria. And it is more than likely that his agents took advantage of the absence of the legitimate sovereigns, Cleopatra and Ptolemy XV, to replace the old administration with a more compliant one. That is the real reason Caesar kept the royal couple in Rome.

Cleopatra's stay in Caesar's gardens outside the city on the banks of the Tiber was marked by a romance—and its hero was not her host. Old-time historians relate that she bore a son, sometimes called Caesarion, and according to some accounts he was Caesar's son. Today M. J. Carcopino has been able to demonstrate by a meticulous interpretation of Egyptian inscriptions, that attributing the son to Caesar was a falsehood trumped up by

Cleopatra and Antony for propaganda purposes. Caesarion could not have been Caesar's son; he was born in all probability about April twentieth, 44, while, in and around July, 43, Caesar was in Spain. But he could have been the son of Antony—or of someone else!

Taking advantage of the confusion into which Rome was plunged after Caesar's assassination, Cleopatra, once she had recovered from the birth of her child, returned to her kingdom. Once back in Egypt she did not hesitate to get rid of her brother-husband Ptolemy XV by poisoning him, so that she could be the sole ruler of the country. The fact that she was a mother exempted her from the necessity of taking a husband. Caesarion was proclaimed King under the name of Ptolemy XVI, but Cleopatra held the reins, alone.

She was soon to revenge herself on Caesar, and, by gambling with the love she was able to arouse in the breast of Antony, became a threat to the master of the civilized world.

However awkward it may have been after so many centuries to interpret what, in those far distant times, men felt in the secret places of their hearts, it is not hard to believe that although Caesar, while he did not refuse the love affairs that came his way, was never enslaved by them. Amorous passion had no more hold on him than others he tried hard not to give in to: neither anger, nor the desire for revenge; not even ambition ever prevailed against his reasoned judgment. Whenever possible his love affairs advanced his projects; in any case they never ran counter to his plans.

The story of his marriages is no less revealing. It starts with a broken engagement—with a young woman of cavalier rank. Her name was Cossutia, and her only merit, apparently, lay in the fact that she was very rich.

This engagement was imposed on the youth before he had taken the *toga virilis,* and he doubtless had no choice in the matter. The woman he did select, later, in 84, two years after her father's

LOVE AND POLITICS

death, belonged to an illustrious family. She was the daughter of Cornelius Cinna, who at that time held absolute power, who served the interests of the "popular" party and continued the policies of Marius, and who became Caesar's uncle by marrying the latter's aunt Julia.

By his marriage Caesar placed himself unequivocally in the ranks of the enemies of the senate. But if he had counted on his father-in-law's support, he was soon disappointed, for Cinna died shortly afterward, and this was followed by the triumph of Sulla and the revenge of the aristocracy.

Sulla's first move was to disrupt the family alliances that tended to form factions he considered dangerous. We have already told how Pompey was obliged to repudiate his first wife, Antistia, and marry Aemilia. Caesar was less submissive. After two years of marriage he resolutely refused to give up Cornelia, in spite of the dictator's threats and the steps taken to harass him. Stripped of his priestly rank, his wife's dowry, and his patrimony, he had to flee in order not to be put to death as an "enemy of Sulla." Was it love that made him resist? Obstinacy? Pride? Or a quite legitimate desire not to submit to the tyrant and to proclaim his freedom? Or the wish to keep a door open on the future, foreseeing that the backlash that had carried Sulla to power would last only a while, and that the Roman people would be grateful to him one day for not giving way before the chief? His indomitable determination not to go back on his family ties with the *populares* was to make him pick up Marius' gauntlet, and very likely this was responsible for his determination to stick with Cornelia.

The first marriage lasted until Cornelia died, in 68. She left a daughter, Julia, whose part in her father's political career has already been described.

Not long after Cornelia's passing, Caesar married Pompeia, the daughter of Quintus Pompeius Rufus, and Sulla's granddaughter. The marriage was no doubt nothing more than a political maneuver, an attempt to line up some necessary alliances within a party that still had to be reckoned with. It was in the same spirit that Pompey, on his part, had married Mucia, which allied him with the clan of the Metelli and indirectly with the Claudii, two of the most powerful families in the senatorial hierarchy. But just as Pompey's marriage was not to last (Mucia, as has been said, was seriously compromised with Caesar himself), neither was Caesar's any too solid: Pompeia yielded to the advances of young Publius Clodius, and the scandal of the "rites of the *Bona Dea* [Good Goddess]" was so shocking that Caesar could not avoid repudiating her.

It is harder to understand the reasons that led Caesar to marry in 59, the same year that he was Consul, the daughter of Calpurnius Piso, who does not seem to have been a powerful political figure. Maybe Caesar felt so strong that he could make alliances but did not have to seek them. Calpurnius Piso immediately became one of Caesar's deputies; the latter had him elected to the consulship in 58, which aroused a protest on Cato's part.

Forgetting that marriage had played a predominant role in political careers for a long time, Cato complained that the election was scandalous, that the supreme power was being "prostituted," and that administrative positions and military commands were now reached via the womenfolk. Piso remained loyal to Caesar as time went on. His activities as Censor in 50 showed him to be a modest man, able to rally public opinion to Caesar's support. When the Civil War broke out, he tried in every way to intervene between Caesar and the senate. When all is said and done, the choice of Piso as a father-in-law was not a bad one.

And the selection of Calpurnia was not a mistake either. She was Caesar's companion during the Ides of March; an attentive, loving, and respected mate. Obviously, she did not hold her husband's infidelities against him. Most of them went back to the years before their marriage. The affair with Servilia had settled down into friendship. As for the others: Cleopatra and the Queen of Mauretania, these were after all only episodes in the life of a soldier fighting in far-off lands.

Caesar spent the night before the Ides of March with Calpurnia. Once the wind suddenly blew the door open and by the light of the moon Caesar saw that his wife was tossing and sighing in her sleep. She finally woke up and told him her dream. It had seemed to her as if the triumphal decorations on top of the house had been torn off and hurled to the ground.

The dream seemed a bad omen, and she begged Caesar not to attend the senate session scheduled for the Ides. It was the first time Calpurnia had given way to womanly superstition, and Caesar was upset. He consulted the soothsayers, and what they told him increased his anxiety to such an extent that he decided to stay home that day. But Decimus Brutus persuaded him to change his mind. His clever talk, his arguments, and his irony prevailed over Caesar's instinctive feeling that he should heed Calpurnia's forebodings. And the destiny of which she warned him, of which the soothsayers warned him, was fulfilled.

It was nothing new on either Pompey or Caesar's part to expect successful marriages to further their careers. It would be easy to give examples of other unions that were decided on at the start from the same motives. But how can one distinguish between a "marriage of reason" or "convenience" as was customary in noble families, and a union that was purely political? Fundamentally, everything depended on the goal that had been set. When two families joined in this way were equal in power and rank, no one could take exception. Public opinion was aroused only if the stratagem showed through, if it seemed to be a maneuver that might adversely affect the customary balance between the magistrates and the tasks to be done. But the public was no less shocked if some great personage was weak enough to show his love for his spouse too openly.

Cato, who had been so indignant over Pompey's marriage to Julia, and Caesar's to Calpurnia, had been deeply insulted in his youth, or so he thought, by Aemilius Lepidus, who had first promised him and then refused him the hand of his younger daughter, Lepida. His pride was so deeply injured that he avenged himself by composing satirical iambics in the style of Archilochus!

The affront had been directed not so much to the man as to the representative of the gens Porcia. Disappointed by the Aemilii, Cato had sought a fiancée from the Atilii, who were no less noble, and ended by marrying Atilia, daughter of Atilius Serranus. The union was not a happy one. Atilia bore him two children, but behaved so badly that he was obliged to divorce her. He then espoused Marcia, the daughter of Lucius Marcius Philippus. It was said that he chose her on the strength of her excellent reputation. And this marriage concluded in the spirit of the old-time Romans as Cato imagined them to be, had some strange consequences that throw an unexpected light on the conception of marriage prevailing at the time.

The orator Hortensius admired Cato greatly, and wanted to be even more than a friend. After his wife died, he tried to persuade Cato to give him his daughter's hand in marriage. The latter, Porcia, was already the wife of Bibulus, but this did not seem to bother Hortensius. In a bizarre speech to Cato, he maintained that after a wife had given her husband all the children he wanted, she should not be condemned to a life of voluntary sterility. It would be better, he said, to pass her on to other husbands who really wanted children. Everyone would gain by it: first of all, the City-State, by the increase in fertility; a virtuous wife could only have children that resembled her; and the proliferation of alliances between families would strengthen the ties between personages of high degree and help to ensure peace.

If, Hortensius added, Bibulus really wanted to keep his wife, that could also be arranged: he himself would give her back after she had provided him with a child. Cato thought the plan absurd and refused. But Hortensius would not admit defeat. He suggested marriage not to Porcia but to Marcia herself, Cato's own wife. He remarked that Marcia was as virtuous as Porcia, that she was still young enough to bear children (and in fact she was about to give birth to one), that Cato was now sure enough of having descendants. In view of all these reasons, he wanted her for a bride himself. Cato realized that Hortensius was perfectly serious, and thinking over his arguments and finding them quite reasonable, ended by accepting, on the sole condition that Philippus, Marcia's father, give his consent. The old man also agreed; he asked only that Cato should be present at this peculiar marriage, and give Marcia to Hortensius. So the weird exchange took place.

It is hard for us to believe in the authenticity of this account. Nevertheless, there is no reason to think it is false. Plutarch avers that it came from a friend of Cato who was his confidant, and witnessed most of the events of his life. Lucanus, who in the *Pharsalia* shows a veritable cult for the stoic hero that Cato became, repeats the story in turn, and not only excuses but explains and justifies the conduct of the man he considered the greatest of all Romans.

Malicious gossips did not hesitate to answer that a dishonorable motive was hidden beneath the surface appearance of the arrangement. Old Hortensius was very rich. When he died, not long before the Civil War, Marcia inherited the greater part of his fortune; she went back to her first husband and remarried him. It would not take much to convince us that what took place was really a legacy-stealing. But Cato could hardly be suspected of such a contemptible act. The marriage, in fact, was for him, as Lucanus reminds us, merely a way of making sure of descendants. Everything that smacks of pleasure, even including the most banal expressions of affection, gave way to the exigencies of duty. And the arguments brought up by Hortensius were just the ones to convince Cato. In 56, when the marriage took place between Marcia and the old orator, it was more desirable than ever for the nobility to counter the ambition of the triumvirs with a common front. Everything that could strengthen the bonds between the great families who dominated political life became an imperious obligation. And how could Cato for an instant have allowed the satisfaction of a personal desire, no matter how legitimate, to counterbalance what he considered the supreme good of the state? On this point his Stoic principles were in harmony with his old Roman maxims. The oath taken before the Censor required him only "to marry in order to have children." Having achieved this, he was free to renounce a union that had proved fertile. He was all the more willing to do this in that he was still more eager to uphold that other liberty which freed him from the bonds of human affection, to submit to the dictates of reason. A deliberate sacrifice for the good of the City-State, the "ceding" of Marcia could seem, if not judged from outside the social structure, rather like one of those multiple divorces sanctioned by custom. But while "ordinary" divorces originated in the desire to ensure or preserve personal satisfaction, this one was as it were sanctified by its noble motive, and the suffering it entailed made it more legitimate. There is no doubt that Cato was attracted by the oddity, the uniqueness of the experience. This proud philosopher had a taste for paradox and a complete scorn for common prejudice. But it would be a serious mistake to ascribe egotistical or even selfish motives to him. In the hierarchy of responsibilities, those he had contracted with Marcia were far below the duties he admittedly owed the state. In the same way, a century later, Titus would repudiate Berenice.

So Cato's attitude was not as extraordinary as it may have pleased him to think. His perfect self-mastery, his detachment from the most justifiable affections, both based on philosophical convictions, do not run counter to the Roman tradition that subordinated "the rights of the heart" to one's duty toward the state.

In this domain as in many others, Stoicism justified a law of life sanctioned by instinct and imposed by ancestral custom. Nevertheless, Cato's "sacrifice" was all the more remarkable in that it occurred at a time when the moral code in effect tended more and more to reject the old-time austerity, and when tender feelings, as the poets have shown, played an even greater role in the relations between men and women and between husbands and wives.

An extreme instance of the approval of a rigidity already rather out-of-date, his repudiation of Marcia was meant to have symbolic value. And that was the way Lucan understood it when he recounted the incident in full. The *Pharsalia* shows Marcia complying with this peculiar observance, sacrificing her woman's sensitivity to be worthy of someone who was not only her husband but her spiritual guide.

Later, after the death of Hortensius, Marcia returned to Cato and asked him to take her back. According to Lucan, she said to him: "Give me the privilege of having 'Marcia, wife of Cato,' inscribed on my tomb." Which signifies that the union of their two wills was indissoluble, and stronger than all the bonds of the flesh. This new marriage between Marcia and Cato was not a "carnal" one. Cato did not want it to be, and Marcia surely could hardly have wanted it that way.

On a higher plane than a "common" marriage, it consisted in an understanding that no longer owed anything to sensual satisfaction but was based on mutual agreement as to the same moral values.

Thus, and rather paradoxically, it was Cato who taught how a "political" marriage—even the principle shocks us somewhat today, and seems like a profanation—could grow into one of the highest forms of agreement between two human beings convinced that their duty to the state meant more than the orientation of their own personal lives. We saw, it is true, that certain wives sought above all to satisfy their instinct for domination, their love of riches, or their taste for intrigue.

But we can now see that many others wanted to be the *spiritual* equal of the man who was their companion, even if he did not give them much of an opportunity.

In spite of what one might think, Cato and Marcia were not the only couple in a Rome where the poets were beginning to sing the praises of only the most free and most passionate love. Many women wished to share, even to their cost, the dangerous life of a husband determined not to neglect his political commitments.

The period of the Civil War abounds in examples of conjugal devotion. Appius, for example, enjoyed collecting edifying episodes that showed how wives of men who had been proscribed refused the chance to be safe—without their husbands. And it was the wife of Apuleius who threatened to turn her husband over to the triumvirs if he continued to forbid her to join him in exile; or the wife of Coponius, who sacrificed her virtue to Antony, asking him to spare her husband's life as the reward for her favors. Elsewhere Appius, again tells how the wife of Ligarius, having failed in her efforts to save her husband, chose to die of hunger rather than survive him.

Even more famous is the story of Porcia, Cato's daughter, who was Brutus' second wife. Not long before the Ides of March, 44, she perceived that her husband was haunted by a secret he did not dare reveal to her. So she wounded herself with a knife, on purpose, and when Brutus hastened to take care of her, she said: "Brutus, I am the daughter of Cato. I was brought into your house not like the common women who do not want to be more than concubines, to share only your bed and board, but to share your happiness and your misfortune."

And she wormed his secret out of him. During the tragic hour when the counterplot was being carried out, she was so profoundly overcome that she fainted and was thought to be dead.

When Brutus was obliged to leave Italy, Porcia followed him to the ship. She bravely tried to conceal her sorrow, but her eye happening to fall accidentally on a painting showing the farewell of Hector and Andromache, she burst into tears. Acilius, a friend of Brutus, then began to recite the well-known verses from the Iliad:

" 'Hector, you are a father to me, and a respected mother; a brother also, and a potent companion in bed. . . .' " At this Brutus smiled and added: "Yes, but I could not use, with Porcia, Hector's words: " 'Return home and take care of your household duties, your loom and your distaff, and give orders to the servants . . .' for Porcia has the heart of a man where her country is concerned. . . ."

Porcia, one might say, was a worthy daughter of Cato. Yet she was not exceptional, in those troubled times. A famous inscription—unfortunately damaged—tells the story of a Roman lady long called Turia by historians but whom we must be content to leave unnamed. After she became engaged and her fiancé had to leave to rejoin Pompey's forces, she showed the stuff she was made of, during several family tragedies. First, when her father and mother were assassinated, she tracked down the criminals herself and had them punished. Then, when wicked relatives tried to break her father's will, she succeeded in blocking the maneuver single-handed, and when her fiancé returned, he found their fortune intact. But how many difficulties occurred after they were married! Proscribed, her husband owed his life only to the cleverness and calm audacity of his wife, who knew better than he how to keep him safe, how to provide him with money and with the means of subsistence. Ready for any sacrifice to obtain the revocation of the edict of proscription, she threw herself at the feet of Lepidus, who roughly repulsed her. So she went back to her husband at last, only to find that he had been pardoned, no doubt largely thanks to her efforts.

It would seem that after so many trials, this model wife deserved an entirely happy life. The couple seemed quite content: they had wealth and they loved each other. But they had no children. The wife was desolate. She blamed herself for being sterile, and offered to retire from the scene. Let her husband marry a younger and luckier woman! In the funeral eulogy he later delivered in her honor the husband said: "Doubting your own fecundity, and broken-hearted over my having no children, you spoke of divorce and of going away, leaving your home to someone else who would be fertile, so that I would not lose the hope of having children by keeping you as my wife and be miserable on that account. Your only aim, since it is well known how fond we were of each other, was to find someone worthy of me yourself and bring the marriage about. You declared that the children to come would be shared and that you would think of them as yours. You did not expect to apportion our heritage, which until then had remained undivided, but would leave it at my disposition as before, and under your management if I wished. You saved nothing for yourself, you kept nothing as your own, you were prepared to devote a sister or a sister-in-law's care and affection to me."

Overwhelmed by such an offer, the husband, less "virtuous" than Cato, less concerned to put the interests of society above individual affection, showed himself adamant to the last in refusing to accept his wife's sacrifice.

"You remained with me, since I could not have acceded to your wish without dishonor and without contributing to our mutual misfortune."

Dishonor—here was a worldly consideration that would never have bothered Cato. Turia's husband, who was more human, bore in mind the opinion of his equals, who would probably have found his conduct reprehensible. And he did not have the strength, either, to destroy a happiness of whose value he was fully aware, and that he placed, in spite of ancestral "prejudices," above the concern for the continuation of his race.

The *laudatio* of Turia, more than the harangues of phrasemakers, makes it possible to know the true state of Roman opinion on the question of marriage during the last years of the Republic and the beginning of the Empire. The energy of the wives, able to cope with the gravest crises, their confidence in their husbands, whom they put in control of their property when the law allowed them to administer it themselves, an utter devotion and self-denial that led them to forget their feminine pride—there is nothing in this that contradicts the picture we may have of the Roman women, for whom the marital bond was not merely, as Porcia said, the relationship of a lover to his mistress. On his part, the husband made every effort to conserve his wife's personal fortune, and substituted his generosity for hers when it was a question of helping relatives; showed her boundless affection and esteem, and protected her from the excesses into which her heroism might lead her.

It would seem that the example of a married life "maintained, without clashes, for forty-one years," indicates the harmonious balance which the Roman moral code had attained. It managed to reconcile what would appear to be irreconcilable: women's independence and their tractability; the structure of society and devotion; the privileges of the heart and the dictates of reason. The scene sketched here may be somewhat idyllic, but its significance is clear. To be sure, all unions were not like this one, and the husband who had this inscription engraved knew it better than anyone: "Rare are the marriages so protracted that they are broken up by death rather than divorce."

But it is enough that this particular marriage was considered exemplary, for us to be able, in spite of Ovid, and later, Juvenal, to consider a society irredeemably perverted and decadent that could not give rise to such phrases.

VIII

IMPERIAL AMOURS

AT the end of the Roman Republic marriage had become a tool of politics. Power, which was divided among a few families, jealous of their prerogatives and firmly determined to protect them against intruders, belonged to those whose birth or the alliances of their gens destined for the magistracy. These unions, therefore, were arranged deliberately, and without the heart's fancies being taken into account. And for the same reasons, no one hesitated to get a divorce when the public interest required it. As the result of a contradiction that was to have dire consequences, these same marriages, held together by such a tenuous bond, were nonetheless considered essential to the survival of a society that could not completely forget its patriarchal tradition. One of Augustus' first tasks when he undertook to reorganize the state was to force the citizens to assume this obligation, which they were anxious to dispense with. Under the Empire senators were required, come what might, to take wives—not just anyone, but a mate of their own rank—in order to keep up an aristocracy that Caesar had no doubt weakened, but to which Augustus and his successors intended to reassign a part of its traditional responsibilities.

Nevertheless, the fact of marriage was not in itself a guarantee that the couple would be on terms of intimacy. It is not hard to believe that there were many men and women who looked for happiness or satisfaction outside a marriage that they did not find in it. Seneca could write his mother: "Immorality, the greatest sin of this century, did not lure you into joining the majority." And it would certainly appear, if one is to believe the rhetoricians, among whom the voice of Juvenal predominates, that many wives

IMPERIAL AMOURS

were not faithful to their vows. And on their side, as we know, husbands could have liaisons openly without causing a scandal or being disgraced. Nevertheless, in spite of all, marriage in itself remained an institution honored by the most dissolute. Caste pride was affirmed through marriage, respected or not. As women gained greater freedom they became more aware of their role in the City-State. The best of them expected to share their husbands' responsibilities to the full, to be worthy of their ancestors, and, broadly speaking, of the appellation of Roman. Love, then, took on a new image. It no longer meant, as in the old days, obedience, respect, and self-effacement; it now stood for esteem, devotion, sometimes comradeship—and even complicity. The picture of married life changed: sexual relations and procreation lost their tyranny, giving way to friendship.

In this development the influence of Greek philosophy can be discerned. We have already noted that the relationship between Cato and Marcia revealed an attitude dictated by the imperatives and even the paradoxes of Stoicism, since Zeno and Chrysippus sometimes also took up the cudgels in favor of women in general, at least among the sages. Cato, it is true, was the only man of his time to have carried the principles of the Stoic cult both to sublime and ridiculous extremes. But others in his vicinity and a number of intellectuals in the generations to follow were attracted by Stoic thought, and modeled their way of life on the Stoics.

If it is true that Stoicism contributed a great deal to shaping the doctrines of the chiefs of state, it is equally certain that it influenced many minds—and all the more so in that they had long been prepared to heed its teaching. The great majority of Roman nobles throughout the Empire were Stoics or had at least been indoctrinated with the moral principles of Stoicism.

Now while the Epicureans considered love to be the satisfaction of merely sensual desires, the Stoics gave it a preeminent place in the life of the spirit. However much they distrusted all passion, they were not reconciled to condemning it; they described it as "an attempt to create friendship through beauty." Cicero, who repeats the axiom, rightly emphasizes its Platonic character. Of course the beauty that gives rise to love is essentially moral—the beauty of the soul; but it is revealed in the loveliness of the body, which becomes in a way an intermediary between lover and loved one. Strictly speaking, there is a considerable gap between the "friendship" of the philosophers and sexual love. In practice, the sages tried to keep their followers from the temptation to oversimplify. The perfection of "Stoic" love can be realized in the soul of the wise man alone; only he is proof against love's dangers. Chrysippus and his successors were well aware of the difficulty an insufficiently seasoned soul might have in differentiating between true love and its sexual caricature. Nevertheless they did not consider that they had the right essentially to condemn a type of human relationship that seemed the only one really able to bring about understanding and communion between minds.

The early Stoics, when they spoke of love, were thinking like Plato mainly of the relation between the sage and his disciples, of "philosophical love," which was directed toward young men. But it was not long before their doctrine was applied to more normal love; it came to define, in very general terms, a "philosophical use" of amorous feelings. Thus the case is cited of a Stoic named Thrasonides who respected the young girl he loved, but was careful to keep an ascendancy over her, for fear she would grow to dislike him.

A love founded on mutual esteem, on sharing the same moral outlook—this was the ideal upheld by Stoicism to its Roman devotees. In a society where women wished to assert their independence, "Stoic" love made it possible for them to enjoy complete freedom without jeopardizing the promptings of their hearts. So we need not be surprised when we find that in Stoic circles, under the Empire, there were several instances of women being true to the Stoic code.

The most famous of them all was no doubt Arria, the wife of

Caecina Paetus. In a letter devoted entirely to her, Pliny has described several heroic traits, the memory of which has been reverently preserved in her family.

Both her husband and her son were at one time struck down by the same malady. The son died. Arria managed to conceal the truth from Paetus. She took charge of all the details of the funeral herself, and when in the presence of her husband pretended that the son was still alive. What is more, as Pliny tells it, she made up a thousand comforting details. "He slept well," she would say, or, "He has a good appetite." Then, leaving the room, she would cry freely and not come back until her eyes were dry and her expression serene, as if, wrote Pliny, "she had left mourning outside the door." She did not reveal the truth to her husband until he was strong enough to stand it.

In Illyria, Caecina Paetus had taken part in a revolt against Clodius, and after the defeat of the insurgents he was arrested. As the soldiers were putting him on board a ship for Rome, Arria begged the guards to take her along.

"Look," she said, "you are certainly going to give a man of consular rank a few slaves to feed him, dress him, and put on his shoes. I can do all that for him by myself." When the soldiers repulsed her, she hired a fishing smack and, in that frail craft, followed the ship. During the trial she showed the same indomitable spirit. When, in her presence, Vibia, the wife of Scribonius, the main instigator of the revolt, agreed to reveal what she knew, Arria cried out: "Do you expect me to listen to you? Scribonius was killed in your arms, and you are still alive?" And when her husband was condemned to die, she took the dagger first and plunged it into her bosom. Then, drawing it out covered with blood, she handed it to him, saying: "It does not hurt, Paetus."

During the trial her children wanted to dissuade her from killing herself. When her son-in-law, Thrasia, said to her, "Would you want your daughter to die with me, if I had to go?" she answered, "Yes, if she had lived with you as long and in such perfect harmony as Paetus and I." Nonetheless, Arria could have lived out a few more happy years. She was an intimate friend of Messalina, and no one would have thought of bothering her if she had not gone out to meet death herself.

It would be unfair to such women to attribute their conduct to a surge of emotion. They were not motivated by despair but by honor. To survive the shipwreck of their entire lives would have dishonored them. They put fidelity to an undertaking freely entered into above any other virtue, and the death of their mate would not be taken as releasing them from it. Their attitude was both analogous to that of the old-time matrons, obliged by their code of honor to remain *univirae*, and not to marry a second time if their husband died. At the same time it differed entirely in its approach: in sacrificing what was left of their lives, they were not submitting to the pressure of popular opinion or to the dictates of an essentially negative moral code. They felt that they were exercising a free choice.

The "friendship" uniting them with their husband caused them to share totally and continuously an ideal they could not renounce even when faced with death. This is no doubt the meaning of the word "concord" Arria used in explaining to her son-in-law her desire to die. She was certainly not thinking of the bourgeois understanding that spares couples from the minor bickerings of daily life, but rather of the identity of souls that truly defines Stoic friendships.

It happened that the greatest philosopher of the day, the Stoic Seneca, also experienced such a love, at least during the latter part of his life. Married to Paulina, a very young woman, after returning from exile, when he himself was past fifty, he had with her a happy, intimate relationship. She looked after his health, which had always been delicate, so carefully that Seneca even complained that she was too attentive in her loving-kindness to him. But he added: "Since I cannot get her to love me with less fervor, she is making me concentrate on loving myself even more." One could be skeptical, most people would think, of such assertions, dictated surely by the vanity of an old man flattered by the love of a young woman. Nevertheless, a few months later, a dramatic incident was to prove that they were true.

It was Tacitus who described Seneca's last moments. Implicated in Piso's conspiracy, and already nearly totally disgraced, Seneca was ordered by Nero to take his life. Then Paulina declared that she refused to outlive him, and asked for "a hand to strike her down." Whereupon, Seneca, moved by the deepest affection and not wishing to oppose her, replied in these words, so that the woman who had loved him so tenderly would not be defenseless against unjust calumny: "I showed you how your life could be pleasant, but you prefer the honor of death; I shall not refuse you the privilege of setting an example to others. Even if our demise now demonstrates that our courage is equally firm, it is your death that will be the more resplendent."

After these words, simultaneously, they opened veins in their arms. Seneca's body was old and worn thin by his ascetic way of living; the blood flowed slowly, so he opened veins in his legs and in his knees. Then, exhausted by the intense pain, and afraid that his own suffering might weaken his wife's resolve, and also that he might not be able to stand the sight of her suffering, he persuaded her to go into another room.

But Nero, who felt no personal animosity toward Paulina, and did not wish to whet public opinion by giving the impression of being cruel, gave orders that the young woman be resuscitated. Directed by the soldiers, the slaves and freedmen put a ligature on her arm and stopped the bleeding, without knowing whether she was aware of what was being done to her. As the common herd is always inclined to put a malevolent interpretation on things, many persons assumed that as long as she had been afraid of Nero, she had wanted the glory of dying with her husband, but when a more helpful opportunity was offered to her, she had yielded to the desire to go on living.

The Stoics liked to think women could attain to "virtue," and gave them more credit for doing so than they did the men, since they had to restrain temperaments more readily influenced by passion and instinct.

In a treatise on marriage of which only a few sparse fragments have come down to us, Seneca declared that a woman's purity was her chief merit, her cardinal virtue, whose loss spoiled all the others. He gave many reasons for this, some of which were already to be found in the traditional moral code, that is, to ensure descendants, to remain worthy of one's ancestors and one's gens.

But one of these, at least, and the most important, expressed the primordial requirements of the caste—respect for oneself and concern for one's own freedom. A woman who has not held to the standard of honor becomes the victim of her lover's lust; she is no longer free.

It is her respect for her own honor, wrote Seneca, that made Lucretia Brutus' equal and perhaps put her above him, for it was from a woman that Brutus learned not to be a slave.

But it was not just the illegitimate aspect of an adulterous affair in itself that made it immoral. "There are marriages," added Seneca, "that are essentially adultery. To love one's wife with an ardent passion is to commit adultery." The dictum was taken from one of Seneca's teachers, the Stoic Sextius. Seneca made it his own, adding, "The wise man should love his wife by a deliberate action of the will, and not by the promptings of passion."

This integral and coherent Stoic theory of marriage, perfected in Rome itself, goes back to and justifies the ancient precepts of ancestral tradition. Here, as there, one finds the same distrust of passion, of the blind forces of instinct, the same ideal of chastity for both man and wife. But the Stoic philosophers added another requirement: the husband, too, must respect his wife and remain faithful to her. It is only by paying this price that "friendship will be achieved." This lifts marriage above distressing everyday vexations and gives it its true value. The example already cited, and those we could add to the list, lead us to believe that this concept of marriage was not mere theory but could be found in real life at least among a few of the couples. Pagan spirituality, by itself, rises to an ideal that prefigures that of Christian marriage, yet remains faithful to the ancient code, at least formally. But what was until then only a simple norm of conduct became a spiritual attitude, finding in itself its justification and its reward.

Once this requirement has been set forth, it is easier to understand the frequently mordant censure Seneca applies to the women of his day, as when he accuses them of "reckoning the years not by the consuls but by their successive husbands." And he is no more lenient in regard to men who let themselves be led astray by other passions, equally prejudicial to their soul's betterment, such as greed, ambition, and love of luxury. All these attractions are especially blameworthy, but for women, lapses from chastity are the chief danger. The first requirement of a "happy life" should be to acquire mastery over what must be called "the curse of women," the lure of the senses against which a woman often cannot defend herself. Let us not speak here of "contempt" for women. Seneca did not scorn either Marcia, Helvia, or Paulina. But he knew that the ideal he set before them was high and hard to reach, that they would need unusual strength of character to overcome unreasonable desires and, transcending love, to attain to the apogee of friendship.

While the Stoic aristocracy, helped by the philosophers, was thus engaged in working out a moral code for legitimate love that was singularly exalted and "modern" in its implication, other tendencies were making themselves felt, fostered by new conditions that the accession to power of a monarchy brought in its train. Like Roman civilization as a whole, the history of love reveals simultaneous contradictory influences, some of which came down from the most authentic national traditions, while others were derived from the East, where Hellenism had brought about a synthesis of diversified moral codes and spiritual attitudes. In Rome these influences rubbed elbows with each other. If we are surprised to learn that a woman like Arria was an intimate friend of Messalina, we should put aside moral indignation and foreswear applying criteria—without distinction—that although hallowed by custom are nonetheless anachronistic. Finally, the scales of Western morality were tipped in Arria's favor.

Listening to the poets, especially Propertius, shows that sensual love has not always been explicitly condemned, but has been regarded as a quasi-divine exaltation of the human soul, a kind of mediator between human and superhuman planes. This tendency could be found at the very core of Roman religious thought, in spite of all the efforts of Puritanically minded senators to hide it and attenuate its consequences.

It was natural that after the defeat of the senate on the battlefield of Pharsalus, a violent reaction set in, and some Romans thought the time had come to reestablish living patterns which condemned the traditional moral code. Such reaction was the more understandable in that it came after the anguish of civil war. In every epoch moments of national tension have been followed by a general relaxation of morals.

The hero of this new morality (or, if you prefer, of this immorality) was Mark Antony. He was drawn to it by his temperament, which led him into excesses of all kinds. And also the family tradition, which had it that the Antonines were descended from Hercules, the "sacred monster" whose exploits were heroic and imposing, free from the criteria of ordinary morals. He could strangle a lion with his bare hands, or give the fifty daughters of Thespius fifty sons, all in one night.

Plutarch relates how Antony always tried to imitate Hercules in his attire and in his bearing. While Caesar was still fighting in Spain to subdue the last remaining members of the party, Antony was traversing Italy with mimes and dancers, stopping by the side of the road to hold banquets, in the course of which he drank to excess, and they would degenerate into orgies.

For a while Fulvia's influence and perhaps Caesar's remonstrances restrained his intense yearning for sensual enjoyment that deeply shocked public opinion—at least that of the aristocrats, for the plebeians seemed to adulate him as a hero.

In an Italy instinctively "bourgeois," it was hard to endow one's image with the dimensions of a myth. Caesar, who tried to do so more subtly than Antony, did not succeed, and paid for his failure with his life. But Antony stayed in the East, where the spiritual descendant of Hercules would try to live out a legend of his own.

In the partition of the civilized world following the establishment of the second triumvirate, Antony was given the East. Octavius found this an easy decision to make, since he was only too happy to keep his untrustworthy ally away from Italy, where the future of the world would really be decided.

From 41 on, Antony was in Asia Minor. He played the role not of Hercules, as might have been expected, but of Dionysus.

In the mythology of those times, Hercules had more than one element in common with the god of the Maenades. Both were conquering heroes, both had gone down to Hades and discovered the secrets of the beyond. (It is well known that the Ptolemies claimed a dual ancestry according to which they were descended both from real kings and from the gods.).

(This was a time when the old myths were interpreted sometimes critically—though subtly—, at other times flatteringly, in ways that could be made to support any political aims.)

Now the kingdoms of the East had witnessed the birth and rise of brotherhoods of Dionysus' devotees that had taken a stray hold on men's minds. These confraternities were revived mainly from the *dionysiastes:* musicians, singers, and dancers whose calling required them to take part in the city festivals honoring this very god. So we see Antony, on his arrival in Asia Minor, surrounded by such artists, and letting them influence his decisions—which aroused Plutarch's indignation. When Antony entered Ephesus, he seemed to be celebrating not a Roman but a Dionysian triumph. Women disguised as Bacchae and men and youths disguised as satyrs and the god Pan headed the procession. The city was abundantly decorated with ivy and thyrses, and full of lyres, syrinxes, and flutes; the people acclaimed Antony, calling him Dionysus the Beneficent and Dionysus the Bringer of Joy.

Beneath this apparent frenzy lay a hidden political motive: to win popular sympathy and backing. Nothing could serve Antony's interests better than the support of Dionysus' votaries—the god he was pretending to incarnate. Heir to Caesar's dreams, Antony hoped to undertake an expedition to India, beyond Parthia—and who could not recall the triumphal "military" procession led by Dionysus as a conquering hero as far as the bank of the Ganges?

In Rome this undignified masquerade would have been considered nonsense. In Ephesus, to the sound of flutes and tambourines, it may have been a wise move.

This was the moment Cleopatra chose to go to the future world conqueror. During the war against Caesar's assassins she had taken Cassius' part, and Antony, after becoming victorious, intended to ask her for an explanation. He sent orders to her by messenger to come to Cilicia to exonerate herself if she could. Cleopatra, who knew Antony well as a result of meeting him— and perhaps having an affair with him—in Rome, decided to go to Tarsus and have a tête-à-tête that would settle matters in her favor. Her informers had told her of his conduct since his arrival in Asia. She knew what his expectations were and the means he employed; she thought she could beat him at his own game. When she went up the Cydnus it was in a royal vessel, with a gilded poop and purple sails; the oars were encrusted with silver, and the count was given to the oarsmen by flutes accompanied by lyres and pipes of Pan. Lying under a gold-embroidered canopy, she resembled the goddess Aphrodite, while cupids like those to be seen in paintings, standing here and there beside her couch, cooled her with their fans. Young and beautiful serving maids, mingling with the crew, represented Graces and Nereids; incense burners spread sweet-smelling perfumes on the banks. From all over the throng hastened to enjoy the spectacle—so that Antony was soon left alone on his bench in the middle of the marketplace. And the rumor spread everywhere that the goddess Aphrodite had come to make merry with Dionysus, for the benefit of Asia.

That night there was an extraordinary festival on the river. Antony, forgetting that he was the master and that the Queen was then his puppet, accepted her hospitality on the Olympian galley. And from that moment began an "inimitable" romance (that was the word the lovers themselves used to describe the life they led from then on) between the new Dionysus and the new Isis. Together they returned to Alexandria, and while Fulvia was unleashing civil war in Italy, her husband was indulging in a thousand capers unworthy of a Roman, but which delighted the Egyptian populace. Together Antony and Cleopatra ran through the streets by night, in disguise, pestering the passersby, who insulted them in turn and sometimes beat them. The rest of the time, Cleopatra threw dice with him, or watched him make weapons, went hunting with him, and drank with him. It was a delightful honeymoon.

Cleopatra was marvelously clever at teasing Antony and flattering him at the same time. One day he went fishing, but had no luck; this angered him greatly, for Cleopatra was watching and he felt humiliated. So he secretly asked some fishermen nearby to dive and tie some of the fish they had caught to his line. Antony thought he had gotten away with it, and Cleopatra, pretending to be taken in, showered him with compliments. But on her side, she meditated revenge. She organized another day's fishing and invited many courtesans. Then, before Antony's arrival, she ordered a diver to attach a dried herring to Antony's line.

When Antony raised his line, everyone began to laugh, and Cleopatra cried out: *"Imperator,* leave fishing to us, the people of Pharos and Canopus. Let your game be cities, kingdoms, and continents!"

But it would be a mistake to think that Antony was completely under the Queen's thrall. He had not become in her hands the willing tool she had dreamed of. When the news came from Italy of the difficulties Fulvia had entangled him in without his knowing it, he did not hesitate to leave Alexandria, pass through Greece, and return to Brundisium, where he made his peace with Octavius. And for three years, without giving another thought to Cleopatra, Antony was to play the part of faithful husband to his new wife. Even when he had to go to Syria to direct operations against the Parthians, in the spring of 38, he did not take advantage of his presence in the East to seek out the Queen. Obviously his love for her, and the memory of that wonderful winter with its inimitable love affair had no place in his thoughts, and this has proved rather embarrassing to chroniclers who would like to explain the whole history of the times in terms of Cleopatra's sex appeal.

There are writers, on the other hand, who minimize the Queen's role, and declare that Antony's policy where she was concerned, and the allocation of territory he agreed to in her favor, did not exceed the limits of honors usually bestowed on vassal kings to attach them to the cause of Rome. Antony was well aware that these transfers of suzerainty could only be temporary, and that sooner or later Rome would take these provinces back. What is more, these same historians point out, in conformity with early accounts, that Cleopatra was anything but young at the time, and Octavia had infinitely more appeal than she did.

The issues at stake, in fact, are not as clear-cut as they might seem, and are not explainable in terms of passion alone. Octavia and Cleopatra symbolize two paths between which Antony had to choose, two "temptations of Anthony" but more political than sexual. And it would be rather strict, morally, to think, remembering Prodicus, that one of the two was the path of virtue and the other the path of lack of will. On the side of Octavia there was Rome, with its tradition of political marriages, of cleverly contrived alliances and the sharing of power with Octavius, which, as Antony well knew, could only be temporary. On the other side was Cleopatra, whose backing could change the Roman General into a Hellenistic sovereign—an old temptation that the *imperatores* who had acquired a taste for the East had found harder and harder to resist. The path toward the Queen had already been more than half traversed; in 40, twins were born, the fruit of their love affair, Alexander Helios and Cleopatra Selene, whose celestial names (the Sun and the Moon) are a fair indication of the religious atmosphere in which they were brought up. In 37 Antony was indeed at the crossroads, and it must be admitted unequivocally that the situation in Italy, where Octavius was patently trying to wipe out his colleagues in the triumvirate, his associates and accomplices during hard times, and now his detested rivals, did not favor inactivity on his part. His only hope lay in complete victory in the East, the triumph of a grandiose undertaking that would have nullified Octavius' crafty machinations. Now this increased prestige he needed so badly, and without which he would be certainly eliminated from the political scene, could be obtained only by tightening the bonds of the alliance with Cleopatra.

On her part, Cleopatra was not idle either, and she was not influenced particularly by the love she felt for Antony. During his absence she set on foot a thousand intrigues in the East. Her aim was clear: to restore the "greater Egypt," that in earlier days included part of Syria under the crown of the Ptolemies. To reach it, she had to be free of anxiety regarding Rome's activities. Her scheme was to maintain as best she could the portion of the Empire that, in Caesar's time, had almost swallowed up her kingdom. Better still, to have the power of Rome serve her ends—which, thanks to Antony, she did not despair of accomplishing.

In diplomacy of this sort, love is not the only element: it is one of many. Octavius' propaganda has popularized the image—and it has become legendary—of an Antony at the mercy of sensual desires, turning traitor to his country to oblige the Queen, a new Hercules following in the footsteps of Omphale. Here was an excellent pretext for a conclusive break with the ruler of the East, around whom a growing "Republican" opposition continued to gather. But this was not the truth—at least not all of it.

After the meeting between Octavius and Antony at Tarentum in the spring of 37, the latter returned to the East. He had made his decision. After a three years' interval, he was going back to his plan of making war against the kingdom of Parthia, and the first step, he decided, was to rejoin Cleopatra. Octavia remained in the West, watched over by her brother. Antony spent the winter of 37–36 in Syria. While the preparations for war were going ahead, the intimacy between him and the Queen was resumed. The two children born in 40 were officially recognized. This made Antony essentially the Regent of Egypt and bound him more closely to the legitimate dynasty—a very clever solution of the Egyptian question.

Governing Egypt was no easy task. Face to face with each other, Antony and Cleopatra found themselves radically opposite in everything they stood for. The Queen was trying desperately to maintain an anachronistic kingdom in a Roman world. Antony was trying harder than ever to link that same kingdom with Rome's lot; to rally its forces without running the risk of open annexation. These rivals with their two distinct policies could realize their projects only by loving each other. And the marvel is that neither one nor the other was repelled by the idea.

Antony was apparently quite aware of how things stood. He felt that he had been called to a transcendental destiny. He liked to repeat that he was not entrusting his race to the womb of one woman; that Solon's laws did not apply to the legitimacy of his descendants; he could let nature take charge of originating, of founding any number of dynasties.

The god within him, who drove him to love, to be unsparing of ever-renewed embraces, was his guide and his strength.

Had not Dionysus been both a conqueror and the god of orgies, of unrestrained sensuality? As for Cleopatra, she was Mother-Isis, the personification of femininity, of fecundity—as her frequent confinements proved—the mystical image of the wife who by her caresses preserved her husband's life, an existence that the forces of Evil tried to wrest from him in vain. In Egypt, the Ptolemies had invented a new god, Serapis, in whom the ancient Osiris merged with the Hellenic Dionysus. This god had rapidly become popular throughout the Mediterranean world to such a degree that even in Rome the poets sang his praises. All was ready for the "inimitable" liaison between the two lovers, united for better or worse in a political situation whose problems could be solved only by their love, and also by the legends that had been woven for them, and which bound them like the magic net in which Hephaestus in very early times caught and held Aphrodite and Ares as they were making love.

This extraordinary arrangement lasted six years. Octavia, who understood what Antony was driving at and was as loyal to him as Fulvia had been before, did her best to provide him with what he expected from Cleopatra: arms and money. She came all the way to the East with these gifts, which she had got from her brother. Antony had the courage not to succumb to this temptation, and to follow his destiny. What were two or three thousand men compared to the resources of a kingdom? And then Cleopatra, sensing the danger to her aims, became more importunate, and played the comedy of love more insistently than ever. Soon Antony's break with Rome was complete, and, having become the Hellenistic King in fact as well as intent, found himself forced into a war with Rome. Thus, in the seas off Actium, ended the drama whose outcome, if Fate had bestowed victory on Antony's fleet, would surely have changed the face of the world. But this could certainly not have been attributed to Cleopatra's withered charms.

Yet Antony's defeat, the end of that "inimitable life," which ended by bringing the lovers together in death, did not end an experiment—did not do away with a mystique of the "Dionysiac royalty" that would find other ways to survive, in the heart of Rome itself.

The night before Antony died, toward midnight, while the city of Alexandria was in the grip of an anguished silence, supernatural music suddenly filled the air. It seemed to be the sound of myriad instruments of different kinds, accompanying the songs and cries of a horde of Bacchae. This tumult filled the streets in an instant, without anyone being seen; after which it moved away and reached the gate that opened out toward the enemy. There it became twice as loud, and then suddenly ceased, as if the invisible throng had left the city. All the citizens of Alexandria had heard it and had understood: Dionysus was abandoning Antony.

It was also, in fact, the end of an epoch: the law of Rome was to replace the orgiastic mystique of which Antony and Cleopatra were the last votaries to occupy the throne of the Ptolemies.

As a conqueror, Octavius, the new master, cut a sorry figure. He dragged Roman Puritanism along with him; he pretended to practice its austerity without having its virtues. He had for a long time been trying to arouse Roman opinion against Antony, by unmasking what he called his "turpitudes." And Antony, in letters destined to be read by the public, answered him offhand and without any false modesty: "Why have you changed toward me? Is it because I sleep with the Queen? She is my wife. Is it because I have begun now, or because this has been going on for nine years? And you, do you sleep only with Drusilla? I congratulate you if, when you read this letter, you haven't already slept with Tertulla or Terentilla or Rufilla or Salva Titisenia or all the others! Do you think I want to know where and with what woman you have intercourse?"

And it is quite certain that Octavius' personal conduct was not above reproach. The reproofs he laid at Antony's door rang false.

The accounts of his affairs were at the beginning rather like those of all young noblemen. He was engaged for the first time to the daughter of Publius Servilius Isauricus, who belonged to the clan of Servilia, since she was the latter's granddaughter. This union

IMPERIAL AMOURS

had clearly been planned by Caesar, it was part of his plan for shoring up the regime. But when the second triumvirate was established, after the Modena War, the soldiers of Antony and Octavius demanded that the alliance of their generals be sealed by a marriage. So Octavius broke his engagement to Servilia the younger, and took the hand of Claudia, one of the daughters of Fulvia and Publius Claudius, and consequently, at that time, Antony's granddaughter. Claudia was still a child; she was "hardly nubile," according to Suetonius. The marriage was not consummated. Octavius used the pretext of his disagreement with Fulvia to repudiate the young woman at the time of the war against Perusia.

In the same year, during a very serious crisis that looked as if it were on the point of destroying Octavius' chances once for all, he tried to resume friendly relations with Sextus Pompeius, who appeared to be master of the situation. As proof of good faith, he offered to marry Scribonia, who was an aunt "by alliance" of Sextus. The matter was arranged with Maecenas acting as go-between, and Scribonia's family eagerly accepted the match. But it was not a happy marriage. Scribonia had already been married twice; she had had children by at least one of these unions (and in particular young Cornelia, whose virtues were lauded and whose premature demise was deplored by Propertius in 16 B.C.). Scribonia quickly started to tyrannize over her husband, who was younger than she (at the time, Octavius was hardly twenty-three years old), and this did not please Octavius at all. Their union might have lasted if he had not suddenly fallen in love with another woman, and had not decided, in spite of all the obstacles in his path, to marry for love.

Scribonia, whom Octavius had married in the last months of 40, perhaps even at the beginning of 39, was expecting a child. This was Julia, whose father was to love her so deeply, and whose affection she was to repay with ingratitude. After the peace of Misenum, arranged at the end of the summer, hostilities had ceased between the triumvirate and Sextus Pompey; Scribonia was no longer "useful" politically. But the conclusion of the peace had another result that was to hasten her repudiation. The exiles had been recalled, and among them were Livia Drusilla and her husband Tiberius Claudius Nero. Both had been on the side of Lucius Antonius at Perusia and, after the defeat, had taken refuge with Sextus Pompey, with whom as a matter of fact they got on rather badly.

Livia already had a son who was later to become the Emperor Tiberius, but she was very young, having been born on January 30, 58, she was not yet nineteen in the autumn of 39. Her portraits give her a calm beauty, with a rounded face and a determined chin. As she was then, she aroused a warm passion in Octavius' heart. But at first blush there appeared to be two obstacles in the way of this love: Livia was married, and she was expecting a second child. What's more, her family had serious reasons for hating Octavius. M. Livius Drusus Claudianus, Livia's own father, had been proscribed and had taken his own life after the battle of Philippi, where he had fought beside Brutus and Cassius. But Octavius was the master; all had to give way before him. As soon as Scribonia had given birth to her child, Octavius repudiated her. Then he succeeded—heaven knows by what arguments, or what pressure—in having Livia's own husband cede her to him—rather like the way, in an earlier day, Cato had himself given Marcia to Hortensius.

But the circumstances then had been entirely different! In one of the insulting letters Antony wrote his rival from Alexandria, he declared that Nero was a witness of his own dishonor. One day during a banquet at which Nero was present in the company of Livia and Octavius, the latter, unable to curb his lust, abruptly left the banquet hall, took Livia with him to a nearby room, and brought her back later with her hair in disorder and her ears red. In these circumstances Nero could only give up the woman the master claimed. And Livia, on her part, could but obey. It appears that she did so with considerable reluctance: a young wife, on the point of becoming a mother for the second time, it distressed her to give up a husband with whom she had shared the dangers of war and the boredom of exile. Nevertheless, she had to leave her husband's house and move to that of Octavius, where, on January 14, 48, her second son, Drusus, was born. Three days later, after the seers had asserted that the gods saw no hindrance in the marriage, she solemnly married Octavius. No doubt Antony had not behaved better either, but at least in his own eyes he could justify himself by feeling that he was a god, and was acting like one, while Octavius simply drifted into a bourgeois kind of immorality.

If, in order to marry Livia, Octavius had brought himself to defy public opinion (no attempt was made to curb wagging tongues), one can assume that love was not the only motive underlying his romance. An alliance with the Claudii, the very aristocratic gens to which Livia belonged, was a kind of ratification of the reconciliation between Caesar's heirs and the persons who had been proscribed in 43. But why should love marriages necessarily run counter to convenience? In any case, Octavius' was most useful to him.

At the end of his life, Augustus still assured Livia of his affection for her. In his final moments he said to her: "Livia, remember our union as long as you live. Good-bye!" They were his last words. There is no doubt—and Augustus vouches for it himself—that this marriage, whose hasty completion was accompanied by violence and scandal, was happy nevertheless. And yet, if it were judged by appearances, how could a marriage be called happy which remained sterile, or almost (a child was born but did not live), when the lack of a direct heir was a tragedy for Augustus that weighed him down all his life, and when, although Livia on her part remained faithful to him, Augustus felt free to have one affair after another, sometimes with Julia's connivance. If Augustus judged it differently than we are inclined to do, that is because he did not feel bound by ordinary rules, and like the other Romans of his day put that *concordia,* that identity of wills which seems to us the great achievement of Roman love, above the "accidental" urges of the flesh.

Even his friends did not deny that Augustus had affairs. They excused them, averring that he did not engage in them from concupiscence, but calculatedly, in order to learn the secrets of the husbands whose wives he seduced. This is hardly a convincing argument, and if true does the Emperor no credit. One of these amours, as a matter of fact, nearly caused his undoing. He had a long liaison with Terentia, the wife of Maecenas, his oldest supporter. Was it to keep a close watch on the latter, who was customarily silent and secretive? It is certainly not impossible, for Terentia was said to be capricious and haughty; no doubt she did not treat her lover any better than her husband. But this same Terentia could not keep a state secret, and told her brother, Terentius Murena, that the conspiracy he had organized had been discovered. This prevented Augustus from finding out all the ramifications of the counterplot, as he had wished.

As for Livia, she never revealed a secret, and her husband often asked her advice. As the years passed her influence apparently increased. It is hard for us today to determine precisely the part she played in establishing the imperial regime. The indications usually set forth cannot always be interpreted with certainty. But one thing is sure: without Livia the Empire would not have been what it was when Augustus died.

Like the matrons of the preceding generation, Livia strove to increase the prestige of her gens. She belonged in the ranks of the Servilii and the Claudii. And her gens, that of the Claudii, did not always have the same aims as that of the Julii. All of Livia's astuteness was to lie in putting the power that Caesar and then Augustus had entrusted to subordinates, into the hands of the leaders. And her cleverness was of a high order.

The verdict her great-grandson Caligula (Gaius Caesar) passed on her is well known: "A Ulysses in skirts." Caligula knew her only when she was old, but her influence began to make itself felt years earlier. Augustus' big problem was not to govern, but to make certain of the succession to the throne, to act in such a way that the system he had built up, that depended on his person, could go on without him the day he died. His power rested partly on the semidivine nature public opinion attributed to him. He was *divi filius,* son of the god Caesar. To whom could he pass on this divine grace, if not a son? Now Livia certainly did not turn out to be a fecund wife. But she had two sons from her first marriage, Tiberius and Drusus.

Could she not persuade Augustus to adopt them, as he himself had been adopted by Caesar, to whom he was not related by blood?

It took Livia many a long year to rescue the Empire from the hands of the Claudii and to give it to Tiberius, that member of the Claudii for whom Augustus felt no sympathy and who, in the depths of his heart, was really a Republican. Perhaps chance favored Livia's plans by having the heirs that the Emperor chose successively disappear one by one: The young Marcellus, in the year 23 B.C., then Augustus' two grandchildren, Caius and Lucius, the two "princes of youth," who died A.D. 4 and 2 respectively. One hardly dares assume that Livia gave Fate a helping hand—but these successive deaths helped her designs so much that one has every right to be suspicious. Finally she won out and forced Tiberius on Augustus through a sheer act of will. Augustus resigned himself to adopting Tiberius because he had no other choice.

Along with these closet dramas, the imperial house of Augustus was plagued with another that also originated in a woman's wiles. Before she had been repudiated, Scribonia had borne the Emperor a daughter, Julia, whom he kept by his side, and whom he brought up in the severe tradition of the old noble families. In her tender years Julia spun wool and wove her father's tunics, which did not interfere with her receiving the choice education and culture of the women of her day. Augustus felt the greatest affection for his daughter, but he presumably hoped, thanks to her, to solve the difficult problem of the succession. Since Livia was not capable of giving him a son, Julia could bring a son-in-law into the imperial house capable of taking over the reins of power when the time came. Many centuries earlier, you remember, the kings of Rome transmitted their authority in this way. It is not an accident if Propertius and Virgil each recalled this ancient custom. And at about the time, Virgil told how old Latinus, King of the Latium had bestowed the hand of Lavinia on Aeneas and his kingdom with it, Augustus chose Marcellus as his son-in-law, who was the son of Octavia, the Emperor's own sister. Marcellus died less than a year later. Julia was then only sixteen. Augustus made an effort to marry her off a second time; her new husband was Agrippa, the Emperor's faithful companion. Agrippa had to break up his own marriage with Octavia's oldest daughter, Marcella (the elder). He was forty-one. This rather surprising choice no doubt imposed itself on Augustus by the recollection of the political crisis that, in 23, had almost caused the downfall of the regime. Seriously ill himself at the moment, he had been obliged to think of making sure of the succession in the immediate future, and the man he had designated was this same Agrippa. It is only natural that he wanted to confirm a selection once for all that had in 23 been no more than a chance improvisation.

The marriage of Julia and Agrippa proved fecund without further delay: Caius Caesar and Lucius Caesar were born in 21 and 17. In between, a daughter was born, the younger Julia. From that time on the succession could be considered safe. In 17 Augustus accelerated the celebration of the centenary games, symbolizing the era of prosperity and peace Julia's son would bring to Rome. But Agrippa died suddenly five years later and now we find Augustus seeking a third husband for his daughter. This time he could not dodge Livia's importunities, and chose Tiberius.

The couple got on well for a few years, and then discord raised its head. The deep underlying reasons have recently been brought to light: Tiberius had been selected only to act as "protector" of the young princes; Augustus had intended him to play a secondary and temporary role. While Tiberius' natural modesty adjusted itself to the situation perfectly well, Julia could not tolerate it; after having dreamed of one day being the companion of great leaders, she could not bear the thought of taking second place. She told Tiberius, and reproached him with what she called his cowardice. In the end, Tiberius decided to leave Rome and live in Rhodes as a simple citizen!

The self-imposed exile of Tiberius, this departure that Augustus tried to prevent by every means, is still a good deal of a mystery.

Probably Tiberius felt that his position was anomalous. The rumor was already abroad in Rome that he was conspiring to throw out Caius and Lucius. It was a calumny, yet there was every reason to believe it. Was it not natural to want to seize the reins, especially when the woman at his side was consumed by ambition, as everyone knew? To be sure, Tiberius did not want power, as we realize or think we do. But in his day he was considered a master of dissimulation, an art he had inherited from his mother, and his denials, his self-effacing attitude, convinced no one.

In retiring to Rhodes, was Tiberius only avoiding an ambiguous situation? Tradition has it that Julia had been unfaithful to him, and that he was also fleeing disgrace. The historians have recounted many scandalous incidents about Augustus' daughter, repeated *ad nauseam* over the years. They speak of her coquetry, that led her sometimes to dress almost indecently, to such a point as to provoke irritated comments from her father. They also report a phrase attributed to her, in answer to the surprise expressed by some friends over the strong resemblance of the children she bore Agrippa to their father: "I don't take on passengers until the hull is filled." In a word, Julia became a symbol of the depravity people like to picture in the shade of the imperial palace, and as a forerunner of Messalina. In such matters it is as difficult to accept as to contradict traditional conclusions, and one can adduce arguments of equal merit for the arraignment and the defense. It might be said that it is most unlikely that Julia could have lived a life of debauchery in a city as eager for scandal as Rome, when all eyes were upon her, and when the imperial police and perhaps a kind of sixth sense on Livia's part would make such licentiousness impossible. But one can also argue that Julia, a wife who kept her dissipation secret as long as she hoped to reach the summit of power, indulged in it openly—and her true nature inclined her in that direction—as soon as she began to lose hope for Tiberius, and that perhaps she began to betray her husband before he left for Rhodes. And it is also possible that for years there was a kind of conspiracy of silence regarding her immorality, no one bothering to inform the Emperor, and Livia patiently awaiting the right moment. After all, Julia was not the only great lady to have clandestine meetings. Augustus himself, as we have mentioned, did not respect the honor of his "matrons," and it has been stated that the laws concerning adultery were imposed by senators who wanted to embarrass him.

It cannot be denied that Julia had several affairs after Tiberius left for Rhodes. She was thirty-three, her beauty was in full bloom, and her violent nature made her commit excesses in all her pleasures. Yet it was not just seeking after enjoyment that led her to surround herself with lovers. The list of her "gentlemen friends" has been drawn up by the historian Velleius Paterculus. One name in particular holds our attention, that of Julius Antonius, the son of Antony and Fulvia, and a son-in-law of Octavius. Tullus seems to have been the favorite, but he shared Julia's favors with a certain Appius Claudius Pulcher and perhaps with one of the sons of Publius Claudius, but that is not sure. There was also Sempronius Gracchus and Cornelius Scipio. In short, we find the young woman surrounded by men bearing the most famous names of the Roman aristocracy.

We should not be astonished to conclude, as everything indicates, that Julia, in drawing young people to her, was seeking not so much to satisfy her senses as to organize a conspiracy against her own father. She wished to reign. Now Augustus had intended to vest the power in Caius and Lucius Caesar, whom he had adopted.

In this way he took them from their mother who could not influence them, even to the slightest degree. In any case, Julia did not hanker in the least for the position of Empress-Mother. She wanted to be the companion of the chief, the "First Lady of Rome," and to take the place of Livia. To accomplish this she could see no other means than to dethrone Augustus, that is to say by assassination. And to succeed in that undertaking, she counted on her ascendancy over the young nobles among whom she distributed her favors. In these circumstances one can understand why she made Antonius her favorite. She thought, rightly or wrongly, that the memory of former days off Actium had not been obliterated, and that there still might be an "Antonine party," ready to go to war for the son of the defeated leader. This opinion was evidently shared by Antonius himself, who was, moreover, spurred on by the wish to avenge his father.

It is not hard to picture the anger and the disenchantment of Augustus when he learned that his own daughter was planning parricide, and that the old coalition between Antonius and a woman—of his own blood—was in the making. Julia's other friends, too, felt that they had grounds for complaint against the regime. They regretted the days of "liberty," when the nobles held power and did not share it with anyone. This was a new counterplot, organized by a coterie of irresponsible young people, probably without very much real influence, but dangerous because they were so rash they dreamed of repeating the Ides of March.

Seneca has left a picture of this conspiracy, which may, one suspects, be exaggerated, but which certainly has some basis in truth, since the witnesses confirm several details: "Lovers brought in in droves, foot-loose races across the city by night in hilarious drunken bands; the Forum itself, the Rostra, from which her father had promulgated the laws against adultery, chosen by the girl for her excesses; daily gatherings at the [statue of] Marsyas [in the Forum] while the adulteress, having become a professional prostitute, assumed the right to try anything in the embrace of an unknown lover."

Julia had accomplices in her own home. These included a freedwoman named Phoebe, who committed suicide when Augustus was informed of her nocturnal escapades.

It is rather surprising that the conspirators should have chosen the Forum, even in the middle of the night, for their confabulations. Perhaps they felt that publicity itself was their best protection. But they particularly enjoyed thumbing their noses at public opinion. Once Julia had decided to break with authority, not to say decency, she wanted to affirm her sovereign right to flout all conventions—this seemed to her a guarantee of status. It is also possible that Antonius, who could not forget the insults proffered his father, drove her to these eccentricities. But Antony transformed Pompey's house into a house of ill fame, and shocked an aristocracy that was just recovering from civil war. He was Antony the conqueror and the dictator's companion. His son Antonius was no more than the heir to a name fraught with danger. His only chance of survival was to join the new regime. It was not for nothing that Rome had lived for twenty-five years under the moralistic rule of Augustus. The time of the "inimitable life" had passed.

Augustus eventually learned everything, although he was the last to know about it, according to Dio Cassius; he was informed only when the true intentions of the conspirators had been found out, and no one was spared his fury. The machinations had gone on some three years; retribution fell in the year 2 B.C. Julius Antonius was sentenced to death. Julia was exiled to the island of Pandataria off the coast of Campania, where she lived as a prisoner with her mother Scribonia, who had requested and obtained the right to share her punishment. After the death of Augustus, Tiberius' first care was to make her lot still harder (she had been transferred to Reggio Calabria) to such an extent that after a few months she died of want and misery. Julia's other lovers were simply moved out of their homes. They were less guilty, perhaps nothing more than supernumeraries, whom the two ringleaders had not thought worthy of being let in on the secret. Their life was spared, and they could live as they wished in the residences assigned to them.

A few years later, in A.D. 8, a new drama again threw the imperial family into confusion. On the surface it was rather like the first. This time the guilty party was Julia the younger, the daughter of Agrippa and Julia. The circumstances giving rise to this scandal are even more obscure than those surrounding the condemnation of the first Julia. Officially the grievances were the same. Following her mother's example, the young woman, who was the wife of Aemilius Paulus, had had an affair with a young noble, Decimus Junius Silanus. But there are indications that this was only a pretext. Her husband, Aemilius Paulus (Suetonius tells us), was executed for having conspired against Augustus. And on the other hand, the exile of Julia the younger seems to have coincided with that of her brother, Agrippa Postumius, who incurred censure as a kind of overweening, cruel brute. It is disturbing enough to see the last two children of Julia and Agrippa deported one after the other, the only ones in whose being the blood of Augustus himself continued to flow and who were not allied to the Claudii. Agrippina the elder, another daughter, was left in peace, probably on account of her marriage to Germanicus, Livia's grandson. Finally, the poet Ovid was exiled the same year; he may well have been involved in some kind of attempt to wrest Augustus' inheritance from Livia's "litter."

Tiberius had finally been adopted by Augustus, at the same time as Agrippa Postumius. The old Emperor was reluctant to disinherit his own issue completely. At that date, A.D. 6, Agrippa Postumius was eighteen. What was later called his "madness" was not yet evident—and there is room for doubt that it suddenly broke out in a few months, to the point of making his exile necessary. One cannot refrain from suspecting, in the tragedy that struck the last descendants of Augustus and Scribonia one after another, the epilogue of the policy Livia had patiently carried out. In spite of Augustus' repugnance, Tiberius was to be left the sole heir. What was to be avoided at any price was to have, when the time came, a "legitimist" party spring up, able to wrest the inheritance of the dead leader—so eagerly coveted—from the hands of the Claudii. And that is why Tacitus, recording the death of Julia the younger among the events taking place in A.D. 28, could write: "At the same epoch Julia died; she had been convicted of adultery and condemned to death by Augustus even though she was his granddaughter, and exiled to an island not far off the coast of Apulia. She lived there twenty years, thanks to the assistance of Livia, who, after having caused the downfall, by means of her secret machinations, of the children of her first marriage when their success had reached its peak, showed them mercy after they were ruined." This was the good, fruitful marriage that had touched Augustus' heart on his deathbed.

The tragedies that rent the house of Augustus asunder and put the Empire into the hands of the "Republican" Tiberius originated in Octavius' passion. He had torn Livia from her first husband—and her union with Octavius could rightfully be called cursed, since it had proved infertile and had as its final result depriving the legitimate representatives of the Julia gens of leadership in favor of the Claudii.

Lust for enjoyment, even for immorality, if you will, played their part in this series of tragedies, but that part was less than the one played by ambition. One woman, Livia, did everything possible to maintain her sway over the man who held the fate of Rome in his hands. For that she was willing to stand Augustus' infidelities—even to encourage them—and later, his senile propensities.

That is what it cost her to be a "good wife," and to bring Augustus, completely subjugated, to disclaim his own issue. Except that it had the imperial house as its setting, this drama is no different from those to which playwrights and novelists of every epoch have accustomed us, whether the stake was the possession of a field, a farm, or the Roman Empire. A man can resist the insidious machinations of the woman he loves but mistrusts for a long time. Then, as old age advances, he gives way little by little and lets himself be outwitted; he ceases to be himself, and agrees to all the betrayals and disavowals, under the illusion that his companion, now aged as well as he, shares the feeling and aims that she really put into his mind. Such was doubtless the story of the marriage that courtiers and some poets applauded as the very picture of a perfect conjugal relationship.

The histories of the two Julias, mother and daughter, are equally cruel and equally rich in moral lessons. The first Julia did not hesitate to organize a criminal conspiracy in order to regain her hold on the reins that were slipping from her grasp. To that end, she bestowed her favors on all the men whose support she needed. Her daughter, following in her footsteps in spite of the fact that the attempt had failed miserably and ended in a frightful bloodbath, thought that she could thwart the intrigues of the all-powerful Livia, using the same means. What conception did these two women have of love? One is inclined to think that they regarded it simply as an instrument, and the worst one can reproach them with, perhaps, is having brought it down to that level. If they had only sought clandestinely the gratifications of debauchery like so many others of their time and in other centuries, they would have grown old peacefully, honored, and no doubt content. But the traditions of Roman women taught them that love was a weakness in itself, that only grandeur and power were worth seeking.

It was only natural that having become scornful of sensual and sentimental attachments and ties—as all women of their class and race innately were—they had reached such depths of decadence. It had already been reached psychologically by the most virtuous matrons of the past, who had grown accustomed to seeing nothing more in their femininity than a means of ensuring the survival of the City-State and the grandeur of their gens. Perhaps this is the profound origin of that "immorality" so often laid at the door of imperial society. It represents a Puritan perversion of natural values, depriving love of its true meaning and taking away its essential character, which is the total identification of two human beings, and trying to subject it to arbitrary restrictions. No doubt the poets, as we have recalled, had known how to find the significance of love once more. But no one listened to them, or, as unfortunately was the case with Ovid, they were accused of immorality. Yet was there ever a more affectionate husband than Ovid, or a more intrinsically perverted couple than Augustus and Livia?

During the reigns that followed that of Augustus, a number of intrigues were hatched that were closely reminiscent of those conducted by Livia and the women of the imperial family: deadly cabals carried on to seize power, and, of course, employing the same means. All those related by the historians may perhaps not be true, but some at least, based on authentic testimony, prove that the Palatine court was not a whit better than the Greek monarchies, while at the same time continuing the traditions of political life at the end of the Republic. It is not perfectly sure that Caligula, when he wanted to obtain the services of Macro, Prefect of the *praetorium,* sought the favors of his wife Eunia. It is still harder to believe that he promised in writing to marry her once he became Emperor. Too many legends grew up around the Julio-Claudian emperors for us to be able to believe in all these anecdotes. But we can perceive, just the same, the part played by certain women belonging to the "Divine House" (*domus divina*) who tended to become increasingly important, as is proved by the honors heaped on them.

In his lifetime Augustus steadily refused to include Livia officially in the divinity with which he surrounded himself, and it was only on his death that she received the title of Augusta. But Tiberius was always against her receiving other honors, and even feigned to avoid all conversations with her that might have suggested that she had any political influence over him.

Caligula, on the other hand, from the beginning of his reign, was far from showing any such cautious restraint. He agreed (and no doubt suggested) that his three sisters be included in the official wishes for his safety put forth by the senate. At the same time he had coins struck that identified them with three symbolic divinities: Securitas, Concordia, and Fortuna. And when the one he loved best of all, Julia Drusilla, died, he agreed that she be considered as a goddess, with the name of Panthea. This amounted to official confirmation of the cult that had already been dedicated to her during her lifetime by the cities of the East, to whom she was the "New Aphrodite." Thus the women of the imperial family became included in the long ascent toward divinity that progressively transformed the hierarchy into a "monarchy by divine right." But this did not prevent their remaining "matrons," motivated by the same desires, ready, as a means of satisfying their thirst for honors and power, to abdicate their moral scruples in the same way their mothers did. Perhaps they were even more convinced that, by belonging to the family of the reigning god, they were above the moral law of humans.

Two names today typify these "wives of the Caesar's" for us: Messalina and Agrippina. Two names covered with shame, and that also would seem to justify history's censorious attitude toward Roman love.

The editor of the *Galerie universelle,* when he included a description of Messalina in the volume, felt obliged to sound a note of warning: "Our readers," he writes, "should not be alarmed simply by the name of Messalina; our respect for morality, the wise supervision of the censors who preside over the publication of the *Galerie universelle* should guarantee that the frightful picture we paint of the shameful excesses of that infamous Empress, the disgrace to her throne and to her sex, has only one aim: that our readers should be appalled by vice, and that by contrast virtue should be admired and should shine still more brilliantly wherever it is found."

These pious expostulations hardly conceal the fascination Messalina exerts. She is the incarnation of what can be called a complete amorality, a licentiousness to which many persons are secretly drawn, though they would never admit it. A century or two ago, everyone could recall Juvenal's lines describing the amorous exploits of the wicked Empress; schoolboys warming benches whispered them to each other.

"Look now at the rivals of the gods; listen to what Claudius endured. As soon as his wife thought he was asleep, preferring a mat to the bed in the Palatine palace, the Empress-courtesan took a cloak to cover herself with in the night and fled, accompanied by a single serving maid. Then, with a red wig hiding her black hair, she often went through an old curtain into a steamy bordello, and thence into an empty cell which was hers. And then, naked, her breasts held in by a golden net, she offered herself, under the false name of Lycisca, and exposed the noble belly that bore Thee, O noble Britannicus. She received and cajoled the visitors, asking them for money; and then, at the time when the keeper managed to get rid of his lodgers, she went off sadly, as late as possible; she was the last one to shut up her room. Aflame with tense convulsions, worn out by men but not sated, she left at last, and, her complexion pallid and wan, her face blackened by the smoke of the lamp, she brought back the stink of the bordello to the holy bed."

The historians Dio Cassius and Pliny (the latter no doubt quoting from his own *Natural History*) are at one in depicting a Messalina wildly greedy for sexual gratification. Juvenal wanted no doubt simply to give a more generalized impression, a brilliant variation on the theme of the Empress-courtesan, contrasting the divine majesty of the Empire with the sordidness of the Roman brothels. One is not likely to believe that the Empress really occupied a smoky cell, above which was inscribed her name: Lycisca, which is the Greek equivalent of the designation *lupa,* meaning simply, in common parlance, whore. On the other hand, one could hardly doubt that she lured the lovers able to satisfy her into the Palatine palace. It is also possible that she held orgies in the palace to which she invited noblewomen accompanied by their husbands. No one would have given the matter a thought if Messalina had not been the Empress. That there may have been a pathological side to her approach to sex should not lead us to condemn a whole social order, not to say a civilization, which was certainly not alone in countenancing such excesses. But what those who censure her have forgotten is that when Messalina yielded to the lusts of the flesh she was not yet twenty, and perhaps much younger still.

Claudius married Messalina one or two years before he became Emperor, in 39 or 40 when, as uncle of the reigning Emperor (Caligula), he was considered at Court to be a clown everyone could make fun of; no one dreamed that he would soon be at the head of the Empire. Claudius had already been married twice; he had been divorced twice, the first time on grounds said to be rather trifling; the second, because his wife had disgraced him by her misconduct, and was even suspected of having killed a man. He could hardly be called young, since, born in 10 B.C., he was nearing fifty. He was Messalina's first husband, and, as we know, girls were customarily married off very young. One would not be far wrong in thinking that in 39 Messalina was hardly even an adolescent. In February, 41, she gave birth to a boy, little Britannicus. There may have been a girl before him, Octavia, or she may have been his junior.

The marriage was happy at first. Claudius was very fond of his child-wife, and was delighted to be a father. Apparently everything began to go wrong after Caligula died and Claudius became Emperor.

The new Emperor was very easily influenced, and the freedmen of his household soon began to exercise authority in his name. One of them in particular, the famous Narcissus, seems to have used the young Empress to further his ambitions. Messalina, involved in the endless intrigues of the Court, tired of a lecherous husband who ran after her serving maids (as young as could be obtained for him), and who found self-interested and servile collusion everywhere when he sought to gratify his fancies. She would have to have been exceptionally virtuous not to have taken advantage of her complete liberty. She would have had to have a very strong character indeed, and, in her childhood, better examples of conduct than Domitia Lepida, her mother, gave her.

The early historians charge her not only with taking part in countless acts of dissipation, but also with having instigated the murder of several great personages on whom she wished to revenge herself, or simply because she wanted their worldly wealth.

Debauched, cruel, greedy—she has been pictured as a monster at an age when many young girls are still thinking of their dolls. But it is highly likely that after her downfall all the crimes committed by others around her were attributed to her. Narcissus, especially, who after having been her ally was responsible for her death, would have found it very much to his advantage to reverse their roles, and pretend that he had only obeyed Messalina, when he had really called the tune. In Nero's time the informer Suillius, who had been one of his cronies, had to give an account of himself. Seneca, one of Claudius' victims, happened to be in power, and the trial started. At first Suillius wanted to hide behind the shadow of Claudius, and insisted that he had only obeyed the Emperor. Nero demolished this defense by asserting that Claudius had never accused anyone, as his memoirs showed. Then Suillius argued that, if Claudius was innocent, the responsibility for all these crimes could be laid at Messalina's door, well knowing that no one would come to the defense of the infamous Empress. Should Suillius' claims be accepted blindly?

In fact we can glimpse a kind of clique around Messalina, which was not attached to her merely by a craving for debauchery, but which made use of her undeniable influence over the Emperor for political ends. Prominent in this group was Vitellius, the father of the future Emperor, who played the role of a great "lady's man," while, on the other hand, placing gold statues of imperial freedmen in his *lararium*. And this coterie revenged itself on all those who opposed its maneuvers. Messalina was "on Antony's side," bound to him by her ancestry in both the male

IMPERIAL AMOURS

and female lines. And since Augustus' reign, a veiled rivalry had brought that branch of the family into conflict with the "legitimate heirs," represented by the descendants of Germanicus. So it is not surprising that one of its first victims was Julia Livilla, one of Germanicus' daughters, who had conspired with Agrippina against her own brother under Caligula. While the latter, made cautious by her preceding failure, kept in the background and waited for her hour to strike, Julia tried to seduce Claudius and eliminate Messalina. She managed to have long private interviews with the old Emperor, who had never been able to resist a woman's charms. So Messalina accused her of having let Seneca seduce her, and of having been his mistress. Julia was sent into exile, and put to death not long after that. Seneca was treated with clemency. The charges against him were not too serious, and he had been no more than a supernumerary in the party of Germanicus' daughters, while his eloquence and influence in the senate were highly appreciated. It was deemed enough punishment to deport him to Corsica, without depriving him of his fortune.

The trial and execution of Valerius Asiaticus figure among the most frightful of the crimes Messalina is blamed for. The current version of Book XI of the *Annals* of Tacitus begins with an account of it. There we see how the Empress, jealous of Poppaea Sabina, became annoyed with Asiaticus; no doubt she had hoped to become his mistress. And as if this was not a strong enough motive, greed was added to her pique: not content with desiring the man, she coveted the gardens and the wonderful park designed by Lucullus which had become one of the most magnificent domains in Rome. Vitellius, Suillius, and some others took it on themselves to bring charges. Claudius, we are told, was inclined to favor an acquittal, but Vitellius was able to get around him; he acted as if he were defending the accused, and eventually asked, as a form of clemency, that the latter be allowed to choose the way he would die. Claudius stupidly agreed, and Messalina, who had not been able to hold back her tears during Asiaticus' defense, finally obtained his death sentence, which was what she wanted.

That is the way Tacitus told it, but his account smacks a little of the improbable. Doubtless Asiaticus was not the harmless character he has been painted. He had taken an active part in the assassination of Caligula, and he was the leader of the conspirators who had sworn to restore the Republic. Far from showing leniency toward him, Claudius was relentless in his hate, and a long time after he was condemned to death, proliferated insults to his memory in the speech recorded in the *Claudian Tables*. Should it be thought that the Emperor was in this simply following blindly and stupidly an attitude imposed on him by Messalina? May not Asiaticus' disgrace have had deeper causes than the pique and cupidity of a shameless woman? May it not rather be one episode in the constant struggle maintained under all the emperors of the Julio-Claudian dynasty, the party of the freedmen, the leader's gens, and the champions of the senate, who sought to prevent the supreme power from being kept under the influence of the bureaucrats? Asiaticus, who was much in favor at Court at the beginning of the reign, who was the Emperor's companion on the expedition to Britain, who was made Consul for the second time in 46, could be considered the most legitimate representative of those who, deep in their hearts, regretted the years of the Republican oligarchy, and strove to reinstate their faction, together with its privileges. Asiaticus himself was the victim of this duel to the death, which began before him and was to continue, with various ups and downs, during Nero's reign and after.

That Messalina was responsible is highly probable—let us recognize at least that she shares the blame with those who soon came to regard her as an instrument not pliable enough in their hands, and began to plot her death.

During the summer of 48, probably on August 15, Claudius, who was about to end his shining career as Senator, made an inspired and almost revolutionary speech which has been preserved in the *Claudian Tables*. The plan was to make the senate more accessible to men of the provinces, and especially to leaders among the "long-haired" Gauls.

At the same time Claudius was particularly kind to the senators: instead of bluntly using his power as Censor to exclude such members as deserved it from the order, he left it up to them to retire voluntarily.

It might seem that a turning point had been reached in the reign when the balance between the influence of the bureaucrats and that of the senate was about to be upset. The feeling that this was so resulted in a motion highly flattering to the Consul Vipsanius Agrippa who proposed naming Claudius "Father of the senate." Claudius refused the honor, which confirmed the general estimate of his moderation and his "Republican" feelings—favorable to the senate, in any case. This is also the impression gained from reading the *Claudian Tables* themselves and by the bonhomie of their style, which was no doubt intentional.

There was enough in all this to upset the freedmen of the palace, who struck back with incredible audacity, and succeeded in turning the tables on the "Republican" elements.

They took advantage of a new imprudence on Messalina's part, and by a clever maneuver, managed to make the Emperor distrust at least some of the senators, while getting the Empress, who had become a threat to their plans, out of the way.

For some time Messalina had been in love with a young man, who, according to Tacitus, was the handsomest of all the Romans: a Senator named Gaius Silius. To please Messalina, he agreed to break off his marriage to a great lady, Junia Silana, since Messalina, with the obstinacy of youth and the pride of a spoiled Empress, would not share him with anyone else. She gave herself unreservedly to the love affair. Claudius looked the other way. Possibly, of course, he did not know about it, but it is more likely that he had decided to allow Messalina her freedom, and deliberately avoid knowing how far she overstepped its bounds. The affair at any rate had become a public scandal: Messalina went to Silius' home accompanied by a large retinue; without concealment, her slaves and freedmen were at home in her lover's house, and used the silverware, dishes, and other treasures of the imperial furnishings for the gatherings and celebrations she organized.

As for Silius, he was well aware of the danger, but what was he to do? How could he oppose an imperious mistress, overjoyed to live her life to the point of satiety and to fill her lover's cup to overflowing? For this descendant of Antony it was a way of beginning the "inimitable life" over again, by playing the roles of Antony and Cleopatra both. And Silius reflected that Messalina's extreme boldness in facing danger made possible daring solutions: since he had taken over the Emperor's wife, why not also take over the reins of power? So he began to put pressure on Messalina: since Claudius was old, why wait for him to die a natural death? Had not Silius already been designated Consul, and was he not, at least for a while, one of the leaders of the state? He had partisans who would be happy to promote his accession to the throne, once Claudius was out of the way. Since the death of Caligula, how an emperor came to power was a matter of common knowledge. No one believed in their "Divine Right" any longer. Then, going one step further, Silius pointed out to Messalina that he had no family ties, no obstacle to marrying her when the death of Claudius set her free. He promised to adopt her children—which meant Britannicus, whose bloodline would guarantee the Romans (at least those who cared) that power had not quite been taken out of the hands of Augustus' descendants.

Messalina herself had not originated this project, and reacted coolly to it. Tacitus declares that all she wanted was to satisfy her passion; then too, these proposals of Silius made her uneasy about the future of her romance, which is not surprising if one agrees with the characterization of Messalina as extremely dissipated, hurrying from one gratification to another, incapable of a deep attachment, a slave to her sensual desires and nothing else. She was afraid, apparently, that once Silius had attained power, he would discard her, like a tool that has become useless, and might end by accusing her of their common crime. One may also think, and here Tacitus himself only supplies some hypotheses, that Messalina was shocked to find how "practical" Silius was, and that she was reluctant to entertain the idea of having her husband assassinated. It was natural, too, that loving Silius as she did, she should be distressed to discover that he could regard her as the means for satisfying his ambition, instead of simply loving her. Of all that her lover told her, only one thing stuck in her mind: that he wanted to marry her. They decided to have the wedding in the absence of Claudius, who had to go to Ostia for an official ceremony. And it duly took place. All the rites were observed; omens were read; sacrifices were offered up; the signing of the marriage contract was witnessed, and the couple then withdrew to spend the night together.

All this seems incredible to us today. The early historians who were antagonistic to Claudius and Messalina have emphasized the scandalous nature of this "marriage," in order to bring out the Emperor's weakness of mind and his wife's perversity. But a few sparse accounts make it possible for us to understand the significance of the episode and explain how, for better or worse, it could happen. First of all, Suetonius tells us that Claudius was aware that the marriage with Silius had taken place, and that he had even signed the contract as a witness. But he had been led to believe that it was nothing but a joke, that sinister portents threatened "the husband of Messalina"; Silius had offered to play that role in order to ward off the anger of the gods. Claudius had agreed, and had left for Ostia in a tranquil frame of mind.

But his illusions were short-lived. Narcissus, one of his freedmen, took on the job of shattering them and making clear the true state of things. In our day, the marriage with Silius may seem like a shocking comedy, devoid of any real meaning. But in Claudius' time things were different: the wife had a perfect right to put away her husband. Claudius was obliged to consider himself as repudiated, even if all the legal forms had not been strictly observed—and that was exactly the way Narcissus explained the situation to him.

"But perhaps," he said to Claudius, "you know about your divorce? Silius' marriage has been witnessed by the people, the senate and the army; if you do not act fast, Messalina's husband will be the master of Rome."

Would he have spoken this way if the marriage had no legal sanction? Had the Empress brought her new husband the Empire as a dowry? She could do it; she too belonged to Augustus' family; it would be enough for the praetors, the people, or the senate to confirm Claudius' downfall for the revolt to become an accomplished fact. And things would no doubt have turned out that way if Messalina had really wanted it, if she had been willing to take the necessary steps, or let Silius take them. Appointed Consul, he had distinguished himself the preceding year by violently attacking Suillius and becoming the spokesman of the "Conservatives." The senators would have backed him up, if he had called on them for support. Narcissus knew this well, since he lost no time in bringing Claudius into the praetors' camp, the same ones who had prevented the senators from reinstating the Republic. They respected the Emperor because he was the brother of Germanicus, whose memory they cherished.

Messalina, while Narcissus was conspiring against her, paid little attention to politics. Delighted to have married Silius, and not caring to take any thought for the morrow, she organized a bacchanalian orgy. For it was then the twenty-third of August; the day the festivities in celebration of the grape harvest started. Whole parts of the imperial palace had been transformed into a stage set; winepresses full of grapes could be seen; the must filled the vats, and, hither and yon, women disguised as Bacchae, their bodies only half-concealed by panther skins, indulged unrestrainedly in the wild dances dear to Dionysus. Messalina herself, her hair disheveled, brandished a thyrsus, playing the part of Ariadne, beside Silius disguised as Bacchus, with his garlands of ivy and his buskins. In the meantime a friend, Vettius Valens, climbed a tree and pretended to scrutinize the horizon; when asked what he saw from up there he answered that he perceived "a violent storm near Ostia." He was not deceived, since at that very moment Claudius, aroused by Narcissus, had taken his place in a litter, where no one had access to him, and was reluctantly returning, more disturbed and unhappy than angry, to face the *coup d'état* that according to strict logic Silius should at least have tried, with some chance of success.

As long as Messalina was a tool in the hands of the "liberators," one could harbor the delusion that she was clever enough to carry on an intrigue, and ensure her triumph. But the fact was that once having given way to her passion for Silius, and no longer in a position to be guided by the advice of Narcissus and the others, forced to rely only on her own powers, she went down into defeat. Exaggeratedly self-confident, she believed too long in her ascendancy over Claudius—she did not deceive herself in this respect but had not reckoned with the cunning of Narcissus, who prevented her having access to Claudius, who would have given in after a few moments of tête-à-tête. It never occurred to her for a moment that the freedman, staking all on one throw, would give orders to have her executed without even consulting Claudius.

She had retired to the gardens she liked so much, which had belonged to Valerius Asiaticus, and she was preparing to write out a petition when a troop of soldiers arrived, led by one of Narcissus' henchmen. Her mother Lepida, who had been on bad terms with her for a long time, had hastened to her side on learning of her disgrace. Realizing more clearly than her daughter that the situation was desperate, she advised her not to wait for the executioners. But Messalina did not have the courage to take her own life; she was but twenty after all, and only a few hours before had been at the height of amorous joy, possessed by that Dionysiac force that had once under similar circumstances bewitched Antony, and that in a way justified her ecstatic raptures in her own eyes. Tacitus, ever severe, condemned her in a phrase. "Corrupted by passion," he said, "her soul no longer had any feeling for honor." Nevertheless, she went through the motions of killing herself when she saw the soldiers, but they were quicker than she: the Tribune transfixed her with his sword.

What was regarded as Messalina's conspiracy, but which had really been that of Silius, was put down—as was customary—by a series of executions. The severity of the sentences indicated the desire to strike at the most active representatives of the senatorial party. Narcissus had triumphed. There was no longer any question of a rapprochement between the Emperor and the senators. One last time, the freedmen had made use of Messalina to further their ends, and the senators humbled themselves to the point of tendering Narcissus the insignia of the Quaestor, thereby ratifying their own defeat.

It was in these circumstances that Agrippina attained to power. It was essential to put someone in the place left vacant by the death of Messalina. Claudius could not get along without a wife, and each clique tried to make sure of their hold on him by providing him with one who was on their side. A thousand intrigues buzzed in the Emperor's antechamber, of which a few weak echoes have reached us via Tacitus; the choice finally fell on Agrippina, who was beholden to every party. She had been selected because the blood of Augustus flowed in her veins, and because she was the daughter of Germanicus, and the freedmen knew she could be bribed. In a word, everyone hoped to get something out of the marriage. It was a scandal as well, since Claudius was Agrippina's uncle, but public opinion was induced to swallow it by the passage of a special law legitimizing such unions, which had until then been considered incestuous.

But those who had expected Agrippina to be as docile as Messalina were soon disillusioned. The fact was that a second Livia was now in command, and she did not have to face the will of a man like Augustus. Abandoning the freedmen, she soon got ready to follow policies of her own; she began to flirt with the senatorial party. She had Seneca recalled from exile, entrusted him with the task of bringing up young Nero, and let it be known that when the time came she would be prepared to give the Empire a leader who would give greater heed to senatorial privileges. It took her five years to destroy Claudius' authority completely and build up a party of her own. But in the end she had no difficulty whatever in imposing Nero, when Claudius' death, which she was accused of having caused—and that is far from unlikely— paved the way for a successor. Her foresight and her resourcefulness had smoothed out all the difficulties. Praetors, senators, and plebeians approved the accession of Nero to the throne. She had been able to achieve what had rarely been accomplished in the three previous reigns: political unity in the Roman Empire.

After her success, attained in the face of her husband's opposition, she had to maintain her sway—this time over a son, but before that, over the coterie of followers who had helped her during the first stage of her project. For the first time the men with whom she had surrounded young Nero were to keep her in abeyance: she had wanted to win the support of the "Conservatives," and in this Seneca had helped considerably. But in so doing she had unwittingly raised an insurmountable obstacle. An "old Roman" would never let a woman openly influence political life and affairs of state. But Agrippina was unwilling to keep out of sight. She had the same desires as all the women of her race; Livia's blood flowed in her veins, but she did not have Livia's caution. She knew that she could make a success of the biggest projects as well as or better than a man. She wanted to be more than the mother of the Emperor; she wanted to be a real Empress. But, although Roman tradition had long permitted women to influence men's decisions, this very tradition—and the men on whom she leaned followed it—forbade her to appear on the scene.

The conflict broke out in the early days of Nero's reign when, one day, a delegation from Armenia was received in an official audience by the Emperor. Agrippina prepared to go up onto the platform and sit beside him. All the spectators were stupefied. Agrippina drew near the tribunal, and none dared stop her by as much as a gesture, when Seneca had the presence of mind to suggest to Nero that it was his duty to precede his mother. The session broke up; disgrace had been avoided, but the incident marked the beginning of a long crisis. Agrippina understood that she had certainly not won a complete victory, and that she had to keep up the fight. And this time it was a son she must dominate, it was no longer an old man who could be won over by a caress.

For four years she was to continue the unequal struggle, in which every weapon would be used on both sides. Nero had the courage to fall in love: in itself, it was an inconsequential affair with a freedwoman named Acte, but Seneca saw in it a way of separating the son from his mother. He encouraged the liaison. One of his friends, Serenus, the Prefect of the night watch, at first tried to cover up the scandal. He tried to take the credit for the gifts the young man bestowed on his mistress, and made it a point to be seen in her company. But Agrippina was not deceived. She flew into a rage. Then they deprived her of one of her allies, the freedman Pallas, one of the "great stewards," a holdover from the preceding reign during which his affairs had prospered. Then she began to threaten. Britannicus, the son of Claudius and Messalina, was always there, a kind of symbol of remorse.

Agrippina knew, in fact she boasted openly, that she could summon the praetors to support her. Britannicus died, so opportunely that everyone was convinced that Nero had him assassinated (although that is far from certain). Then, Agrippina herself was banished from the Palatine palace. But this did not cause her to abandon the struggle. It was even alleged that she considered becoming the mistress of her own son, and was prevented from perpetrating such a crime only by the intervention of Seneca. Nero was also protected by his love for Poppaea whom he had pirated from a friend, Salvius Otho, and whom he finally married.

IMPERIAL AMOURS

And it was Poppaea's influence that finally made him decide to commit that other crime: the murder of his own mother.

With Agrippina and Nero a line comes to an end. The imperial family, descended from Augustus, had raised tragedies of lust and political intrigue to heights never before known, ending in a veritable paroxysm. They were certainly not new to Rome, but they had never reached such intensity nor had they been carried on so uninterruptedly. Historians have provided so many details on the sexual perversions of the last of the Julio-Claudians, that we are tempted to think they let their imaginations and sensual curiosity run away with them. The same historians have told how tenderly Nero loved Poppaea, how overjoyed he was at the birth of a daughter, the only child he ever had. They add that the Emperor caused Poppaea's death by once kicking her so hard in the stomach that the young woman, who was pregnant, died shortly after. But doubt is shed on the authenticity of this account when one remembers that a rumor was current among the people that Nero had poisoned her.

What is sure, however, is that he cherished the memory of his wife, to the point of "replacing" her with a young boy whose features were similar to hers. And it should not be forgotten either, to complete the picture of what may have been Nero's real image —the Emperor who began to reign at the age of seventeen—that his first mistress, Acte, remained faithful to him, and that it was she who buried him when everyone had abandoned him, when he was proscribed, when the senate had declared him a public enemy, when he had died carrying with him the fate of a whole dynasty.

IX

ROME AND LOVE

It would seem, in the course of this history that has taken us from the origins of Rome to the end of the Julio-Claudian dynasty, that the Romans had an ambivalent attitude toward love: they distrusted it as a passing aberration, a kind of madness, but at the same time they were spellbound by its force, which gave them an intimation of its divine nature. Love is so intimately bound up with the drama and mystery of life that its existence cannot simply be denied. But it is also the destroyer of cities and souls. Men are less apprehensive of its coming within reach but women can so easily let themselves be overpowered by it, and thus—in a moment of aberration—jeopardize the purity of their race! Though men can permit themselves to regard the act of love lightly, as of no consequence, it is for a woman an overwhelming initiation that transforms her whole being. The entire moral code and the practice of the art of love in Rome can be explained by these two conceptions.

The sociological aspect of the communities that grew with the Roman state interprets only some components of the love ethic, but not the whole. For instance, it explains why for Roman men there were several categories of women: those who had to be protected at any cost against themselves and against the initiatives of the God of Love, and those whose purity was of no account. But it does not explain the repugnance felt by the Romans of all epochs toward "Greek love," nor the sense of sin they attached to the pleasures of the flesh. Plutarch asked why, in Roman marriage, custom required that on the wedding night the newlywed husband must draw near to his wife in the dark, without any light whatsoever. He answered his own question, recalling that the Romans felt a deep respect for their wives, and he added that this custom emphasized the shameful aspect of the act of love, even when it took place between husband and wife. "Shameful" is no doubt too strong a word. The term shows the astonishment and the bewilderment, in a sense, of Plutarch before a feeling that was rather unfamiliar to the people of his nation. The Romans were no more shocked than the Greeks by nudity, and their bodies never struck them as "damned," but they had kept the sacred character of that nudity more than the Greeks—the nudity that discloses the most intimate essence of a human being. It was a Roman, Valerius Maximus, who recalled that the moral code forbade men of the same family to bathe together, because, he said, "One respects the affiliations of blood and family relationship as much as the immortal gods themselves . . . and it is forbidden to remove all men's clothes in a holy place." Just as there are rules for the celebration of sacrifices, similarly love, the holy art par excellence, calls for secrecy, and must not be profaned by human sight. Love, like death, is not inconsequential in the eyes of the gods. We have already noticed the taboos applied to impure women and in particular to the *paelex* (concubine) in the heart of the house.

But this magical attribute could also be beneficial. Courtesans danced at the feast of Flora, and the peasants, during the *Liberalia,* still perpetuated in Virgil's time ancient phallic rites consecrated to Liber, the god of "all sowings." In primitive times love was related to morals only to the extent that the latter simply codify beliefs that were essentially religious or magical for the early Romans. And its early character would persist even after the beginning of "disinterested" reflection, and when human personality, freed from collective controls, would tend to have its rights recognized. Even when the love relationship became a matter preeminently "between persons," the Romans did not forget, in the search for pleasure and the flowering of their tenderness, that it was a god who intervened.

And this concept or feeling was fraught with consequences. It prevented amorous conquest from being oriented solely toward sexual satisfaction, and from making the man forget his companion's dignity. We have observed several times to what extent women were regarded with respect, even with veneration, in ancient Rome and then in Classical Rome. No doubt this respect sometimes seemed very like a safeguard against woman's complaisance, which the men always feared. But it would be a mistake to believe that all the Romans thought about was shutting their wives up in prison, no matter how gilded the cage was. Respect for women was for them a value in itself, confirmed in many situations—as well in the extraordinary privileges accorded the vestal virgins as in certain legal prohibitions such as the one exempting matrons from the *manus iniectio* (laying on of hands) when they were brought before the bar. The free woman was essentially sacred, as untouchable as the tribune of the plebeians. It is because he failed to understand this fundamental principle of this Roman moral code that the *Decemvir* Appius Claudius brought on the revolution we have previously mentioned.

It may be said that this argument is valid in regard to freeborn women, whom men married, and often did not love. But there were the others, who existed only for pleasure—courtesans and slaves. Were they respected? Was the feigned "love" proffered them anything more than the animal satisfaction of an instinct that drove men to enjoy and then discard them?

It is true that the courtesans in Plautus' plays were thought of only as instruments of enjoyment, and that in them, one might say, femininity was profaned. It is also true that this state of affairs lasted a long time, and we can hardly maintain that eventually *all* Romans reached a plane on which they experienced true love.

Who could claim that this would be true of any social system at any time? But what we want to establish here is whether Roman morals on the whole excluded sentimental love. We are certainly obliged to admit that they did not. Remember how in Terence the picture of "love life" grew into something entirely different from what it had been in Plautus' time. In the middle of the second century B.C., under the Hellenistic influence, but also because of a natural evolution of Roman moral custom itself, the sentiment of love became more subtle and freed itself from traditional taboos and rules. And, one unexpected result, it was not married love that was degraded, but that other love, freed of all restraint, became more introverted, more concentrated, and also more respectful.

It seemed as if respect for women was extended to cover a whole category of girls to which it was not supposed to apply. And this respect did not make its appearance among men only, but among women as well. The latter, who until then had not given a thought to the feelings they could arouse in the hearts of male companions, began to hesitate—at least the best of them—to yield their bodies alone. And on their part the adolescents began to expect more from marriage than a form of servitude and austere duty, and also from a liaison that it would be more than ephemeral. For all of them, the feeling of love became a psychological reality, separate from mere instinct—which is possible only to the extent that woman assumes dignity. All genuine love is based on mutual respect, but especially on respect for the woman, not only on her own part but on the part of her companion. And it was because they were prepared by tradition and a kind of instinctive feeling to treat women with respect, even with a kind of religious awe, that the Romans were destined, perhaps more than any other people, to discover love.

It is significant that among all the divinities associated in Roman religion with the love relationship, first place was given to a goddess, Venus, instead of a god. It was as if the Romans thus implicitly recognized that love was essentially "woman's affair," and that it was the woman who conferred its full consecrated value on sexual union. It is also significant that the God of Love is not to be found in the list of Roman divinities. Rome has no character among the gods comparable to the Greek Eros, who, according to this epoch or that, was either a cosmic principle or a wayward child. When Lucretius wanted to give a name to the universal force of love, it was Venus that he chose, and not that of a masculine daemon. It is easy to contrast the Greek Eros—the spirit of adventure and conquest, the son of expediency and poverty, according to Plato—with the Roman Venus, the "good goddess," on whose breast Mars came to rest, vanquished beyond a shadow of a doubt. In other races and other eras, the man was supposed to accomplish feats of valor for the loved one. In Rome, love disarmed the hero. In this struggle, the woman has the upper hand, and always wins. The Greek Eros, nervous and anxious, cares nothing for what comes after his victory. But the Roman Venus looks forward more or less openly to maternity, and is repelled by infertile marriages.

In spite of all joking about it, marital love was the Romans' most precious ideal, for which everyone had a nostalgic feeling. In Augustus' own family, where passion caused so much havoc—but more the passion for power than love—history has preserved the recollection of the tenderness that Drusus and his wife Antonia felt for each other. It was exclusively on account of his love for her, it is said, that he renounced all other sexual adventures. Thus, at the very moment when, we are assured, morals were becoming daily more corrupt, a noble Roman made the discovery of the value of being faithful to one woman. And at about that same time Propertius found out somewhat the same thing: that a love like his needed to be based on *fides*. In the olden times the moral code required a woman to be *univira,* that is, to have only one man. At the beginning of the Empire we find a similar obligation expected of men. Two or three generations earlier this would have been unthinkable. And it was the men themselves who, because of love, sacrificed the freedom that traditional morals gave them: Catullus, who wanted to become "husband" of Clodia; Tibullus who wanted to share the solitude of the country with Delia. The mistress tended to become the *domina,* who ruled over the lover as the mother of a family reigns in her home over the slaves. The lover has no other will than that of his companion.

The submission was real; it was not just a literary legend. This is proved by the example of unbelievable political power exercised by women at the end of the Republic and during the first years of the Empire. At that epoch, Rome was making woman into a divinity, and the feeling a lover vouchsafed to his companion became a kind of adoration.

Under the Empire, women were fully aware of this reverence and of their supreme power over men, which they did not hesitate to use. The "old Romans" (or those who talked as if they were) could grumble that morals were becoming corrupt as much as they liked, that all was lost because men no longer knew how to keep women in the strait and narrow path, that those they wanted to be "madonnas" had become she-devils. This is the theme Juvenal embroiders on freely in the sixth *Satire:* women have a perverse instinct which drives them to look everywhere for sensual satisfaction no matter what the cost. "Impelled by the tyranny of sexual desire, they commit the worst crimes, and debauchery is the least of their sins." Juvenal dug this pessimism, this affected mysogyny, out of the records of the earliest centuries, but by now it was out of date. And of course it might have been provoked by pique, by the disappointment of a man who had aimed too high. Juvenal's rhetoric echoes Catullus' deplorable poems attacking the unfaithful Clodia, Tibullus' lament after being deceived by Delia, and the reproaches proffered Cynthia by Propertius. Romans would not have complained about women so much if they had not insisted on dreaming that they were different.

Under the Italian sky it would have been quite surprising if love had not dominated every aspect of life. The profound peace generated by the Empire was a favorable climate for these games, and nothing occurred to interrupt them. The romances the historians relate are those of the aristocracy, and even if they no doubt resemble those of the common people, they also show some striking differences. Aristocratic customs were more subject than others to traditional moral regimentation; when they broke loose, they created more of an uproar. Augustus' laws restricted only the two chief upper orders, senators and nobles. They did not apply to those who were practically excluded from public life. Moreover, a large section of the lower classes did not belong to the old Italic stock. It was unfamiliar with the religious and family traditions that weighed heavily on the Roman bourgeoisie or the lesser Italian cities. Eastern elements had infiltrated them long ago and had brought customs unaffected by the old taboos that continued to haunt the consciences of real Romans. Campania was the principal place where this mixture took place, this synthesis of East and West that contributed so much to perverting Roman morals, to causing Rome—apparently—to abandon the old values, but in fact to deepen them and give them a new meaning.

Campania was the setting for a section of Petronius' novel, or at least those parts of the *Satyricon* that have come down to us. Now the episodes of which it is composed are highly licentious, and it is certain that the author (no doubt the Senator of that name who was Nero's friend and was forced at a later date to kill himself at the order of the Emperor) enjoyed depicting scenes we would call indecent. In it two students, having escaped from school, wander freely among the mixed social groups of the cities in the rural areas. They have committed a mysterious crime against both a god, Priapus, and against a lady, a member of the bourgeoisie, who, in her anger, pursues them. The lady loses them and finds them over and over again; each time she comes upon them she makes them satisfy her erotic desires. There are plenty of frankly libidinous episodes. Apparently the pleasures of the flesh were primordial in the lives of the young men and the women they encountered.

This picture of rural life is reinforced by the erotic paintings, and many inscriptions and graffiti found on the walls of the little city buried by the ashes of Vesuvius in 79 B.C. Already in Plautus' day, the public places and streets of Rome were full of young men, and mature ones as well, who had nothing to do but watch the women go by and make all sorts of advances to those they thought were amenable. This is the picture of Rome painted by Ovid in his poetry. As one leaves the upper classes and meets the common folk, it is apparent that morals become even freer. The women have less to lose; the men are less restrained and do not find sexual satisfaction in their own homes. So they try their luck on the streets, and the walls of Pompeii have immortalized their love episodes.

A number of these amorous inscriptions have recently been collected, and give a strikingly vivid tableau of rural customs. The people of Pompeii considered love the dominating sentiment that gives the souls of human beings their true beauty: *Nemo est bellus nisi qui amavit* which means, more or less: *"A* person who has never loved is incomplete." The God of Love can perform miracles; he can melt stones and draw human speech from them: *Iam docui silices verba benigna loqui* ("I have taught the stones to speak in benevolent terms"). But he is also a cruel god, and Venus too torments human souls: A disappointed lover declares that he would like to "break the ribs of the goddess with the blows of a stick." Another curses all lovers for enjoying the happiness that is denied to him. Venus was the patron goddess of the city; it was to her that lovers addressed their prayers, and it was she they insulted when she did not favor their designs.

The names that appear on the inscriptions show that they were written by "little people": slaves fired by love for some little serving wench, artisans, freedmen whose names indicate their Eastern origin, or citizens of nearby cities who came to have a good time in Pompeii, far from prying eyes. But even these simple folk thought a lot about the love that occupied all that we know of their lives. They knew that pleasure did not last and that "as soon as Venus has joined the bodies of two lovers, she separates them." But they also knew that sensual pleasure was only the beginning, in the union of two human beings: "The soul," according to an inscription on a column near the amphitheatre, "is accustomed to take what is due to it, and return it later: if you follow this rule, may Venus, who reciprocates—*Venus Syntropos*—make your dreams come true." Perhaps this remarkably "altruistic" maxim may owe its origin to some odds and ends of philosophy imported from Greece. But it corresponds so closely to what the Roman poets proclaimed that it is hard to think that the love affairs of even the humblest denizens of Campania did not have a romantic side.

The last of the great literary works bequeathed to us by pagan literature of the Latin tongue, Apuleius' *Metamorphoses,* sums up in a picturesque fresco the different aspects of the life of love as it was lived in the second century A.D. in Roman provincial cities. The theme of the novel was borrowed by Apuleius from a Greek "novel," written, perhaps, by one Lucian of Patras. It is the story of a young man called Lucius, who, wishing to become initiated into certain magical practices, employs by mistake a salve which he thinks could change him into a bird, but which actually transforms him into a donkey. And now we find Lucius involved in a thousand adventures, now comic, now tragic. In particular, he witnessed many scenes that usually take place in the intimacy of the household but which it was thought did not need to be kept hidden from this animal (who nevertheless was so different from the others).

Before he became a donkey, Lucius was a young man whose sensual desires were easily aroused. He was certainly not a ne'erdo-well like Petronius' heroes; on the contrary, he was of good family, respected the established order of things, was scrupulously polite, extremely obliging, and on his good behavior with hosts. If he entertained the unseemly idea of seducing the little serving maid who did all the work in the house where he was welcomed, in a little town in Thessaly to which his desire to see some genuine sorceresses had led him, he would certainly abstain from doing it. But the serving maid, Photis, is young and anything but shy; a word, a trite compliment, would be enough for her to give in, and there could be no doubt, moreover, that if he had not spoken she would herself have made the first advances. At the beginning of the romance, Lucius also had an ulterior motive, to be sure; he had guessed that the lady of the house was a sorceress, and he counted on the aid of the serving maid to ferret out her secrets. But he quickly found the affair to his liking, and gave himself unreservedly to enjoying her favors, which she on her part did not hold back in the least.

But once the first heat of passion was over, Lucius returned to his project. He begged for the disclosures he had been dreaming about, and Photis, in spite of her reluctance, was obliged to show him the "laboratory" of the witch. She went even further and purloined the salve that could change him into a bird, but she was so disturbed that she made a mistake, and Lucius turned into a donkey before her very eyes. At this point, before Photis could change him back into his human self by making him eat attar of roses (this was the philter capable of counteracting the spell), a band of brigands arrived on the scene, pillaged the house, and, in order to transport their booty, took with them all the beasts of burden in the stable, including Lucius. Soon he arrived in their mountain lair with them, and there met a prisoner, a young girl they had abducted on the eve of her wedding, and who spent the time bewailing her lost love. And while the brigands were off on one of their expeditions, an old woman who acted as a servant, tried to console the young girl by telling her a marvelous story, the tale of Cupid and Psyche.

This legend is a strange one. Essentially it is the same as the story well known in all folklore, of "Beauty and the Beast." But it also contains other elements that indicate that Apuleius wanted to do more than entertain his readers by inserting it in his "picaresque" novel. Psyche was a King's daughter; she had two sisters who were very lovely, but she herself was marvelously, transcendentally beautiful. While her sisters married kings, she lived on alone in her father's palace, no one having the presumption to ask for her hand. The King, grievously distressed, decided to consult the oracle, who ordered him to expose the girl on a mountain top, dressed as for a wedding, and to abandon her there; a monster would seek her out and hold her in his power. Although broken-hearted, the King obeyed, and Psyche was taken up the mountain. But when she was alone, a breeze came up, and she was gently wafted through the air and carefully set down on the lawn of a wondrous garden. Psyche had fainted from fear, but when she opened her eyes, was delighted to find a shining gold palace in front of her. She entered the palace; although it was deserted, she could hear voices and music. The voices informed her that she was the mistress of the domain, and that they were there to serve her. Psyche bathed, decked herself out, dined peacefully, and when night fell withdrew to her room. But before she had time to fall asleep, she felt a presence near her. In the total darkness she was afraid, but the being beside her was persuasive enough to overcome her scruples, and Psyche experienced her first night of love.

Next day and the following days her life was the same. During the day attentive voices catered to her slightest desire, and each night her unknown spouse came back to her side. And he explained to her that she must not try to find out who he was, or the most dire misfortunes might result. Psyche was able to contain her curiosity for a while, but as time went on she became unhappy; her loneliness, far from all human presence, weighed on her terribly. She begged her spouse to allow her to have her sisters join her. At first he objected, warning her that such visits were fraught with danger for their happiness. But Psyche, through tenderness and by persistence, overcame his opposition. The sisters were sent for. They came once and they came again, and were devoured by envy of Psyche's good fortune. They found unjust a Fate that had given treasures to her that they could obviously have turned to better account. As they were jealous, they tried to sow the seeds of doubt in Psyche's soul. Who was this "husband" of which she could tell them nothing? Might it not be a horrible monster who was fattening her in order to devour her? And Psyche, bewildered, listened to their perfidious counsel. The following night she hid a lighted lamp under a bushel, and provided herself with a sharpened razor. When her husband was asleep, she lifted the bushel and took the lamp in one hand, the razor in the other. She was about to strike when what she saw took her breath away. It was no monster that was stretched out on the bed, but the most adorable, voluptuous god, a youth with a body like marble, half-enveloped in two quivering wings. Psyche understood that she had had Cupid for her companion during all these nights of love. She leaned over to give him a kiss, but awkwardly let fall a drop of burning oil from the lamp. Cupid cried out, awoke, and saw that she had learned his secret. Immediately he flew off, escaping from Psyche's embraces, and telling her that he would never see her again.

Then a long series of tests began for the poor child. She would not resign herself to giving up her love. She looked everywhere for him, but the gods and goddesses themselves repudiated her. Venus, Cupid's mother, sought her everywhere to punish her. She had always been jealous of the girl; she had asked her son to torture her, and now she had seduced the person who was to have been her executioner. So Venus was furious. Psyche, repulsed on every side, went to her enemy of her own accord in the secret hope of thus coming nearer to the one she loved. Venus tormented her in a thousand ways, and subjected her to trials she thought impossible, but all nature joined forces to come to Psyche's aid.

At the end of the last test, nevertheless, which consisted in going down into Hades, Psyche would have died if Cupid himself had not taken pity on her because of all the constancy and affection she had shown, and he persuaded Jupiter to consecrate their union with due solemnity. And Venus and her daughter-in-law became reconciled.

That was the story the old woman told the brigands' prisoner. Lucius, still in the form of a donkey, was all ears. Then the novel itself took over again, and events followed one another rapidly. The captive was saved and the brigands wiped out, but other dramas were played: lovers united, were separated by jealous persons, someone died of love, someone else wreaked a horrible vengeance—all this before the eyes of the donkey. Elsewhere, among the villagers, and in the most humble dwellings, incidents took place worthy of the "fables in verse." There was a succession of deceived husbands, perfidious women—sometimes criminal, unusually cruel stepmothers who poisoned the children of a previous wife, or who were in love with their stepsons, and when the latter resisted their advances, took steps to have them done away with. The entire repertory of the "Milesian" tales and of the most sombre tragedies passes before our eyes. It would appear that Apuleius exercised his wits to devise a kind of Inferno of love, where comic adventures and tragic episodes rubbed elbows. And the climax of this pageant of Hades was a highly perverted incident of which the donkey himself was the hero. A great lady desired him (and her immoderate ardor recalls the excesses of the characters in Petronius and the vices denounced by Juvenal) so he became the instrument of a monstrous, unnatural satisfaction. But Divine Grace now entered his sad life to change it for the better. The goddess Isis herself appeared to him on the beach at Corinth one night when the moon was full, and told him what to do to break the spell. The very next day Lucius found the roses that had eluded his search until then, and presto! regained his human form. Initiated into the mysteries of the goddess, converted to her religion, cured of his sacrilegious curiosity about magic practices from then on, Lucius lived a happy and holy life.

No doubt we are not well informed about the model for Apuleius' novel. But we know that he added to the two main episodes that give the *Metamorphoses* its moral and religious significance: the legend of Cupid and Psyche, which occupies the central place in the novel, and the "Book of Isis," which constitutes its mystical conclusion.

Psyche, as her name clearly indicates, is the symbol of the human soul which is fixed by a love for the divine, and laboriously attains happiness after going through a thousand painful tests.

Apuleius, in elaborating the legend, transposes it into a setting provided by a theme from folklore, a doctrine of love that we have already quite near to hand in classic Platonism, and this had been illustrated and popularized in bas-reliefs and paintings in both Roman and Hellenic art. Psyche is one of those little winged girls to be seen in small pictures—tormented or sometimes consoled by Eros, also wearing wings—who burns them with his torch, wounds them with his arrows, or triumphantly draws them harnessed to his chariot—when he himself is not portrayed as the one who is defeated. Apuleius made these images his own, and built a readily understandable allegory, using them as a theme that he has placed at the core of the whole novel. So the *Metamorphoses* contains a true "doctrine" of love. One can recognize a rather flattering enumeration of the rawest types of the feeling or the instinct of love, those that threaten the soul's very existence, and, on the other hand, the novel extols love's force and its saving virtue. The soul attains salvation through a love purified by a knowledge of the sacred mysteries. Apuleius teaches that love is closely bound to the World Soul, which the philosophers of that time readily identified with Aphrodite. It is the daemon that keeps everyone in communion with the universal life principle. Is it not love that gives that which is mortal the means of triumphing over its own death and perpetuating itself in its race and in its works? That is what Isis provided her devotees; she is herself the "feminine" principle in the universe, the mother that receives the fecundating seed and brings forth a forest of forms.

All the hymns in honor of Isis give her the credit for having taught the art of love to humans. She is the protectress of women, who partake especially of her divine attributes. She guarantees the validity of their love, and gives their amours their whole meaning. In the Roman forms of this religion of Isis, it is to be remarked that she is no longer in subjection to Osiris. It is she who decides for her husband where the cult is to be observed. And it is noteworthy that the religion of Isis triumphed in Rome at the same time that the moral code definitively accepted the emancipation—for some, even the "deification"—of women. It should not be forgotten that the Emperor Caligula, who was so ready to erect altars in honor of his sisters (to such a point that he was suspected of having an incestuous passion for one of them —in the Egyptian mode) was a votary of Isis. Many women too assiduously frequented the temples dedicated to the worship of the goddess, specially the *Isaeum* in the Plain of Mars. Isis watched over their behavior, imposed penance and a period of ritual chastity, but also consoled them and secretly revealed to them their dignity and power as women. Let the "old Romans" grumble! No one listened to them anymore. For several generations Rome had been ready to harken to the gospel of Isis, and Cleopatra had been forgiven.

In the same epoch there was a proliferation of decorative paintings: on the walls of houses, mythological scenes representing the marriage of the gods: those of Adonis and Aphrodite, Dionysus and Ariadne, Mars and Venus were the most often portrayed. In this way the decorations satisfied the taste of a clientele for whom marriage was coming to have an ever greater mystic significance. A large number of weddings were also to be found on the sarcophagi of the Roman epoch: marriage was considered an initiation into sacred mysteries and an image of immortality. The famous frescos of Boscoreale could be interpreted, with some justice, as a Dionysiac symbol of marriage. Roman tradition, according to which Dionysus had never ceased to be a living god, used motifs brought from the Hellenistic East. The Boscoreale fresco was no doubt painted about the time when Messalina and Silius also celebrated their marriage by imitating the legend of Ariadne. From that time on, love was regarded as a source of the life of the spirit, and customs conformed exactly to what Apuleius taught a century later.

Despite all the individual excesses and aberrations which Roman historians were only too happy to pass along; despite the lewdness of Petronius, we should not think of Rome as no more than the depraved Babylon, characterized by unnatural loves, that is too often conjured up before our eyes. Rome tried to reconcile the exigencies of society and morals, with which love so often conflicted, and the profoundest aspirations of the human soul, which it is dangerous to distort. Did she quite succeed in resolving this problem? Probably not, but that is doubtless because it cannot be solved. Has there ever existed a social system anywhere in the world that can be credited with finding a complete solution?

SELECTED READINGS

Babcock, C. "The Early Career of Fulvia." *American Journal of Philology* 86 (1965): 1–32.

Baldson, J. P. V. D. *Roman Women: Their History and Habits.* London: Bodley Head, 1962.

Best, E. E. "Cicero, Livy and Educated Roman Women." *Classical Journal* 65 (1970): 199–204.

D'Avino, M. *The Women of Pompeii.* Naples: Loffredo, 1967.

Durry, M. "Le Mariage des filles impubères dans la Rome antique." *Revue des Études Latines* 47 bis (1970): 17–25.

Finley, M. I. "The Silent Women of Rome." *Horizon* 7 (1965): 57–64.

Fitton, J. W. "That was No Lady, That was. . . ." *Classical Quarterly* 64 (1970): 56–66.

Gagé, J. *Matronalia: Essai sur les dévotions et les organisations cultuelles des femmes dans l'ancienne Rome.* Collections Latomus 60. 1963.

Gordon, H. "The Eternal Triangle, First Century B.C." *Classical Journal* 28 (1933): 574–78.

Hallett, J. P. *Fathers and Daughters in Roman Society.* Princeton, N.J.: Princeton University Press, 1983.

Highet, G. *Poets in a Landscape.* New York: Alfred A. Knopf, 1957.

Hoffsten, R. *Roman Women of Rank of the Early Empire, as Portrayed by Dio, Paterculus, Suetonius, and Tacitus.* Philadelphia: University of Pennsylvania Press, 1939.

Kiefer, O. *Sexual Life in Ancient Rome.* Translated by G. Highet and H. MacInnes. London: Routledge and Kegan Paul, 1934; Panther Books, 1969.

Kitto, H. D. F. *The Greeks.* New York: Penguin Books, 1951.

Lilja, S. *The Roman Elegists' Attitude to Women.* Annales Academiae Scientiarum Fennicae, Series B, vol. 135, Fascicle 1. Helsinki: Suomaleinen Tiedeakatemia, 1965.

Luck, Georg. *The Latin Love Elegy.* London: Methuen, 1959, 1969.

MacMullen, R. *Roman Social Relations: 50 B.C. to A.D. 284*. New Haven: Yale University Press, 1974.

Motto, A. L. "Seneca on Women's Liberation." *Classical World* 65 (1972): 155–57.

Pomeroy, S. B. "Selected Bibliography on Women in Antiquity." *Arethusa* 6 (Spring, 1973): 125–57.

———. *Goddesses, Whores, Wives and Slaves*. New York: Schocken Books, 1975.

Rawson, B. "Family Life Among the Lower Classes at Rome in the First Two Centuries of the Empire." *Classical Philology* 61 (1966): 71–83.

Seltman, C. *Women in Antiquity,* 1956. New York: Collier Books, 1962.

Treggiari, S. "Libertine Ladies." *Classical World* 64 (1971): 196–98.

Williams, G. "Some Aspects of Roman Marriage Ceremonies and Ideals." *Journal of Roman Studies* 48 (1958): 16–29.

INDEX

Acca Larentia (Romulus and Remus's foster mother): 11
Aeneas and the *Aeneid:* Amata, 8; Anchises and Aphrodite, 1–2; Anna, 7; Ascanius, 2–3, 8; Creusa, 2–3; Dido, 3–5, 7, 9; Latinus, 6, 8; Lavinia, 6–8; Nisus and Euryalus, 9, 179–81; Turnus, 8
Agrippa and Julia: 268
Agrippina: 277, 288–89; Nero and, 289–91
Alkmene and Amphitryon: 92–95
Antony: and Cleopatra, 256–61; and Dionysus, 255–57, 260–62; and Fulvia, 213–20; and Hercules, 254–55
Appius Claudius, engagements and political power of: 73
Apuleius (*Metamorphoses,* or "The Golden Ass"): 46, 108, 206, 300–306
Arria and Paetus: 248–49
Art of Love (Ovid): 136–46
Augustine: 27, 29
Augustus (Octavian): and Agrippa, 268; and Claudia, 263; and Julia (daughter), 268–73; and Julia (grand-daughter), 273–75; and Livia Drusilla, 264–67, 270–71, 273–76; and Marcellus, 268; marriage legislation of, 114, 156–58, 161; promiscuity of, 262, 266; and Scribonia, 263; and Servilia, 262; and Tiberius, 268–70
Aurelius, Marcus: 115

Bacchantes: 30–32
Bachelors, taxed: 82
Bona Dea: 34, 236
Brothels: 128
Brutus and Porcia: 242–43

Caesar, Julius:
  engagement to Cossutia: 234
  love affairs of: 226–27
  marriages of: 235–37
  mistresses of: Cleopatra, 231–34; Servilia, 227–31
  reputation as "the rooster," "baldy": 226
Canuleian Law: 61, 67
Carmenta (Niostrate, Themis, Tamandra): 16–17
Catiline: and Aurelia Orestilla, 206–207; and Fulvia, 208–

209; and Sempronia, 207–208
Cato the Elder: 83–85, 102, 109–10, 113–14, 116–17, 134–35, 137, 143–44, 182–83, 185
Cato the Younger, Marcia, and Hortensius: 237–41
Catullus and Clodia ("Lesbia"): 148–56, 296, 297
Cicero: 186–87; attacks Antony (the *Philippics*), 213–18; death of, 218; famous trials of, 203–12; philosophy of, 248; Publilia, later marriage to, 200–202; Terentia (wife), 191–200; Tullia (daughter), 196–97, 202
Cleopatra: and Antony, 256–61; and Julius Caesar, 231–34
Clodia ("Lesbia"): 149–56, 296–97
Cluentius and Cicero: 203–205
Coemptio (ritual of marriage): 57, 59–60
Concubines, "concubinage" (*contubernium*): 112–18
Confarreatio (marriage ritual): 52, 57–59
Contraceptive, wine as: 66
Corinna (Ovid's love): 138
Coriolanus: 183–84
Cornelia (Augustus's daughter-in-law): 177–78
Cornelia (mother of the Gracchi): 186–91
"Cupid and Psyche" (love story by Apuleius): 301–304

Cynthia (Propertius's love): 165–77
Delia (Tibullus's mistress): 158–65
Dido (Queen of Carthage, lover of Aeneas): 3–5, 7, 9
Digest (compendium of Roman Law): 51
Dio Cassius: 272, 278
Dionysus (Bacchus): 30–32; impersonated by Antony, 255–57, 260–62
Divorce: 63–69
Domina ("mistress"): 141–43
Dowry: 71–72
Drusilla (Livia, wife of Augustus): 264–67, 270–71, 273–76

Emancipation of women: 146–47, 186; political importance of, 194–95
Engagements: 74–78; age of, 77–81; consent to, 75–76
Epicureans: 247
Eros: 47, 295–96
Etruscans: 15–17
Evander: 16
Extramarital affairs, adultery: 102, 107–109

Fascinus (phallus, penis): 28–29, 33
Fidelity (*Fides*): 64, 296
Fire and water, in marriage ceremony: 57
Flamen and *flaminica* (priest and priestess): 52–53

INDEX

Flammeum (bridal veil): 55
Fortuna Muliebris, temple to: 184
Free love: 102–103
Fulvia (Antony's wife): 213–20
Fulvia (Catiline's): 208–209

Gaius and Gaia (marriage vow): 51, 57
Gellius, Aulus: 82
Genius (male organ): 28, 33; see also *fascinus*
Gracchus, Tiberius: engagement of, 73

Hadrian: 42
Hair, the bride's: 55
Hannibal: 41
Hercules: impersonated by Antony, 254–55; "knot of" (bride's belt), 55
Heroism of women: 85
Hesiod (*Works and Days*): 160
Homosexuality, Roman stories of: 103–107
Horace: 110–11
Hortensius, Cato, and Marcia (an unusual triangle): 238–41

Impotentia muliebris (woman's "lack of control"): 206
Isis: 304–306; Cleopatra as, 257, 260

Julia (Augustus's daughter): 267; conspiracy against Augustus?, 270–72, 275; debauchery of, 269–70; exile of, 272; marriage with Tiberius, 268–70; marries Agrippa, 268
Julia (Augustus's grand-daughter): 273
Juno (goddess of marriage): 50, 55
Juvenal (Roman satirist): 246, 297; *Sixth Satire,* 278

"Kissing cousins," right of (*ius osculi*): 66
Knot of Hercules: 55

Lena (madam, procuress): 129
Leno (pimp, procurer): 121–24
Liber (Latin god of wine): 29–30, 293
Liberalia (festival of Liber): 293
Livia (wife of Augustus): 264–67, 270–71, 273–76
Livy (Roman historian): 12, 15, 21, 184
Love: free love, 102–103; marital love idealized, 146, 296; mutual love, 145; in public life, 183
Lucan (epic poet of the civil wars, *Bellum Civile* or "Pharsalia"): 224, 241
Lucretia, her rape and the driving out of the Tarquin kings: 21–25
Lucretius (didactic poet): 44–45, 296
Macrobius: 79
Marcia (wife of Cato the Younger) and Hortensius: 237–41
Marriage: 48; ceremony, 54–57;

in comedy, 87–89; family alliances, 72–74, 80–81, 185, 203, 227, 237, 246; happiness in, 81; legal categories of, 59–60; *manus* (husband's authority over wife), 60–61, 67; men's views on, 82–83, 87, 182, 266; and money and property, 62–63; soldiers limited to one, 102

Mars and Rhea Silvia: 1, 9
Matrimonium: 50
Matronalia: 34
Menander (writer of Greek Comedy): 86, 134
Messallina: 277–78; wife of Claudius, 279–88
Metella, Caecilia: 54
Minos and Scylla (a parallel for Tarpeia and Titus Tatius): 20
Modestinus (Roman legal writer on marriage in the *Digest*): 51, 77
Mutunus Tutunus (god in the form of a penis): 27–28

Naevius's *The Young Girl of Tarentum:* 124
Nemesis (Tibullus's mistress): 164
Nero and Agrippina: 289–91
Numa Pompilius (second king of Rome): 15, 79–80, 83, 112
Numitor (grandfather of Romulus and Remus): 9

Ocrisia and Servius Tullius: 28
Oppian Law (against extravagance): 84–85

Ovid: 136–46; exiled by Augustus, 137–38; *Heroides,* 146; *Metamorphoses,* 146

Paelex: 112
Paraclausithyron (serenade of the shut-out lover): 126–27
Paterfamilias: 71
Pervigilium Veneris ("Venus's Vigil"): 46
Petronius: 118–19, 298
Phallus: 28–29
Philemon and Baucis: 146
Plautus (Roman writer of comedy): Amphitryon and Alkmene (*Amphitryon*) of, 92–95, 185; *Casina,* 88; courtesans and, 130, 294; *Curculio,* 121–22; marriage, negative view of, 87; Menander adapted by, 10, 86; *Poenulus,* 127–29; and older Roman view of women, 295, 298
Pliny the Elder: 278
Pliny the Younger: 114, 249
Plutarch:
  Parallel Lives of: *Antony,* 215, 254; *Caesar,* 227–28; *Cato the Younger,* 239; *Lucullus,* 209–10; *Marius,* 104–105; *Numa,* 79–80, 83; *Pompey,* 225–26; *Romulus,* 64; *Tiberius Gracchus,* 73
  on husbands returning from a trip, 91
  teen-age boys, 106–107

INDEX

on wedding gods, 56
on wedding night, 292–93
Pompeia (wife of Julius Caesar): 235; affair with Clodius, 192–93
Pompeii (Roman city): 299
Pompey: 220–26; and Cornelia, 224–26; and Julia (Julius Caesar's daughter), 222–24
Porcia and Brutus: 242–43
Praecia and Cornelius Cethegus: 209–10
Priapus (god of fertility): 32–33
Propertius and Cynthia: 165–77; *Elegy to Cornelia,* 177–78
Pudicitia ("modesty," "purity"): 89
Punic Wars: 39

Rhea Silvia (mother of Romulus and Remus): 1, 9–11
Romulus and the "Rape of the Sabines": 11–15
Romulus and Remus: birth of, 10; and wolf, 11

Sabines (Sabine women): 11–15
Sallust's *Conspiracy of Catiline:* 207–208
Scylla and Minos: 20
Sempronia (wife of Scipio Aemilianus; supporter of Catiline): 207–208
Seneca: exiled to Corsica, 281; on the debauchery of Julia, Augustus's daughter, 271; on honor in marriage, 252; praises maternal purity, 246

Servius Sulpicius (Roman legal writer): 74
Servius Tullius (sixth king of Rome): 28
Sextus Tarquinius: 21–25
Social War: 204
Stoicism: 240, 247–48, 252–53
Stuprum (blood tainted by illegitimate intercourse): 103, 107
Suetonius on Julius Caesar: 231
Sulpicia (wife of Q. Fulvius Flaccus): 41
Sulpicia, her poems among Tibullus's *Elegies:* 120

Tacitus: 281–82
Tanaquil (wife of Tarquinius Priscus): 16
Tarpeia (vestal virgin who betrayed Rome for love): 18–21
Tarquinius Superbus: 21; his son rapes Lucretia, 21–25
Terence: *Adelphoe,* 122–23; *Andria,* 97–98; contrasted with Cato the Elder, 134–35; contrasted with Plautus, 96–97, 130, 133, 294–95; *Eunuch,* 131–33; *Heauton Timoroumenos,* 133; *Hecyra,* 99–100, 130–31
Terentia (wife of Cicero): 191–200
Tiberius (successor to Augustus) and Julia: 268–70
Tibullus (Roman love poet) and Delia: 158–65, 296–97
Titus Tatius (king of the Sabines) and Tarpeia: 18–21

Tullia (daughter of Cicero): 196–97, 202
Turia (praised in the *Laudatio Turiae*): 243–45

Ulpian (Roman jurist): 78, 79
Usucapio, usus (common-law marriage): 57, 59–60

Valerius Maximus: 71–72, 293
Varro, Marcus Terentius, on the duties of a husband: 83
Venus: as Aeneas's mother, 1–2, 4–5; and Aphrodite, 35–36; at Eryx, oriental worship of, 39–40; Calva, 37–38; and the Greek Eros, 295–96; Genetrix, and Julius Caesar, 43–44; Obsequens, 38–39; *Pervigilium Veneris,* 46; Syntropos, 299; Verticordia, 41; Victrix, and Pompey, 43; Viriplaca, 68
Villa of the Mysteries: 32
Virgil: *Aeneid* of, 3–6, 8, 179–81; Dido and Aeneas of, 179; Nisus and Euryalus of, 179–81

Wine, as a contraceptive: 66
Women of the city of Rome: emancipation of, 146–47, 186; heroism of, 85; importance of, in politics, 194–95; in religion, 16–17; marital love an ideal for, 296; public activism of, 84–85; respected, 294–95